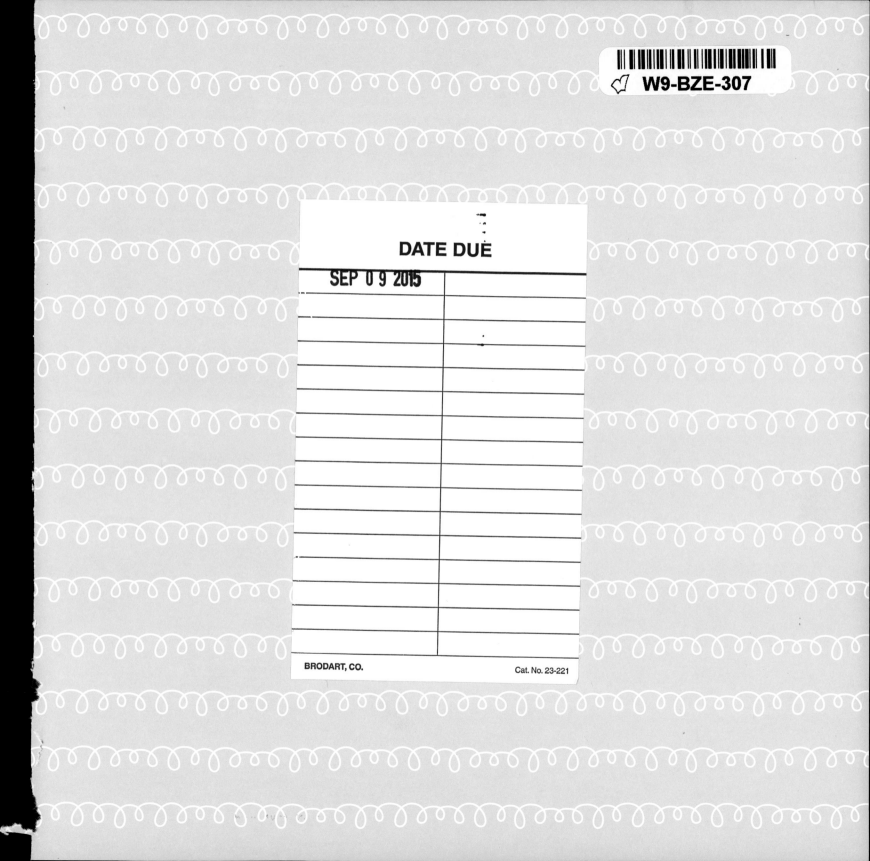

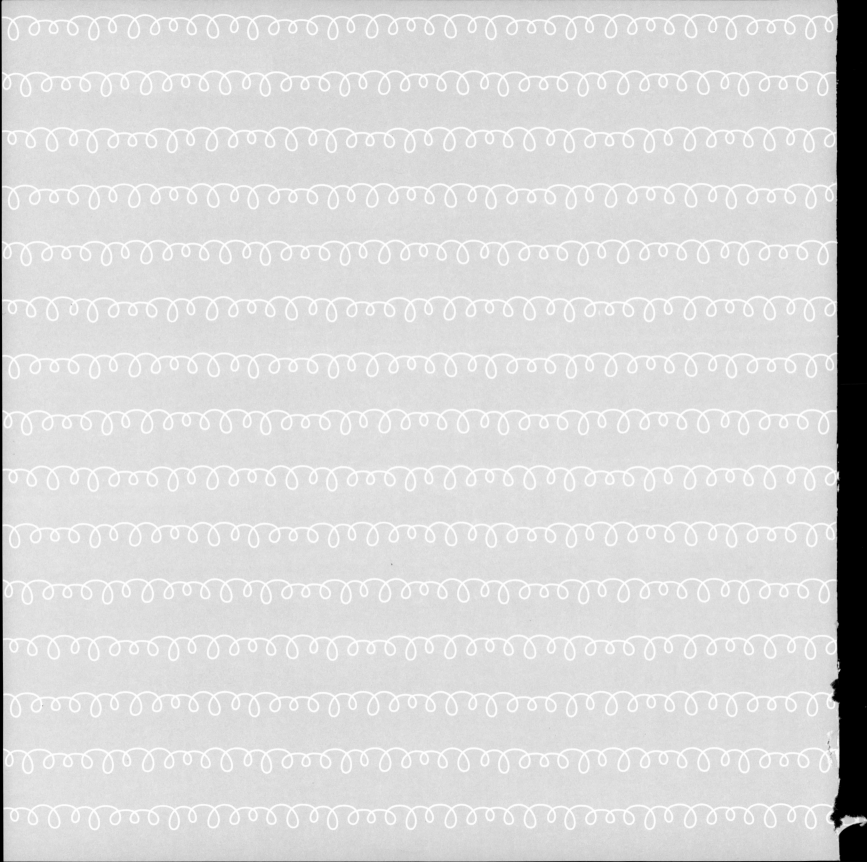

bake it *like you* mean it

you mean it

GESINE BULLOCK-PRADO

PHOTOGRAPHS BY *Tina Rupp*

Stewart, Tabori & Chang   New York

Published in 2013 by Stewart, Tabori & Chang

An imprint of ABRAMS

Copyright © 2013 Gesine Bullock-Prado

Photographs copyright © 2013 Tina Rupp

Cataloging-in-Publication Data has been applied for and may be obtained from the Library of Congress.

ISBN: 978-1-61769-013-6

Editors: Natalie Kaire and Dervla Kelly
Designer: Alissa Faden
Production Manager: Tina Cameron

The text of this book was composed in Archer, Chalet Comprime, Gotham, and Walbaum.

Printed and bound in the U.S.A.

10 9 8 7 6 5 4 3 2 1

Stewart, Tabori & Chang books are available at special discounts when purchased in quantity for premiums and promotions as well as fundraising or educational use. Special editions can also be created to specification. For details, contact specialsales@abramsbooks.com or the address below.

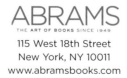

115 West 18th Street
New York, NY 10011
www.abramsbooks.com

FÜR OMI

contents

INTRODUCTION

Allow me to introduce my sweet friend, Cake. Cake, meet my fellow bakers. Fellow bakers, meet Cake. You've met her before—perhaps in chocolate or vanilla, possibly presented to you in a sheet or sliced from a small round. But now we've got an opportunity to ask her a few questions, so let's go!

BAKER: You can't attend a celebration without cake appearing at some point, surrounded by fanfare and flickering candles. Have you always been so popular?

CAKE: Yes. But don't hate me because I'm beautiful and delicious. I've been around since ancient times, the delicacy of pharaohs and reclining Grecians. Back in the day, I was most likely a honey-and-nut confection, a bit more breadlike than fluffy. And when all things sweet were a genuine treat, too expensive for common folk to get ahold of, I led a rarified life among royalty and fancy people. Once sugar manufacture became mechanized and efficient, I was made available to all and sundry, and now anyone at any time can be graced with my delicious presence. You're welcome.

BAKER: What constitutes a "cake," exactly?

CAKE: How dare you! Don't try to pigeonhole me with such a question; I'm multi-faceted and complex! Just think about this: When you assemble a birthday cake, you layer *cake* with a luscious filling, and then usually you ice the whole thing. And what do you call the lovely creation you just made? That's right: *cake*. So I'm an element of the whole *and* I'm the whole. Existential, ain't it? And I come in many guises: cupcake, round layer cake, single-slab sheetcake. I can be made fluffy by whipping eggs into a frenzy, or springy by adding baking powder or baking soda. Some of my brethren even use natural yeast to get high and mighty. That's right! Yeast, in cake! Sometimes I'm composed of layers of meringue instead of spongy pastry, and sometimes I'm a jewel-toned mousse. Some of my family members are gluten-free; others are chock-full of flour. Some people call me a gâteau or a torte. I am all these things—and more.

BAKER: Aren't you a symbol of all that's wrong with modern cuisine, an instrument destined to make our children obese and sick?

CAKE: Anything in excess is dangerous. Confine your diet to a strict regimen of kale and carrots, and you'll be sick in no time. I'm pretty irresistible; of this I am acutely aware. I'm tasty, contain very few nutrients, and am very hard to say no to. I'd rather you save me for special occasions and even then, savor me in moderation. I hate to be thought of as "common," so keep me special and use me with care.

BAKER: Is this a decorating book or a baking book?

CAKE: First, let me just say that every cake should be beautifully made from the inside out. When you embark on a cake journey, you should approach it with care and thoughtfulness. Remember, I'm multifaceted—a feast for all the senses—and I'm not going to let you forget it. Above all, you should strive to make me outrageously delicious. But as you go about developing my flavors and luscious textures, you must also take care to make me visually sumptuous. My purpose in life, after all, is to be eaten, and for this to happen, you must come upon me and *see* something on the outside that entices you. And then you'll take a knife to me and scar me permanently…but that's a story for my pastry therapist and not something we need discuss any further. The bottom line is, baking and decorating need not and *should* not be mutually exclusive. If you approach cake making as simply an exercise in advanced arts and crafts without paying heed to the fact that your intended audience will also be ingesting your visual masterpiece, you've missed the point of my existence entirely. By all means, dress me in edible haute couture, but never lose sight of the fact that it's what's inside that really counts.

BAKER: Is this book for the beginner?

CAKE: This book is for everyone. Some recipes are easy peasy. Some are complex. As you become more adept at the simpler techniques, you can start taking on the recipes that once intimidated you. Each chapter is devoted to a technique of making cake (me) and will begin with my most streamlined iteration. As the chapter progresses and your confidence grows, you will see how complex I can become, and then you'll be able to mix and match as you see fit. And you can always visit me at https://www.facebook.com/bakeitlikeyoumeanit for extra help!

BAKER: So what do I need to start?

CAKE: Beautiful ingredients and a stand or hand mixer. Most people have a cake pan or two; you'll need a few of those. But most important, you have to "bake it like you mean it." If you've got the right attitude, you'll make great cake.

My baking philosophy—my mantra—has always been "bake it like you mean it."

To bake with an eye for the details and the pleasure of the process. To bake with the intent to create desserts that are delicious and beautiful from the inside out.

And I'm finding that home bakers are chomping at the bit for new and amazing ways to work with cakes and pastries. If popular cookbooks geared toward designing ever more extravagant treats are any indication, it's obvious that both serious and occasional bakers are seeking out the different and challenging. What's even more exciting is that it's possible to make a visually stunning masterpiece without complicated carving and manhandling of cake layers. *Bake It Like You Mean It* is a compendium of gorgeous cake recipes and techniques that will yield glorious pastries for everyone, from the bakers who want to impress without breaking a sweat to those who want to challenge themselves and expand their baking skills.

It is my firm belief that a cake isn't worth making if it isn't going to be beautiful in every way: from the exterior décor, to inside the slice, to the glory of scrumptious flavors and perfect textural balance in your mouth. *Bake It Like You Mean It* is the next wave in making, baking, and building cakes that are masterpieces from the inside out. From deceptively easy recipes to incredibly fun and challenging cake art, there's no reason your next cake can't be just such a masterpiece.

WHAT YOU'LL NEED

1 A STAND MIXER Yes. It's essential. The art of making great pastry is inextricably linked with proper technique, and the technique most important for great cake is the proper aeration of the batter—which is just a fancy way of saying you beat the hell out of certain ingredients until they are full of air and have increased in volume. For hearty doughs, such as those for brioches and croissants, where mixing takes up to ten to twenty minutes to develop the proper structure, a stand mixer is heaven sent. And while it's not impossible to make some of these recipes by hand, it is very, very hard. Yes, you can go old school and use your hands, but you'll be kneading for what will seem like days (great workout, though). A sturdy hand mixer can be substituted for less hearty applications.

2 MEASURING CUPS You'll need both dry and wet measuring cups, as well as small measuring spoons. A scale is awfully handy, but not essential. To measure dry ingredients, such as flour, I utilize the spoon-and-scrape method: With a large spoon, scoop the flour into the dry measuring cup. Use the back of a knife to level off the flour. Don't wiggle the cup and don't pack it down, as this will result in an improper measure.

3 AN OVEN These recipes utilize *conventional,* not convection, temperatures—this way anyone with an oven can participate. If you prefer convection baking, reduce the heat stated in the recipe by 25°F (15°C). I'd also recommend quite earnestly that you get yourself an oven thermometer to check the accuracy of your oven. I mean no offense, really—I'm sure you've got the best oven ever—but I can tell you from experience that they are notorious fibbers when it comes to accurate temperatures. I've worked in every type of oven imaginable, from a $20,000 professional oven to a microwave-convection-tabletop thingy, and they've all lied to me. To illustrate how important accurate temperature is, an oven that runs hot could cause your gorgeous cake to rise too quickly, leaving the inside uncooked. The weight of all that unbaked batter will take its toll and the whole cake will collapse. Too low a temperature, and the cake can come out leaden and dry. Oven thermometers are cheap—much cheaper than replacing wasted ingredients when your cake collapses. And they are available in most grocery stores, so you really have no excuse.

4 CAKE PANS You don't need a large array of cake pans. Three 8- or 9-inch (20- or 23-cm) rounds will get you started. A Bundt or loaf pan will also be helpful. I'll also give you some ideas on how to employ household items in your baking so you don't have to purchase costly professional individual molds (Hint: Start saving all your tuna cans, cat food cans, coffee cans, tomato soup cans . . .).

5 GREAT INGREDIENTS:

- Use the best-quality unsalted butter you can afford. Always use unsalted. Salt is a preservative, ergo salted butter is always older than unsalted. Salted butter also suffers from what I like to describe as "butter funk," an unpleasant taste that can ruin anything in which it is used. I also like to dictate exactly how much salt goes into my goodies and don't want a stick of salted butter to mess up my hard work.

- Fine-quality chocolate and cocoa powder are also essential to the best results. I'll always tell you the exact type of chocolate I've used in my recipe and will also suggest alternatives. Using inferior chocolate or cocoa guarantees the recipe will not live up to its chocolaty potential. I use Cacao Barry/Callebaut and Valrhona chocolates and cocoas most often, but grocery stores are carrying a vast array of lovely chocolates for baking these days. Scharffenberger, Lindt, and Green & Black's Organic chocolates are a few brands to try that are readily available. Look for labels that specify the percentage of cacao. I stick to chocolates in the 60% to 70% cacao range.

- **Flour** is another crucial ingredient on which I never compromise. I am lucky enough to live around the corner from King Arthur Flour (I teach there as well), and I use their flour in all my baking. They didn't pay me to do so or to say this—I swear. Their flour is the only one that comes with a guaranteed gluten percentage. Most flours aim at a specific percentage but usually err by 10 to 20 percentage points, so two bags of all-purpose flour from the same manufacturer can contain vastly different gluten percentages. This can make an alarming difference in your finished product. I'll talk more about gluten later.

- Keeping your **eggs** at room temperature will go a long way in making your cakes and meringues come out beautifully, as the warmth allows the proteins to integrate into the sugars more quickly. However, if you need to separate eggs, separate them as soon as you take them out of the fridge, then allow them to come to room temperature. When the egg is cold, the whites and yolks are firmer, making it less likely that the yolk will break during the separating process. Note that all the recipes in this book use large eggs.

- And finally, use *real* flavors and extracts. I'll know if you use imitation ones; I have baking fairies scouting the world, and they bring me news of baking infractions. (The use of imitation vanilla is right there at the top of unforgivable violations.) You'll also notice that I use something called "vanilla bean paste" in many recipes. Vanilla bean paste is vanilla bean suspended in a thick extract. It imparts wonderful flavor, more than a traditional extract, and it is a superior alternative to scraping out beans from an expensive pod. But if you have a hard time finding vanilla bean paste, you can substitute an equal amount of vanilla extract.

6 PATIENCE Baking requires your undivided attention and patience. Read each recipe twice before tackling it. Get your ingredients and equipment ready before you start. Give yourself plenty of time to play. Allow your butter and sugar to cream until light and fluffy, take the time for your eggs to double in volume, and make sure that the ingredients are at the temperature called for in the recipe. Let your cakes cool completely before assembling. Make sure that when the ingredient list states "1 cup sugar, divided," you don't add the entire cup at step 1, only to read further and discover you were supposed to save ½ cup for step 10. We've all done it, but a little patience and attention would have kept us from making the mistake.

7 KINDNESS —to yourself. Bakers are notoriously hard on themselves, expecting perfection each time. When it takes so much time to transform raw ingredients into a beautiful pastry, it's frustrating beyond measure when the pastry doesn't come out as planned. We bakers employ a craft that's as close to alchemy as anything in this world. We take whole ingredients—eggs, flour, sugar, butter—and transform them into something entirely different from their origins. When you cook a meal, you can still see the individual ingredients you've utilized in the completed product: "There's a tomato! There's some garlic! There's the beef!" But in baking, the transformation is complete, and it lends a satisfaction totally unlike that of cooking a lovely dinner. It's magical. So to go through the entire journey only to find it all having gone pear-shaped is disheartening and depressing. But let me tell you something: Every important lesson I've learned in baking has come from a mistake. Let me rephrase that: Everything I've learned in baking has come from *learning* from my mistakes. If you know how it can go wrong, then you're well on your way to mastery. So give yourself a break.

8 LOVE —it's an essential ingredient, and you'll taste the difference when it's there. Put your heart and soul into your baking. Bake it like you mean it.

Chapter 1

AIRY
&
MARVELOUS

MERINGUES

FOR A CONFECTION THAT AT ITS SIMPLEST consists of just two ingredients, egg whites and sugar, meringues inspire some outsize devotion. In my family alone, the sight of a crunchy cloud the size of a melon elicits unladylike squawks of delight and has led to quite a few flesh wounds in our scramble to get our greedy paws on the stuff. Then there's that flavor, a sweetness that's front-loaded and hazardous to your well-being, but it's tempered by the mellowness of the egg white, giving you the sense that you're doing something more sophisticated than upending supersized Pixy Stix into your maw. And that texture—good golly, that texture. A simple meringue, baked slow and low, has a crunch and crumble paired with a sticky chew that leaves snack-tastic reminders lodged in your teeth. A pie meringue is at once elastic and crisp, an outer skin of campfire marshmallow happiness giving way to a heartbreaking, melting smoothness.

Amazingly, a meringue is so fine it can stand on its very own, like My Big Fat Creamsicle Meringue Moment (page 16), or can easily be combined with yummy extras, as in an Nussbuserln Torte (page 19). Or the meringue can act as a component of a larger dessert, giving a soufflé or a cake a lighter-than-air texture that plain baking powder or baking soda just can't deliver. Take the meringue process a few technical steps into the fancy and you can whip up a glorious layered creation like a dacquoise, or even a macaron tart beautiful and tasty enough to put Ladurée on notice. But even a simple mound of spiky white meringues stacked high to the heavens is a beauty to behold.

MY BIG FAT CREAMSICLE MERINGUE MOMENT
A SIMPLE MERINGUE MADE BEAUTIFUL

Makes 8 meringue tarts

MY FAVORITE SHOP WINDOW IS in a side alley in Venice. Walking around with friends one summer day, in search of lunch, I was stopped in my tracks by a sight of such unadulterated beauty that I began to tear up in wonder: meringues the size of a pug's head, from winter white to pastel pink and Easter yellow, piled into lovely pyramids. I had stumbled onto the Valley of the Pastry Kings, the Giza of sweets. Before our hungry group could move along, I insisted on purchasing one of each flavor, and all during lunch I stole bites from those cumulus clouds of sweetness, scattering crunchy white crumbs about me and finishing my sack of meringues before I'd touched my pasta. *Mamma mia!* What a meal.

Today, I make meringues with the same splendid taste and texture that I enjoyed as a kid, but I also take the time to make them beautiful. Here I combine two meringue flavors in one pastry bag and pipe them into rose shapes. (Other times I paint the sides of my pastry bag so a swirl of color descends as I pipe my little masterpieces.) Taking just a little extra time for details—like piping instead of plopping—goes a long way in creating a memorable cloud of deliciousness. Sandwich two crunchy beauties around a touch of fluffy meringue-based seven-minute frosting, and you've just made the Cadillac of meringue pastries.

FOR THE MERINGUE:

4 egg whites, at room temperature

¼ teaspoon salt

¼ teaspoon distilled white vinegar or cream of tartar

½ teaspoon vanilla bean paste

1 cup (200 g) superfine or baker's sugar

¼ teaspoon orange extract (*not* orange oil)

2 drops orange food coloring (optional)

FOR THE FILLING:

5 egg whites, at room temperature

1 cup (200 g) granulated sugar

2 tablespoons light corn syrup

1 teaspoon vanilla bean paste

pinch salt

½ teaspoon orange extract

Make the meringue:

Preheat the oven to 225°F (107°C). Line two half sheet pans with parchment paper.

Transfer the egg whites to the bowl of a stand mixer fitted with the whisk attachment. Whisk on high until just foamy and add the salt, vinegar, and vanilla bean paste. (The vinegar acts as a protein stabilizer, helping to maintain the integrity of the protein networks and prevent overmixing.)

With the mixer on high, add the superfine sugar a scant tablespoon at a time, letting it trickle in slowly (I count to ten). This is crucial; you must ensure that the superfine sugar completely melts into the meringue (the friction of the whisking causes the sugar to melt). If the sugar isn't properly integrated and melted into the egg white mixture, your meringue will break and begin to weep while baking.

Beat the egg whites and sugar until *very* stiff, white, and glossy.

Place half of the meringue in a clean bowl, leaving the remaining half in the mixing bowl. Place the orange extract and orange food coloring (if using) into the mixing bowl and whisk on high until fully incorporated.

Baryshnikov Tartlets

My Big Fat Creamsicle Meringue Moment

Lemon-Rosemary-Blackberry Vacherins

Carefully transfer the plain meringue to a pastry bag fitted with a large star tip, working the meringue into the bag so it fills up only one side (you don't have to be perfect). Spoon the orange meringue into the other side of the pastry bag. On the prepared pans, pipe the meringue into rosettes, starting in the center and carefully spiraling out until you've created a 3-inch (7.5-cm) rosette.

Bake for 2 hours, or until the exterior is crisp and sounds hollow when you tap the underside. You can store the meringues in an airtight, moisture-free container for up to 2 weeks.

Make the filling:

In the heatproof bowl of a stand mixer, combine the egg whites, granulated sugar, corn syrup, vanilla bean paste, salt, orange extract, and ¼ cup (60 ml) water. Place the bowl over a saucepan of simmering water and whisk constantly until the temperature of the mixture reaches 180°F (82°C).

Transfer the bowl to a stand mixer fitted with the whisk attachment and whisk the mixture until you achieve very stiff, white, glossy peaks.

To assemble:

Pipe a silver dollar–size dollop of the filling onto the flat side of a meringue rosette and sandwich with a second meringue. Serve the assembled meringue tarts immediately.

OPTIONS!

FLAVOR! Meringue is beautifully adaptable to flavors. You can replace the vanilla bean paste with lemon extract or orange extract for a citrus spike; however, you *cannot* use oil-based flavors: The oil will deflate the meringue. You can also add a few tablespoons of fruit purée for both a flavor punch and a color splash. Or fold in 2 tablespoons Dutch-process cocoa powder once the meringue has reached the stiff-peak stage.

COLOR! For stripes of color on your meringues, dip a very small pastry brush in the food color of your choice and paint the inside of the pastry bag with stripes, starting as close to the tip as possible and continuing up the sides. Continue replenishing the color on your brush every few strokes. If you want uniform color, simply add 2 to 3 drops of color to the egg whites before you start whisking and adding the sugar.

A NOTE FROM THE SWEET TALKER: Is it meringue or the European Union? The European Union or meringue? You'd be hard pressed to guess which one when you read that there can be a French, a Swiss, or an Italian meringue. The country of origin refers not to an egg white's birthplace but to the manner in which the sugar is integrated into the fluffy stuff. A French, or dry, meringue is one made by simply adding sugar in a steady stream to egg whites as they are beaten. It's tasty, sweet, and billowy, but not the most stable of meringues. A Swiss meringue is made by combining the egg whites and sugar from the beginning and whisking the two in a bain marie (a metal bowl placed over a saucepan half filled with gently simmering water) until the sugar has completely melted and the temperature of the mixture reaches at least 160°F (72°C), the point at which any lingering bacteria will be exterminated. The mixture is then whisked until stiff and glossy. Italian meringue is made by combining the sugar with a small measure of water and warming the two in a saucepan until the sugar melts and the sugar reaches the soft-ball stage (234°F to 240°F / 112°C to 116°C) on a candy thermometer. The sugar syrup is then slowly poured into the beating egg whites and whisked on high until stiff, white, glossy peaks form. Italian is thought to be the most stable of all meringues; it is luscious and very smooth.

NUSSBUSERLN TORTE

NUT-KISS CAKE

Makes 1 (10-inch / 25-cm) cake

LEAVE IT TO THE AUSTRIANS to invent a delectable dessert at a health resort. In the town of Bad Ischl, you could take in the healing baths and snack on crispy meringue kisses simultaneously. That's my kind of medicine. Traditionally, the meringue batter is dropped in little mounds and baked. But I make this into a splendid little mouthful that is more torte than cookie. It features a luscious dark-chocolate bottom layer studded with walnuts and a pointy *Nussbuserln* meringue for the top, sandwiching a slather of fudgy ganache—a mini cake that's visually delightful, sinfully decadent, and gluten-free.

FOR THE *NUSSBUSERLN*:

1 cup (100 g) finely ground walnuts

¼ cup (30 g) cornstarch

4 egg whites, at room temperature

1 teaspoon vanilla bean paste

¼ teaspoon salt

½ teaspoon instant espresso powder

1⅓ cups (265 g) superfine sugar

FOR THE CHOCOLATE-WALNUT LAYERS:

12 ounces (340 g) bittersweet chocolate, finely chopped (I use Callebaut 60/40)

½ cup (115 g) unsalted butter

¾ cup (65 g) Dutch-process cocoa powder (I use Valrhona)

1 tablespoon vanilla bean paste

5 egg whites

1 teaspoon salt

1½ cups (300 g) granulated sugar

1½ cups (150 g) confectioners' sugar

3 cups (300 g) chopped walnuts, divided

¼ cup (30 g) cornstarch

FOR THE FILLING:

12 ounces (340 g) bittersweet chocolate, finely chopped (I use Callebaut 60/40)

8 egg yolks

1 tablespoon pure vanilla extract

pinch salt

½ cup (120 ml) strong coffee, boiling

1 cup (230 g) unsalted butter, cut into small pieces, at room temperature

Make the Nussbuserln:

Preheat the oven to 250°F (120°C). Line two half sheet pans with parchment paper.

Spread the ground walnuts in an even layer on one of the prepared sheet pans and "toast" in the oven for 15 minutes. Allow to cool completely and transfer to a bowl. Stir in the cornstarch to coat completely. Flip the parchment over to use for baking the meringues.

Combine the egg whites, vanilla bean paste, salt, and instant espresso powder in the bowl of a stand mixer fitted with the whisk attachment. Beat on high until foamy.

Very slowly add the superfine sugar, so that the granules are poured into the beating egg whites in a very slow trickle. This should take a few minutes. Beat until you achieve very stiff peaks.

Gently fold the cornstarch-coated walnuts into the mixture.

Transfer the meringue to a large pastry bag fitted with a large open tip.

Nussbuserln Torte

*Coffee-Hazelnut
Meringue Tartlets*

*Lone-Star
Gesine Torte*

On the first piece of parchment, trace two 10-inch (25-cm) circles on one side and flip the parchment over, so the circles are visible but will not transfer onto the meringue. Starting at the center and spiraling outward, pipe meringue layers to fill the circles.

On the second piece of parchment, pipe the remaining meringue into "nut kisses" 1 inch (2.5 cm) apart. For each kiss, gently press to create a quarter-size round base, then pull up as you stop pressing on the bag to create a point. You should have a few dozen kisses.

Bake the meringue kisses for 30 minutes and the 10-inch (25-cm) discs for 1 hour. Turn off the oven, open the oven door and allow the meringues to sit in the cooling oven until they are completely cool.

Make the chocolate-walnut layers:

Preheat the oven to 350°F (175°C). Prepare two 10-inch (25-cm) round cake pans by lining the bottom of each with a round of parchment paper. (Do not use nonstick cooking spray.)

In a heatproof bowl set over a saucepan of simmering water, combine the chocolate and butter (the bottom of the bowl should not touch the water). Stir until melted.

Remove from the heat and stir in the cocoa powder and vanilla bean paste until completely combined.

In the bowl of a stand mixer fitted with the whisk attachment, combine the egg whites and salt and whisk on high speed. Slowly add the granulated sugar until the mixture becomes light and doubles in volume, about 5 minutes. Slowly fold the chocolate mixture into the egg whites with a large rubber spatula and continue folding until completely combined.

In the bowl of a food processor, combine the confectioners' sugar, 2 cups (200 g) of the walnuts, and the cornstarch and pulse until fine.

Fold the walnut mixture into the egg mixture until evenly distributed, then fold in the remaining walnuts.

Divide the batter evenly between the two prepared pans. Bake for 30 minutes, or until the cake springs back when gently touched. Allow to cool completely. Run a sharp paring knife along the side of the cake pan to release the cake.

Make the filling:

Place the chocolate, egg yolks, vanilla, and salt in a food processor fitted with the blade attachment. Pulse to just combine.

Pulsing continuously, add the boiling coffee in a slow stream.

Add the butter, a bit at a time, and continue pulsing until all the butter is added and the mixture is completely smooth.

To assemble:

Place a chocolate-walnut layer on a cake board or platter. Spread one-quarter of the filling in an even layer over the cake. Place the 10-inch (25-cm) meringue layer on top of the filling. Place one-quarter of the remaining filling on top of the meringue, then top with the remaining cake layer. Spread one-quarter of the remaining filling in an even layer over the top, set the last meringue layer on top of the filling, then spread the remaining filling over the meringue.

Arrange the nut kisses on top of the cake. Serve immediately, or cover with plastic wrap and refrigerate for up to 2 days before serving.

OPTIONS!

NUTS! You can mix it up and use pecans or pistachios instead of walnuts. Steer toward nuts that bring flavor and texture to the mix. If you're feeling adventurous, invite dried fruit or chocolate chips to the party. A pistachio, cranberry, and white chocolate meringue sounds like a fabulous mouthful to me!

CRUSH IT! If you find yourself with leftover meringues, whether plain or with nuts, you can break them into pieces and fold them into lightly sweetened whipped cream as a lovely filling with a bit of texture. Don't let the meringues sit around for long, though; they will get soggy.

A NOTE FROM THE SWEET TALKER: A plain meringue—one made with egg whites and sugar— is naturally fat free! YAY! But it's not calorie free. Not by a long shot. As you may have noticed, meringue requires an insane amount of sugar to come together properly. So you might say to yourself, "Why don't I just swap in a sugar substitute? Now it'll be fat free *and* sugar free!" Not so fast. Not all substitutes are legit when it comes to baking. In addition to its particular flavor and cooking properties, sugar also imparts bulk and flavor to a baked product, something that baked goods made with artificial sweeteners will lack.

Aspartame is heat sensitive and a disaster when it comes to baking. Stevia is a natural sweetener, but in large quantities it imparts a taste that can only be described as "shrubbery-esque." Splenda is a suitable substitute in many baking applications; it works best for sweetening dense and naturally sweet products like fruit fillings and sauces in muffins and pies. However, where a high volume of sugar provides bulk to the pastry, such as in sponge or butter cakes, cutting in a small percentage of Splenda with the granulated sugar is best. In recipes where the amount of sugar is very high, as in soufflés or angel food cakes, only a small amount of Splenda should be substituted, with the bulk remaining granulated sugar. For meringue, sticking to granulated sugar alone is your best bet. With other baked goods, if you feel the need to substitute, use Splenda, and don't do it full-scale: Cut the sugar back just a little, to a proportion of two-thirds sugar and one-third artificial sweetener.

MANDELKRÄNZCHEN
ALMOND WREATHS

Makes 14 wreaths

MY MOTHER'S ALL-TIME FAVORITE PASTRY was a *Mandelhörnchen*, a horn-shaped, marzipan-rich confection that's both delightfully crisp and wonderfully chewy. She loved them to such an extent that she'd have my grandmother ship them in bulk from Germany and would freeze them for safekeeping, dipping into her stash whenever the craving struck her. Considering the glory of those half moons of almondy splendor as a kid, I never understood why bakers couldn't just complete the orb and double the goodness. So I've filled the void and brought this glorious little cake "full circle."

1 pound (455 g) almond paste
¾ cup (150 g) granulated sugar, divided
1 teaspoon vanilla extract
½ teaspoon salt
4 egg whites, divided, plus 1 egg white set aside for finishing
½ cup (70 g) all-purpose flour
2 cups (180 g) sliced almonds, with skins on

Line two half sheet pans with parchment paper and set aside. On each piece of parchment, draw seven (4-inch / 10-cm) circles evenly spaced 2 inches (5 cm) apart. Flip the parchment over so you can still see the outline of the circles.

In the bowl of a stand mixer fitted with the paddle attachment, combine the almond paste, ¼ cup (50 g) of the granulated sugar, the vanilla, and the salt. Slowly add 2 of the egg whites, until a thick, sticky, pastelike dough forms. (An alternative is to mix the almond paste and sugar in a food processor fitted with the blade attachment and add the egg whites with the food processor running.)

In the clean bowl of a stand mixer, now fitted with the whisk attachment, whisk 2 of the remaining egg whites on high speed until foamy. With the mixer running, add ¼ cup (50 g) of the remaining sugar in a slow, steady stream. Continue whisking until the meringue is stiff, white, and glossy. Do not overwhip to the point of dryness.

Transfer one-third of the meringue to the almond-paste mixture. Stir until the mixture has lightened. Add the remaining meringue to the bowl and gently fold into the mixture.

Sift the flour over the mixture and continue folding until completely integrated.

Transfer the mixture to a pastry bag fitted with a large open pastry tip. Pipe 4-inch (10-cm) circles onto the prepared pan.

Using a pastry brush, cover each circle with some of the remaining egg white, reserving enough of the egg white for an additional brushing. Overlap the almond slices all along the top and sides of each circle. Brush the almond slices gently with egg white and sprinkle with the remaining sugar.

Allow the Kränzchen to sit uncovered at room temperature for 3 hours to dry out (this creates a crisp exterior during baking).

Bake at 325°F (165°C) for 25 minutes, or until golden brown. Allow to cool completely.

Store in an airtight container for up to 1 week, or freeze in an airtight container for up to 1 month.

Blood Orange and Lingonberry Bombe

Mandelkränzchen

WHISKING WHITES

I'm sure you've heard it emphatically stated that when whisking egg whites, you should always start with a very clean bowl and a very clean whisk. The reason for this might not be clear to you, though.

The science behind the miracle of the egg white is its composition. An egg white is composed of 90 percent water and 10 percent protein. It's the protein that creates a stable network of bubbles. If you whisk a cup of plain water, you'll notice it might get foamy from the agitation but the bubbles soon subside. With an egg white, the proteins form bonds with one another and ensure that the bubbles stay "alive" to transform into a meringue. When you bake a meringue, the heat causes the protein ovalbumin to stiffen, essentially solidifying the cloud of lovely sweet bubbles into crunchy-chewy perfection. If, however, even a small amount of fat is accidentally introduced into the mixture, such as a bit of egg yolk or a stray bit of oil clinging to your bowl, the fat will deflate the delicate protein structures and undo all of your hard work.

So now that you've made sure that your baking instruments are very clean and ready to accept egg whites, check the weather. Is it humid? Is it raining? If your answer is yes to either question, close shop until it's nice and dry outside. Humidity is meringue's second-worst enemy and takes great pleasure in deflating all your work.

So heed the warning: Always use sparkling-clean bowls and utensils when making a meringue . . . and never use a plastic bowl. Plastic traps fats and all manner of cooking debris, no matter how well you scrub it. And I'm convinced that as plastic is a petroleum—that is, oil—product itself, it will mess with your meringue no matter how clean you get it, therefore your plastic-bound meringue is doomed to fail. And never bake meringue on a soggy day. You'll thank me later.

GRAND MARNIER SOUFFLÉ
WITH BITTERSWEET CRÈME ANGLAISE

Makes 8 individual soufflés

MY FIRST SOUFFLÉ was at a celebratory birthday dinner for my mom's "twenty-ninth" birthday. If you do the math, you'll find that it would have been physically impossible for me to have been present at that occasion. My mother, however, staunchly refused to reveal her age, and all birthdays subsequent to her twenty-ninth were celebrated as . . . her twenty-ninth. This particular dinner must have marked a momentous year (I'm guessing her fiftieth, but my mom would never tell) because we went to an extravagant French restaurant just outside of Washington, D.C., and to my utter delight and approval, we ordered dessert first! I would later realize that this is standard operating procedure for ordering soufflé, but at the time, it was a revelation—and a confirmation of my deeply held belief that dessert was the most important element of every meal. And the fact that it was laced with Grand Marnier made the experience that much more noteworthy.

FOR THE SOUFFLÉ:
½ cup (115 g) unsalted butter, plus extra for buttering the ramekins
1 cup (200 g) sugar, plus 8 tablespoons to coat the ramekins
⅓ cup (40 g) all-purpose flour
1 cup (240 ml) whole milk
7 egg yolks
½ teaspoon vanilla bean paste
½ teaspoon orange extract
½ teaspoon orange zest
pinch salt
2 tablespoons Grand Marnier
8 egg whites

FOR THE CHOCOLATE CRÈME ANGLAISE:
1 cup (240 ml) half-and-half
4 egg yolks
¼ cup (50 g) granulated sugar

1 teaspoon vanilla bean paste
pinch salt
1½ ounces (45 g) bittersweet chocolate, chopped

Make the soufflé:

Preheat the oven to 400°F (205°C). Smear butter onto the sides and bottoms of eight 1-cup / 240-ml (3½-by-2-inch / 9-by-5-cm) ramekins. Add 1 tablespoon sugar to each ramekin and swirl the ramekin to coat the bottom and sides completely. Turn each ramekin upside down and tap gently to remove any excess sugar.

In a large saucepan, heat the ½ cup (115 g) of butter over low heat until melted. Whisk in the flour. Continue whisking until the mixture is smooth and slightly thickened. Add the milk, raise the heat to medium, and continue whisking until the mixture is very thick and starts to pull away from the sides of the pan.

Transfer the mixture to a large mixing bowl. Set aside to cool for a few minutes.

In a separate bowl, whisk together the egg yolks, vanilla bean paste, orange extract, orange zest, and salt. Whisk in the milk mixture and Grand Marnier until smooth.

In the bowl of a stand mixer fitted with the whisk attachment, beat the egg whites on high speed until just foamy. Slowly add the 1 cup (200 g) sugar in a steady stream and beat the meringue until it just holds stiff, glossy peaks. Stir one-quarter of the meringue into the yolk mixture to lighten it. With a large rubber spatula, gently fold the remaining meringue into the mixture until no white streaks remain.

Spoon the batter into the ramekins, filling them just to their rims. Use a small offset spatula to level the tops. Place the ramekins a few inches apart in a large restaurant pan or glass baking dish and add enough hot water to the pan to reach halfway up the sides of the ramekins. Bake the soufflés in the middle of the oven for 20 minutes, or until they are puffed and their tops are golden.

Make the crème anglaise:

In a large saucepan, bring the half-and-half to a simmer.

While the half-and-half heats, in the bowl of a stand mixer fitted with the whisk attachment, combine the egg yolks, granulated sugar, vanilla bean paste, and salt. Beat the mixture on medium-low speed until it lightens and thickens.

With the mixer running, slowly pour the hot cream mixture into the whisking yolks, carefully pouring it down the sides of the bowl to prevent the hot liquid from scrambling the yolks. Continue whisking until all the ingredients are combined.

Transfer the mixture back to the saucepan and whisk over medium-low heat until the mixture thickens and coats the back of a spoon. Remove from the heat and add the chocolate. Allow the chocolate to sit undisturbed for a few minutes, then whisk to fully incorporate. Transfer the cream to a small metal bowl and cover with plastic wrap. Place over a pot of hot water that's just been taken off a simmer to keep warm.

When the soufflés are done, immediately transfer the ramekins to dessert plates. Using two forks, pull open the center of each soufflé and pour some crème anglaise into the opening. Serve immediately.

LEMON-ROSEMARY-BLACKBERRY VACHERINS

Makes 6 individual cakes

A *VACHERIN IS A FROZEN CAKE*, but I'll be honest with you: It's really just an extravagant ice-cream sandwich. Instead of two cardboardy rectangles of chocolate wafer sandwiching anemic vanilla ice cream, this is a chewy nut meringue cradling luxurious tart frozen yogurt. Of course you can mix and match flavors to your taste, but you'll fall in love with the wonderful interplay of these textures. The combination of lemon and rosemary is perfect for a summer treat.

FOR THE FROZEN YOGURT:

2 cups (500 g) Greek-style yogurt

1 cup (250 g) crème fraîche

1 cup (240 ml) lemon simple syrup (¾ cup / 180 ml lemon
    juice and ¾ cup / 150 g sugar simmered together until the
    sugar is dissolved)

½ cup (120 ml) heavy cream

¼ cup (60 ml) whole milk

½ cup (100 g) granulated sugar

zest of 3 lemons

¼ cup (60 ml) fresh lemon juice

FOR THE MERINGUE:

1 cup (140 g) almond flour

1 cup (200 g) granulated sugar, divided

1 tablespoon cornstarch

¼ teaspoon finely minced fresh rosemary

4 egg whites

1 teaspoon almond extract

2 drops yellow food coloring

½ teaspoon salt

FOR THE ASSEMBLY:

1 pint (250 g) blackberries

6 sprigs fresh rosemary

Make the frozen yogurt:

In a mixing bowl, whisk together the yogurt, crème fraîche, and lemon simple syrup. Cover with plastic wrap and refrigerate.

In a large saucepan, combine the cream, milk, sugar, lemon zest, and lemon juice and stir over medium heat until the sugar has completely dissolved. Pour the mixture through a fine-mesh sieve into the yogurt mixture and stir to combine completely. Cover the bowl with plastic wrap again and refrigerate until completely cool.

Process the yogurt in an ice cream maker according to the manufacturer's instructions and freeze for at least 2 hours or overnight.

Make the meringue:

Preheat the oven to 275°F (135°C). Line two half sheet pans with parchment paper. Draw six (4-inch / 10-cm) circles, evenly spaced a few inches apart, on each piece of parchment. Flip the parchment over, so the circles are visible but will not transfer onto the meringue.

Place the almond flour, 2 tablespoons of the granulated sugar, the cornstarch, and the rosemary in the bowl of a food processor fitted with the blade attachment. Pulse just until the ingredients are combined and powdery. (Do not overprocess—the mixture should not become a paste.)

In the bowl of a stand mixer fitted with the whisk attachment, combine the egg whites, almond extract, food coloring, and salt. Whisk on high speed until the egg whites become foamy. Slowly pour in ¾ cup (150 g) of the sugar and continue whisking until stiff, glossy peaks just begin to form. (Be very careful not to overmix—the meringue should not look dry or chunky; it must be very smooth to be properly integrated into the almond flour mixture.)

Sift the almond flour mixture over the meringue. Using a large rubber spatula, gently fold into the meringue until no white streaks remain but the meringue still holds its shape. Transfer the meringue to a pastry bag fitted with a medium open tip.

Starting in the middle of one of the circles drawn on the parchment, pipe the meringue in a continuous spiral until you reach the edge of the circle. Repeat the piping procedure with the remaining circles. Place a little dab of leftover meringue under each corner of each piece of parchment paper to secure the paper to the pan (otherwise it will curl up and attach itself to the meringue).

Bake for 30 to 40 minutes, until the meringue is firm to the touch. Do not allow it to brown. Set aside to cool completely, then gently peel off the parchment.

To assemble:

Place 4 blackberries on 6 of the meringue discs on their side.

Allow the frozen yogurt to sit in the refrigerator for 10 minutes to soften a bit. Scoop about ¼ cup (60 g) of softened frozen yogurt onto the flat side of a meringue and on top of the blackberries. Sandwich with the flat side of a second meringue, pressing gently to adhere but being careful not to break the meringues in the process. Place the assembled *vacherins* on a sheet pan and freeze for 20 minutes before serving. The *vacherins* will keep in the freezer, individually wrapped in plastic, for up to 1 month.

To serve, allow the *vacherins* to thaw ever so slightly, about 10 minutes, and top with a sprig of rosemary.

A NOTE FROM THE SWEET TALKER: Adding sugar slowly to a dry (i.e., French) meringue: Why bother? Must it really take *minutes* to add all that sugar? Yes. Add the sugar too quickly and it doesn't have time to "melt" properly into the meringue, which will leave intact sugar crystals suspended in the egg whites. This weakens the bond between the egg whites and the sugar and leads to fissures in the finished product. The unmelted sugar crystals react to the heat of the oven by attracting moisture to themselves (so selfish). Where the moisture meets the unmelted sugar crystals, the meringue will start "weeping." Essentially your meringue will crack and molten sugar will start leaking out. Not pretty. So take your time when you're instructed to, and you'll be thrilled with the sweet result.

SALZBURGER NOCKERL MIT PALATSCHINKEN
SALZBURGER SOUFFLÉ WITH CRÊPES

Makes 10 servings

A *SALZBURGER NOCKERL* IS actually a very simple souf-flé with a dose of preserves, but it appears as a complex mountain of confectionary beauty. Originally it con-sisted of choux paste (the stuff you use to make cream puff and éclair shells) poached in warm milk, and somewhere along the way morphed into a fluffy soufflé. I know—dessert evolution rarely makes sense. In its natural state today, it's delicious. But add a little struc-ture to the bottom of the baking dish in the form of *Preiselbeern Palatschinken* (Austrian-style crêpes layered with lingonberry preserves) and the venerable dessert is transformed into a smooth, creamy, crunchy masterpiece (if I do say so myself).

FOR THE CRÊPES:
1½ cups (360 ml) whole milk

3 eggs

3 tablespoons granulated sugar, divided

¼ teaspoon salt

1½ cups (185 g) all-purpose flour

½ cup (120 ml) sparkling water, such as Perrier or Pellegrino

4 tablespoons (55 g) unsalted butter, softened, divided, plus 1 tablespoon to coat the baking dish

½ cup (120 ml) lingonberry preserves

FOR THE *NOCKERL*:
4 egg whites, at room temperature

½ teaspoon salt

6 tablespoons (75 g) granulated sugar

½ cup (120 ml) half-and-half

4 ounces (115 g) almond paste

6 egg yolks, at room temperature

2 tablespoons all-purpose flour

1 teaspoon vanilla bean paste

FOR THE FINISH:
¼ cup (25 g) confectioners' sugar

Make the crêpes:

In a large bowl, whisk together the milk, eggs, 1 table-spoon of the granulated sugar, and the salt. Sift the flour over the milk mixture and whisk until just combined. Cover with plastic wrap and refrigerate for 2 hours. Refrigerat-ing the batter allows the gluten to relax and the flour to hydrate, so don't skimp on the time.

Remove the batter from the refrigerator and stir in the sparkling water. (The bubbles help aerate the batter.)

Add ½ tablespoon of the butter to an 8-inch (20-cm) skil-let or nonstick crêpe pan and warm over medium heat to gently coat the pan. Pour ¼ cup (60 ml) of the batter into the skillet and swirl to coat the bottom of the pan in a thin, even layer. Cover the pan and cook over medium-low heat for about 1 minute, just until the crêpe is cooked through. (Placing a lid over the pan gently steams the top of the crêpe, allowing it to cook through without you hav-ing to flip it. It also keeps the crêpe very tender.) Transfer the crêpe to a platter lined with parchment paper.

Continue cooking crêpes and transferring them to the platter, placing a small piece of parchment in between the crêpes to keep them from adhering to one another. Add more butter to the pan as needed to keep the crêpes from sticking.

Coat a 2-quart (2-L) round enamel baking dish with 1 tablespoon butter and sprinkle with the remaining sugar, tipping the dish from side to side to coat the bottom and

sides of the dish evenly with the sugar; invert the dish and gently tap it to remove any sugar that's not clinging to the dish. Line the bottom of the dish with 4 crêpes, over-lapping to ensure the entire base is covered. Spread the preserves over the layer of crêpes and arrange another 4 crêpes to cover the lingonberry layer. Set aside.

Make the Nockerl:

Preheat the oven to 425°F (220°C).

In the bowl of a stand mixer fitted with the whisk attach-ment, combine the egg whites and salt and beat until the whites become foamy. Slowly pour the granulated sugar into the whites and whisk until stiff, glossy peaks form. Transfer the mixture to a clean mixing bowl. (You needn't clean the stand mixer bowl after transferring; it will be reused later, but a little stray meringue won't hurt the batter.)

Pour the half-and-half into the crêpe-lined baking dish and bake for 3 minutes.

In the meantime, break up the almond paste and place it in the stand mixer bowl. Fit the mixer with the paddle attachment. Add the egg yolks, flour, and vanilla bean paste and beat until a soft paste forms. Add one-third of the beaten egg whites and mix to lighten the batter. Using a large rubber spatula, add the remaining egg whites and gently fold into the batter.

Remove the baking dish from the oven. Mound the meringue batter atop the half-and-half. Bake for 40 to 50 minutes, or until the mounds are golden brown and a toothpick inserted into the center of the meringue comes out clean.

To finish:

Sift confectioners' sugar over the meringue and serve immediately.

BARYSHNIKOV TARTLETS

Makes 4 tartlets

A TRADITIONAL PAVLOVA IS a free-form meringue tart, smeared on a baking sheet to form an ersatz bowl meant to hold fillings. The ultimate gluten-free pie! Once it's baked, the meringue is slathered with whipped cream and topped with fruit. In the spirit of order (and parsimony), I prefer to pipe the meringue into small, tight circles and sandwich these tartlets with a lightly sweetened Greek yogurt. I've taken the liberty of naming this new iteration of a venerable confection for my favorite tiny dancer and girlhood crush, Mikhail Baryshnikov. He destroyed my dreams of becoming a professional ballerina when I saw him in person, as I realized that at twelve I already towered over him. This confirmed my suspicion that a tall, knock-kneed, uncoordinated preteen might not make the most elegant dance partner. The presentation here, however, is entirely up to you.

FOR THE MERINGUES:

5 egg whites

1 teaspoon vinegar

pinch salt

1 cup (200 g) granulated sugar

2 teaspoons cornstarch

1 teaspoon vanilla bean paste

FOR THE FILLING:

1 cup (250 g) Greek-style yogurt

1 tablespoon honey

FOR THE ASSEMBLY:

1 pint (250 g) raspberries, cherries, or blackberries

Make the meringues:

Preheat the oven to 225°F (107°C). Line two half sheet pans with parchment paper. Draw six (4-inch / 10-cm) circles, evenly spaced a few inches apart, on each piece of parchment. Flip the parchment over, so the circles are visible but will not transfer onto the meringue.

In the bowl of a stand mixer fitted with the whisk attachment, whisk the egg whites, vinegar, and salt until foamy. In a small bowl, stir together the granulated sugar and cornstarch. With the mixer running on medium-high speed, slowly pour the sugar mixture into the egg whites (this should take a few minutes; be patient). Raise the mixer speed to high and continue to whisk until stiff peaks form. (Be very careful not to overbeat the meringue to the point of dryness.) Transfer the meringue to a large pastry bag fitted with a large open star tip.

Starting in the middle of one of the circles drawn on the parchment, pipe the meringue in a continuous spiral until you reach the edge of the circle. Repeat the piping with the remaining circles. Place a little dab of leftover meringue under each corner of each piece of parchment to secure the paper to the pan (otherwise it will curl up and attach itself to the meringue). Bake for 45 to 50 minutes, until the meringues feel dry. Do not allow them to brown.

Make the filling:

Drain the yogurt in a fine-mesh sieve lined with cheesecloth to remove any excess water. Transfer the yogurt to a bowl, mix well with the honey, and chill for 30 minutes.

To assemble:

Top 4 of the meringue discs with 4 or 5 berries, then spoon 3 tablespoons of the yogurt on top of the raspberries. Top with another disc of meringue. Pipe a small dollop of yogurt onto the center of the top disc and top with fresh berries. Serve immediately.

CHOCOLATE AND SALTED GINGER CARAMEL MERINGUE WHOOPIES

Makes 12 meringues

THIS IS ONE OF THE yummiest little treats to ever grace my pie hole. It's soft, chewy, slightly crisp, and utterly delicious. It manages to be delicate yet with the punch of the gooiest, sloppiest childish treat. You'd never know how outrageously decadent this is until you start chewing on the deep chocolate-caramel ooze. Just when you think you've sunk into a sugar coma, the ginger gives you a fantastic kick in the pants, allowing you to continue noshing away. And then you'll moan like a crazed, sugar-addled nitwit, advertising to anyone nearby that there is something out-of-this-world to be had.

FOR THE MERINGUE SHELLS:

1½ cups (150 g) confectioners' sugar

1½ cups (125 g) Dutch-process cocoa powder (I use Callebaut/
    Cacao Barry Extra Brute or Valrhona Gastronomique), plus
    ¼ cup (20 g) for dusting

1 tablespoon powdered egg white

1⅓ cups (265 g) granulated sugar

1 squirt fresh lemon juice

6 aged egg whites (see Sidebar, page 46)

1 teaspoon salt

¼ cup (60 ml) strong coffee, at room temperature

FOR THE GANACHE:

8 ounces (225 g) bittersweet chocolate, finely chopped

½ cup (120 ml) heavy cream

2 tablespoons unsalted butter

FOR THE CARAMEL:

2 cups (400 g) granulated sugar

½ teaspoon salt

1 squirt fresh lemon juice

1 cup (240 ml) heavy cream, divided

2 tablespoons unsalted butter

FOR THE ASSEMBLY:

¼ cup (35 g) finely chopped crystallized ginger

⅛ cup (10 g) Dutch-process cocoa powder

Make the meringue shells:

Preheat the oven to 325°F (165°C). Line four half sheet pans with parchment. Using a 3-inch (7.5-cm) round, draw six circles on each piece of parchment, spacing them a few inches apart. Flip the parchment over, so the circles are visible but won't transfer onto the meringue. Set aside.

In a large metal mixing bowl, whisk together the confectioners' sugar, cocoa powder, and egg white powder, then sift them together into another large mixing bowl. Set aside.

In a heavy saucepan, combine the granulated sugar, 6 tablespoons (90 ml) water, and the lemon juice, stirring over medium-low heat until the sugar has completely melted. Wipe down the sides of the saucepan with a damp pastry brush to remove any clinging sugar granules. (If left, they could jump back into the sugar and cause your syrup to crystallize.) Attach a candy thermometer to the side of the saucepan and increase the heat to medium-high. Heat until the sugar syrup reaches 240°F (116°C).

Meanwhile, place the egg whites and salt in the bowl of a stand mixer fitted with the whisk attachment. Whisk until the egg whites are foamy and light but not stiff.

When the sugar has reached temperature, decrease the mixer speed to medium and carefully pour the hot sugar syrup down the side of the bowl into the whisking egg whites. Once all of the syrup has been added, increase the

*Raspberry and
White Chocolate
Ganache Macarons*

*Chocolate and Salted
Ginger Caramel
Meringue Whoopies*

speed to high and whisk until stiff white peaks form, but not so stiff that the meringue is dry. The meringue should hold its shape well.

Transfer one-third of the egg white mixture and the coffee to the bowl containing the cocoa mixture. Using a large rubber spatula, stir the meringue into the cocoa mixture until a stiff paste forms. Add the remaining egg whites and gently fold them into the mixture until there are no white streaks remaining. Transfer the meringue to a large pastry bag fitted with a large open tip.

Using the circles on the parchment paper as guides, pipe 3-inch (7.5-cm) discs onto the parchment. Gently but firmly tap the sheet pan on your work surface three or four times to release any air pockets. Place a little dab of leftover meringue under each corner of each piece of parchment paper to secure the paper to the pan (other-wise it will curl up and attach itself to the meringue). Dust with the cocoa powder.

Bake for 25 to 30 minutes, until the meringues crack and are dry on the bottom. Allow the meringues to cool completely.

Make the ganache:

Place the chocolate in a medium-size heatproof bowl.

Place the cream and butter in a heavy saucepan and bring to a simmer, stirring occasionally. When the butter has completely melted, pour the hot cream mixture over the chocolate and let it sit undisturbed for a few minutes. Once the chocolate has melted, whisk the ganache until smooth and emulsified. Allow to cool until the ganache reaches room temperature but is still spreadable.

Make the caramel:

In a large, heavy saucepan, combine the granulated sugar with ½ cup (120 ml) water, the salt, and lemon juice. Stir

over medium-low heat until the sugar has completely melted. With a damp pastry brush, wipe down the sides of the saucepan to remove any clinging sugar crystals. Increase the heat to medium-high and cook the sugar syrup until the caramel turns a medium amber color. Immediately remove from the heat and add 1 cup (240 ml) of the cream and the butter. Be careful—the mixture will bubble vigorously. Once the bubbling has subsided, stir the mixture until the cream and butter are completely integrated. Pour the mixture into a large heatproof bowl and cover with plastic wrap. Set the caramel aside to cool to room temperature.

To assemble:

Spread a heaping tablespoon of ganache onto half of the meringue shells. Sprinkle the chopped ginger atop the ganache.

Divide the caramel evenly atop the ginger on each shell. Place a second shell atop the caramel. Serve immediately.

OPTIONS!

This little tart shell is equally wonderful filled with vanilla pastry cream and topped with raspberries. Or fill it to the rim with orange-infused chocolate ganache. Feel free to make the shells and freeze them, unfilled, in an airtight container for up to 1 month.

THE UNITED NATIONS OF MERINGUE

Meringue, macaron, *vacherin*, dacquoise—what's with all these names? Are they interchangeable? Yes and no. All of them are meringue-based confections: They require the use of egg whites whipped to a frenzy with sugar. A meringue is just egg white and sugar and can be baked all by itself; it can also be piped onto a pie or a Baked Alaska and then lightly browned. A macaron is a meringue-based sandwich cookie, usually made with the addition of almond flour. It is distinguished by its shiny, smooth, and slightly crisp exterior shell and tender middle, and is not to be confused with the American coconut-based "macaroon." The macaron shell must also have what is called a *pied*, or foot—a ruffle that surrounds the edge of the shell. The sandwich can be filled with buttercream, preserves, or ganache. A dacquoise is another nut-infused meringue batter, but it's piped into rounds and can act as the base or the layers of a cake. It is crisper than a macaron and doesn't require a shiny appearance or a *pied*. *Vacherin* describes a specific dessert made of dacquoise rounds and sandwiched ice cream (or in this book, frozen yogurt—see page 30). It may seem confusing now, but you'll get used to the lingo and be an old pro in no time.

BAKED VERMONT

Makes 1 (12-inch / 30.5-cm) dome cake

WHY SHOULD ALASKANS GET ALL the sweet, cold, creamy fun? We've got plenty of snowcapped mountains here in the Lower Forty-Eight, especially in maple syrup country, to warrant a creation of our very own. So why not a "Baked Vermont"? Taking its theme from the dessert named for the forty-ninth state, this beauty features maple-infused meringue encasing a maple-pecan-layered ice cream interior. Baked Alaska was invented by Delmonico's in 1876, to commemorate the acquisition of our northernmost state from the Russians, but I think every state deserves its own delicious version.

FOR THE ICE CREAM (SEE NOTE):
1 cup (100 g) pecans, chopped
3 cups (840 ml) heavy cream
2 cups (480 ml) whole milk
1 cup (240 ml) maple syrup, preferably grade B
1 teaspoon vanilla bean paste
6 egg yolks, at room temperature
¼ teaspoon salt

FOR THE SPONGE CAKE:
1½ cups (210 g) cake flour
½ teaspoon baking powder
6 eggs, separated, at room temperature
½ teaspoon salt
½ teaspoon vinegar
1 cup (220 g) maple sugar, divided
1 teaspoon vanilla bean paste

FOR THE MERINGUE:
4 egg whites, at room temperature
1 cup (220 g) maple sugar
¼ teaspoon cream of tartar
pinch salt

NOTE: For the homemade ice cream, you may substitute 2 pints (900 g) of store-bought maple pecan ice cream that's been slightly softened.

Make the ice cream:

Preheat the oven to 350°F (175°C). Line a sheet pan with parchment paper.

Spread the pecans evenly on the prepared pan and toast for 5 minutes. Set aside to cool completely.

In a large saucepan, combine the cream, milk, maple syrup, and vanilla bean paste and bring to a simmer over medium-low heat.

In the meantime, in the bowl of a stand mixer fitted with the whisk attachment, combine the egg yolks and salt and whisk on high speed until the yolks are pale. Decrease the mixer speed to medium-low, and in a very slow stream, pour the hot cream mixture down the side of the bowl into the beating egg yolks. Continue mixing until all the cream mixture is combined.

Transfer the mixture back to the saucepan, attach a candy thermometer, and whisk constantly over medium heat until the mixture reaches 170°F (77°C). Transfer the custard to a large bowl. Cover with plastic wrap, pressing the plastic directly onto the surface of the custard to prevent a skin from forming. Chill overnight.

Transfer the mixture to an ice cream maker. Follow the manufacturer's instructions to process the ice cream. Stir the pecans into the ice cream and transfer it to the freezer to allow it to firm further, but make sure it remains spreadable.

Make the sponge cake:

Preheat the oven to 350°F (175°C). Line a half sheet pan with parchment paper and spray lightly with nonstick cooking spray.

In a bowl, sift the flour and the baking powder.

In the bowl of a stand mixer fitted with the whisk attachment, combine the egg whites, salt, and vinegar. Whisk just until the whites are foamy. With the mixer running on high speed, slowly add ½ cup (110 g) of the maple sugar, whisking just until the meringue becomes stiff and glossy. Transfer to a clean metal bowl.

In the bowl of the stand mixer (you don't need to clean it; the stray meringue won't harm the proceedings), combine the egg yolks, vanilla bean paste, and the remaining maple sugar. Beat with the whisk attachment on high speed until the mixture thickens and turns a pale yellow.

Sift the flour mixture over the egg yolk mixture. Using a large rubber spatula, gently fold the flour mixture into the yolks.

Transfer one-third of the egg whites to the bowl with the yolks and gently stir to lighten. Add the remainder of the whites; again using a large rubber spatula, gently fold the whites into the batter until no white streaks remain.

Pour the batter into the prepared pan. Using a large offset spatula, gently smooth the batter into an even layer. Bake for approximately 25 minutes, just until the cake starts to pull away from the sides of the pan and gently springs back when you touch it. Allow to cool completely.

Cut a 12-inch (30.5-cm) round and an 8-inch (20-cm) round from the sponge cake. Reserve the remaining pieces of cake.

To assemble the sponge cake and ice cream layers:

Line a medium-size metal bowl (5- to 6-cup / 1.2- to 1.4-liter capacity) with plastic wrap, letting the wrap hang over the sides to help you remove the cake.

Carefully transfer the larger cake round to the bowl and press gently to line the bowl with the cake (it may crack along the way—just make sure there are no large gaps).

Transfer 2½ cups (750 g) of the ice cream into the cake-lined bowl and gently smooth with an offset spatula. Place the smaller cake round on top of the layer of ice cream and press down gently. Place the cake in the freezer for 1 hour to set.

Transfer the remaining ice cream into the bowl, smoothing over the top round with the offset spatula. Place the cake back in the freezer.

Preheat the oven to 250°F (120°C). Line a half sheet pan with parchment paper. Break apart the reserved pieces of sponge cake and spread them evenly on the parchment. Bake for 10 minutes to dry. Set aside to cool completely. Transfer the pieces to the bowl of a food processor fitted with the blade attachment. Pulse until the pieces become fine crumbs.

Remove the cake from the freezer and spread the crumbs evenly over the top layer of ice cream (which will eventually be the bottom!), pressing gently so the crumbs adhere. Freeze the cake until completely set, at least 2 hours or overnight.

Make the meringue:

Place the egg whites, maple sugar, cream of tartar, and salt in the bowl of a stand mixer. Place the bowl over a saucepan of simmering water and whisk constantly until the sugar has completely melted and the mixture reaches at least 160°F (72°C).

Transfer the bowl to the stand mixer fitted with the whisk attachment and beat on high speed until stiff, very glossy peaks form. Transfer the meringue to a pastry bag fitted with a large open tip.

To assemble:

Line a half sheet pan with parchment paper. Remove the cake from the freezer and invert it onto the parchment. Remove the bowl by gently pulling on the overhanging plastic wrap. (If this gives you trouble, gently heat the bowl with a kitchen torch or a blow dryer to release.) Remove the plastic wrap from around the cake.

Pipe the meringue onto the exterior of the sponge cake: Start at the bottom and wind your way around in a continuous rope until the entire cake is covered in a single spiral of meringue. Using a kitchen torch, gently brown the meringue. Alternatively, preheat your broiler to 500°F (260°C), placing the cake back in the freezer during preheating, and broil the cake just until the meringue begins to brown, no more than 2 minutes. Serve immediately.

COFFEE-HAZELNUT MERINGUE TARTLETS

Makes 10 tartlets

ADMIT IT: When the outside world thinks of German beverages, beer is the first thing that comes to mind. But I would submit to you that coffee is as revered a liquid comestible in Germany as the frothy, hops-infused stuff. Match hazelnut with coffee in a dessert and you are creating a splendid homage to that most favored hot beverage. Here, a hazelnut meringue creates a tart shell that holds the filling. The texture of the meringue mellows with the addition of the filling, allowing for just a slight crunch that gives way to a lovely, soft chew once the filling does its work.

FOR THE MERINGUE SHELLS:

1 cup (120 g) finely ground hazelnuts or hazelnut flour

¼ cup (30 g) cornstarch

1 tablespoon very finely ground fresh espresso beans

4 egg whites

1 tablespoon cream of tartar

½ teaspoon salt

1 cup (200 g) superfine sugar

FOR THE FILLING:

6 egg yolks

¼ teaspoon salt

½ cup (100 g) granulated sugar

½ cup (120 ml) very strong coffee

1 cup (240 ml) praline paste (see Sidebar, page 44), or
   1 cup (240 ml) Nutella

1 pound (455 g) unsalted butter, slightly cooler than
   room temperature

FOR THE ASSEMBLY:

1 cup (135 g) whole hazelnuts

Make the meringue shells:

Preheat the oven to 275°F (135°C). Line four half sheet pans with parchment paper. Draw 5 (4-inch / 10-cm)

squares, spaced a few inches apart, on each piece of parchment. Flip the parchment over, so the circles are visible but will not transfer onto the meringue.

In the bowl of a food processor, combine the hazelnuts, cornstarch, and espresso beans and pulse.

In the bowl of a stand mixer fitted with the whisk attachment, add the egg whites, cream of tartar, and salt and whisk until light and frothy. With the mixer running, very slowly add the superfine sugar—this should take more than a minute. Continue whisking until stiff white peaks form.

Fold the nut mixture into the egg white mixture.

Transfer the nut meringue to a large pastry bag fitted with a medium-small open tip. Starting at the outside of the square, pipe a 4-inch (10-cm) square following the outline you've drawn on the parchment. Continue piping smaller and smaller squares until you've filled all the squares on two of the half sheet pans. On the remaining two pans, pipe the meringue along the edges of the circles to make open squares. Pipe 10 small hearts on the empty spots of parchment. Place a little dab of leftover meringue under each corner of each piece of parchment paper to secure the paper to the pan (otherwise it will curl up and attach itself to the meringue).

Bake the squares for 20 to 30 minutes, until they are baked through and dry but not browned. Set aside and allow to cool completely.

Make the filling:

In the bowl of a stand mixer fitted with the whisk attachment, whisk the egg yolks and salt until pale.

Meanwhile, in a heavy saucepan, combine the granulated sugar and coffee and stir over medium-low heat until the sugar has completely dissolved. Attach a candy thermometer to the side of the saucepan and heat until the syrup reaches a temperature of 234°F (113°C).

With the mixer running on medium speed, carefully pour the sugar syrup down the side of the bowl and into the whisking egg yolks. When all of the syrup is added, increase the mixer speed to high and whisk until the mixture has cooled (just touch the bowl to see if it's still warm). Add the praline paste or Nutella and whisk until smooth. Add the butter, 4 tablespoons (55 g) at a time, whisking until the filling achieves a smooth, silken texture.

To assemble:

Transfer the filling to a large pastry bag fitted with a large star tip. Divide the filling evenly among meringue squares. Place the open meringue square on top of the filling and finish with a meringue heart.

A NOTE FROM THE SWEET TALKER: Praline paste is a soft, sweet hazelnut paste not unlike almond paste but *much* softer and often downright runny. It is far more widely available now in the States than ever before. Once you start working with it, you'll become obsessed and want to sneak it into everything from pastry cream to buttercream. If you can't find it alongside the almond paste in the baking aisle of your grocery store, you can easily buy it online. You won't regret it. Be forewarned that the paste will often separate into a liquidy top and a hardened bottom, just as natural peanut butter tends to do. You can stir the two back together, but if that's too difficult, place the entire contents of the can in a food processor and pulse until it's combined and smooth.

RASPBERRY AND WHITE CHOCOLATE GANACHE MACARONS

Makes 8 individual tarts

ONE MAGNIFICENT BIRTHDAY, my husband, Raymond, took me to Paris. As soon as our plane landed, we went straight to Ladurée for dessert. I ordered macarons. "How many?" the waiter asked. "How many can you cram onto a plate?" I replied.

While the small macarons are terribly special there, the larger ones, rimmed with fresh berries, are not to be missed—not only do they give you more macaron per square inch, but the splendor of the berries' jewel tones against the shiny decadence of the macaron shells is a sight to behold. If you don't find yourself in Paris anytime soon, make your own macarons. Just beware: These beauties are famously finicky, responding brattily to small changes in temperature, humidity, and technique. (Hence the necessity for measuring some ingredients by weight, as it is more exact.) It takes a bit of practice and a confident hand to perfect them. But anything this exquisite and delicious deserves a bit of effort.

FOR THE MERINGUE SHELLS:
1½ cups (210 g) almond flour
2 cups (200 g) confectioners' sugar
1 cup (200 g) granulated sugar
5 aged egg whites, divided (see Sidebar, page 46)
pinch salt
3 drops fuchsia food coloring

FOR THE WHITE CHOCOLATE GANACHE:
8 ounces (225 g) white chocolate, finely chopped
½ cup (120 ml) heavy cream
2 tablespoons raspberry purée (I use Boiron, or make my own; see Sidebar, page 48)
1 teaspoon vanilla bean paste

FOR THE ASSEMBLY:
3 to 4 pints (750 g to 1 kg) fresh raspberries

Make the meringue shells:

Preheat the oven to 350°F (175°C).

In a food processor fitted with the blade attachment, combine the almond flour and confectioners' sugar and pulse until very fine. Sift through a very fine-mesh sieve into a large metal mixing bowl.

In a heavy saucepan, combine the granulated sugar and ¼ cup (60 ml) water. Stir over medium heat until the sugar is completely melted. Attach a candy thermometer to the side of the saucepan and heat until the syrup reaches 240°F (116°C).

While the syrup is cooking, in the bowl of a stand mixer fitted with the whisk attachment, combine 3 of the egg whites with the salt and whisk on high speed until the mixture is white and foamy. When the syrup reaches temperature, slowly pour it down the side of the bowl into the whisking egg whites so the syrup doesn't scald the whites. Continue whisking until slightly stiff, shiny white peaks form.

Add the reserved (unwhisked) egg whites directly to the almond-flour mixture along with the food coloring and stir until a thick paste forms. Add one-third of the whisked egg whites and gently stir until combined. Using a large rubber spatula, add the remaining egg whites and this time gently fold them into the mixture until smooth; the batter should have the pouring consistency of thick ketchup.

Transfer the batter to a large pastry bag fitted with a large open tip. Pipe the batter onto parchment-lined half sheet pans in 4-inch (10-cm) rounds. Leave a few inches between the meringues so that heat can circulate around them.

Firmly tap the sheet pans on your work counter to release any air bubbles. Leave the piped meringues at room temperature for 20 minutes so that a skin forms on the shell.

Bake the meringues for 4 minutes. Then open the oven door for 15 seconds; close the door and bake for another 4 minutes. Again, open the oven door for 15 seconds; close the door and bake for another 3 to 4 minutes, until pieds (or feet) have formed and the middle of the meringue is no longer wet. (Take into account that all ovens behave differently and have heat sources in different locations—some above, some below, some in the back. Times and temperatures will vary with each oven, so experiment, and don't be afraid of failing the first few times.)

Allow the shells to cool completely on the sheet pan before filling.

Make the white chocolate ganache:

Place the white chocolate in a mixing bowl. Set aside.

In a large heavy saucepan, combine the cream, raspberry purée, and vanilla bean paste and heat over medium-low heat until barely simmering.

Pour the hot cream mixture over the white chocolate, making sure the cream completely covers the chocolate, and allow it to sit undisturbed for a few minutes to allow the chocolate to melt completely. Using a balloon whisk, gently stir the ganache clockwise until smooth and shiny. Allow to cool just enough that the ganache begins to set to a spreadable consistency but isn't hard.

To assemble:

Turn a meringue shell shiny side down, and place 4 or 5 raspberries along its outside perimeter. Pipe a dollop of ganache into the middle of the shell and gently place a second shell, shiny side up, on top. Repeat until all the shells are filled. Serve the macarons immediately.

A NOTE FROM THE SWEET TALKER: "Aged" egg whites? What on earth could that possibly mean? If you've ever made a French macaron, you've no doubt been instructed to use only aged whites. Do you have to go to a flea market to purchase such a thing? Are you going to end up in an eBay bidding war for turn-of-the-century poultry products? No. The fact is that if eggs sit around too long, their whites become watery, and since most home bakers get their eggs from grocery stores, chances are the eggs will be a little old. To create a perfect macaron shell, you need to eliminate as much excess moisture as possible, and aging egg whites facilitates this process. To age egg whites, first you separate the whites and the yolks. You then place the whites in a clean porcelain or metal bowl. Cover with plastic wrap and poke holes in the wrap. Leave the bowl on your kitchen counter overnight or for up to 24 hours. This allows any excess moisture to evaporate from the whites, leaving a higher percentage of protein to water and giving you a winning chance at confectionary perfection.

PISTACHIO-CASSIS HEART TARTS

Makes 8 tartlets

THIS IS A COMBINATION I find so arresting that I can't help myself from eating every morsel. The meringues are sweet, but the pistachio brings a heady earthiness to the party that makes the shells irresistible in themselves. Then there's the black currant filling—all sweetness and unbridled fruitiness, but with a slight tang that elevates what could be a cloying sugar bomb to an artful bouquet of a dessert. This little tart is, in a word, special. Quite frankly, it's one of my all-time favorites.

FOR THE MERINGUE SHELLS:

1 cup (115 g) finely ground pistachios or pistachio flour

1 tablespoon cornstarch

1 cup (100 g) confectioners' sugar

5 egg whites

½ teaspoon salt

½ cup (100 g) granulated sugar

FOR THE FILLING:

1 generous tablespoon powdered gelatin

1 cup (240 ml) cassis (black currant) purée (see Sidebar, page 48; also see Note below)

1 cup (200 g) granulated sugar

5 egg whites

pinch salt

1½ cups (360 ml) heavy cream

½ cup (115 g) mascarpone

FOR THE ASSEMBLY:

¼ cup (25 g) confectioners' sugar

NOTE: For the black currant purée, you can substitute 1 cup (240 ml) black currant preserves, warmed and thinned with 2 tablespoons water, or 1 cup (240 ml) blackberry purée.

Make the meringue shells:

Preheat the oven to 250°F (120°C). Line two half sheet pans with parchment paper. Draw 8 (4-inch / 10-cm) hearts, evenly spaced a few inches apart, on each piece of parchment. Flip the parchment over, so that the outlines are visible but will not transfer onto the meringue.

In the bowl of a food processor, pulse together the pistachios, cornstarch, and confectioners' sugar. Transfer the mixture to a large mixing bowl.

In the bowl of a stand mixer fitted with the whisk attachment, add the egg whites and salt and whisk until light and frothy. With the mixer running, very slowly add the granulated sugar—this should take more than a minute. Continue whisking until stiff white peaks form.

Combine one-third of the egg whites with the nut mixture and stir until a paste forms. Using a large rubber spatula, gently fold the remaining egg whites into the mixture until no white streaks remain.

Transfer the nut meringue to a large pastry bag fitted with a medium-large open tip. Using the outlines on the parchment as guides, pipe the meringue into filled heart shapes.

Bake the hearts for 30 to 45 minutes, until baked through and dry but not browned. Set the meringues aside and allow to cool completely.

Make the filling:

Bring ¼ cup (60 ml) water just to boiling. Add the gelatin to a heatproof and microwave-safe bowl and pour the water over it, making sure that each particle of gelatin is saturated; stir until the gelatin has completely dissolved into the water. If there are still some undissolved particles, microwave the mixture in 10-second intervals, stirring between blasts, until they are completely dissolved. (You want to time dissolving the gelatin so that it is still liquid when you incorporate it into the whipped-cream mixture but has cooled enough that it doesn't break the meringue or melt the whipped cream. Conversely, if it cools too much, it will set too early and you'll be left with gelatin chunks in the mousse.)

Gently warm the cassis purée to just a little above body temperature (100°F / 38°C, if we're being persnickety) and stir in the gelatin mixture. Set aside.

In a heavy saucepan, combine the granulated sugar with ⅓ cup (80 ml) water. Stir over low heat until the sugar has completely dissolved. Attach a candy thermometer to the side of the saucepan and heat the syrup until it reaches 234°F (112°C).

Meanwhile, in the bowl of a stand mixer fitted with the whisk attachment, add the egg whites and the salt and whisk until foamy. When the sugar reaches temperature, decrease the speed of the mixer to medium and carefully pour the hot sugar down the side of the bowl. Once all of the syrup has been added, increase the mixer speed to high and whip until the meringue is bright white and shiny and maintains a stiff peak when you lift the whisk attachment from it. Transfer the meringue to a metal bowl and set aside.

Using the same mixing bowl (you don't have to clean it), add the cream and mascarpone and whip until soft peaks form. Gently fold the whipped cream into the meringue.

Check the temperature of the gelatin mixture: It should be slightly warmer than room temperature and the consistency of a thick maple syrup. Gently fold one-quarter of the egg white mixture into the purée to temper, then gently fold in the remaining egg white mixture until no white streaks remain.

Spread the mousse onto a parchment-lined sheet pan and freeze until it is set, about 1 hour. Using a heart-shaped biscuit or cookie cutter, stamp out hearts of mousse slightly smaller than the meringues.

To assemble:

Using a small offset spatula, gently transfer one mousse heart to the top of each meringue shell. Gently place a second shell, smooth side down, on top of the mousse, but don't press down.

Refrigerate the tarts until set, at least 2 hours. Gently place a stencil over the meringues and dust with confectioners' sugar. Serve immediately.

A NOTE FROM THE SWEET TALKER: Fruit purées are terribly easy to make. Place your berries (4 cups / 760 g small berries, or 3 cups / 525 g chopped strawberries) or other fruit in a saucepan with ¼ cup (50 g) sugar, or to taste. (Berries such as currants and gooseberries are tart and may require more sweetness—do a taste test.) Simmer the fruit over low heat until the sugar has melted. Allow the mixture to cool. In the bowl of a food processor fitted with the blade attachment, pulse the fruit mixture until smooth (you can use a blender or an immersion blender for this process as well). Strain the purée through a fine-mesh sieve to remove the seeds, and voilà! Purée! Freeze any extra purée in a zip-top bag. Purées are lovely in mousses, as sauces to accompany plated desserts, and as toppings for sundaes! You can also buy fantastic premade purées in an array of flavors from ordinary (raspberry) to exotic (passion fruit). My favorite brands are Boiron and L'Epicerie. Check the internet for availability.

THE LONE-STAR GESINE TORTE

Makes 8 servings

I NEVER WENT THROUGH A "princess" phase as a kid. Empress phase, yes, but not princess. However, had I known that back in the day the most fabulous desserts were created in honor of lesser nobility, I'd have happily played princess, at least until someone presented me with a royal treat. Prince Esterhazy was perhaps the luckiest dude in all of the Hapsburg Empire, not for his vast wealth and political sway (he was a powerful diplomat in the service of his emperor), but for the magnificent nut-meringue torte created in his name. Traditionally, layers of crisp hazelnut meringue sandwich luscious buttercream filling and are topped with a sweet glaze and chocolate. I put a lone-star spin on this treat by replacing the hazelnuts with pecans—and simply shoved Esterhazy's name aside and replaced it with my own. Now I'm just waiting for someone to hand me a tiara and I'm Princess for a Day.

FOR THE NUT MERINGUE:

12 ounces (340 g) toasted, chopped pecans

1 tablespoon cornstarch

½ cup (50 g) confectioners' sugar

6 egg whites at room temperature

1 teaspoon vanilla bean paste

¼ teaspoon salt

1 cup (200 g) granulated sugar, divided

2 teaspoons baking soda

FOR THE FILLING:

1 cup (240 ml) heavy cream

1 cup (240 ml) whole milk

2 tablespoons dark rum

6 egg yolks

½ cup (100 g) granulated sugar

¼ cup (30 g) cornstarch

pinch salt

1 cup (230 g) unsalted butter, cut into small pieces, slightly cooler than room temperature

FOR THE ASSEMBLY:

¼ cup (60 ml) smooth apricot preserves

1 ounce (30 g) bittersweet chocolate, finely chopped

1 cup (100 g) confectioners' sugar

¼ cup (60 ml) whole milk

Make the nut meringue:

Preheat the oven to 275°F (135°C). Line a half sheet pan with parchment paper. Set aside.

In the bowl of a food processor fitted with the blade attachment, combine the pecans, cornstarch, and confectioners' sugar. Pulse in short bursts until the mixture is very fine. (Be careful not to overprocess to the point that the mixture starts to clump.)

In the bowl of a stand mixer fitted with the whisk attachment, combine the egg whites, vanilla bean paste, and salt. Whisk on high speed until the egg whites are white and foamy but not yet stiff. With the mixer running, add the granulated sugar in a very slow stream and continue whisking on high speed until stiff, glossy peaks form. Make sure not to overwhip and dry the meringue.

Sprinkle the nut mixture over the meringue. Using a large rubber spatula, gently fold the nut mixture into the meringue.

Using a large offset spatula, spread the meringue evenly to cover the bottom of the prepared sheet pan. Bake for 20 minutes, or until the meringue turns a light golden brown. Release the meringue from the pan by running a small paring knife along the edge of the meringue. Invert the meringue onto a cutting board slightly larger than the sheet pan. Remove the parchment. While the meringue is still warm, use a very sharp serrated knife to even the edges of the meringue, then cut it lengthwise into four strips, each 3½ inches (9 cm) wide. (If you wait until the meringue has completely cooled, it can splinter when cut.) Set aside.

Make the filling:

In a large saucepan, combine the cream, milk, and rum and bring to a simmer.

In the meantime, in the bowl of a stand mixer fitted with the whisk attachment, add the egg yolks, granulated sugar, cornstarch, and salt and whisk until light and fluffy. Raise the mixer speed to medium and slowly pour the warm cream mixture into the egg yolk mixture. Whisk until well combined.

Transfer the pastry cream back to the saucepan, scraping the sides and bottom of the mixing bowl to catch any stray bits of yolk and cornstarch. Whisk over medium-low heat until the mixture thickens to the consistency of mayonnaise. Transfer the pastry cream to a clean mixing bowl and cover with plastic wrap, pressing the plastic directly onto the surface of the pastry cream to prevent a skin from forming. Refrigerate until cool, at least 2 hours.

Transfer the pastry cream to the bowl of a stand mixer fitted with the whisk attachment. Whisk on high speed until smooth and creamy (it will have become very firm while in the fridge).

Add the butter, a few pieces at a time, and whisk until the filling is smooth and thick.

To assemble:

In a small saucepan, combine the apricot preserves and 2 tablespoons water and stir over low heat until the mixture is smooth. Transfer to a small bowl and allow to cool completely.

Place a wire rack on top of a parchment-lined half sheet pan and arrange the meringue strips on it. Using a clean pastry brush, coat each strip of meringue with the apricot glaze. Set aside the best-looking piece to use as the top of the torte. Allow to set, about 15 minutes.

Place the chocolate in a microwave-safe bowl and microwave at 50% power for 30 seconds at a time, stirring gently in between, until completely melted. Transfer the chocolate to a coronet (a parchment-paper cone) and snip the tip of the coronet. Set aside.

Stir together the confectioners' sugar and 2 tablespoons of the milk. Keep stirring and adding milk as needed until a smooth glaze forms that has the consistency of ketchup.

Using a ladle, pour the glaze over the reserved strip of nut meringue. Using a small offset spatula, smooth the glaze so that the entire strip has a thin, even layer of glaze. While the glaze is still wet, use the chocolate-filled coronet to pipe horizontal stripes on top, 1 inch (2.5 cm) apart. Take a toothpick and drag it down the far edge of the pastry across the lines of chocolate. Allow the glaze and chocolate to set completely, about 30 minutes.

Transfer the filling to a pastry bag fitted with a large open tip. Place one of the meringue strips on a serving platter. Pipe the filling onto the meringue until the meringue is completely covered. Top with another meringue. Continue piping and layering until you reach the final layer. Carefully place the decorated meringue strip on top of the last layer of filling. Using a small offset spatula, smooth over any excess pastry cream on the sides of the pastry. Refrigerate until the filling is set, about 1 hour. Use a very sharp serrated knife to cut 8 even slices (or *Schnitten*) from the torte, and serve.

BLOOD ORANGE AND LINGONBERRY BOMBE

Makes 1 (10-inch / 25-cm) dome cake

I GET A KICK OUT of dome-shaped desserts, especially when there's a bombe within the bombe! There's something so lovely about cutting into an already unusually formed frozen dessert to find that there's a hidden treasure inside. The blood orange plays its citrus cards openly and allows just a whisper of bitterness into the picture, while the lingonberries lend an open sweetness and a soupçon of tartness. Layer all this together with a moist cake and a crisp yet chewy foundation, and this frozen bombe will explode with flavor in your mouth.

FOR THE *MANDELKRÄNZCHEN* LAYER:
½ recipe *Mandelkränzchen* (page 24), prepared to just before the
    dough is piped from the pastry bag into wreaths

FOR THE BLOOD ORANGE CAKE LAYER:
⅓ cup (65 g) granulated sugar
¼ cup (60 ml) almond oil (you can substitute olive oil)
2 eggs
½ cup (60 g) all-purpose flour
1 teaspoon baking powder
¼ teaspoon ground cardamom
½ teaspoon salt
¼ cup (60 ml) sour cream
juice and zest of 1 blood orange

FOR THE BLOOD ORANGE FILLING:
2 cups (480 ml) heavy cream
½ cup (125 g) crème fraîche
¼ cup (60 ml) blood orange preserves, sieved
2 tablespoons confectioners' sugar

FOR THE LINGONBERRY FILLING:
3 cups (720 ml) heavy cream
1 cup (250 g) crème fraîche

½ cup (120 ml) lingonberry preserves, sieved
3 tablespoons confectioners' sugar

FOR THE ASSEMBLY:
¼ cup (60 ml) lingonberry preserves

FOR THE MERINGUE TOPPING:
1 cup (200 g) granulated sugar
5 egg whites
pinch salt

Make the *Mandelkränzchen* layer:

Preheat the oven to 325°F (165°C). Line a 10-inch (25-cm) round cake pan with parchment paper and spray with nonstick cooking spray.

Pipe the *Mandelkränzchen* dough from the pastry bag into the prepared pan. Bake for 25 to 30 minutes, or until the top of the cake is golden brown and the layer is firm to the touch. Set aside to cool.

Make the blood orange cake layer:

Preheat the oven to 350°F (175°C). Line a 9-inch (23-cm) cake pan with parchment paper and spray with nonstick cooking spray.

In the bowl of a stand mixer fitted with the whisk attachment, combine the granulated sugar and almond oil. Whisk until just combined. Add the eggs, one at a time, whisking until each is completely combined.

In a separate bowl, whisk together the flour, baking powder, cardamom, and salt. Add one-third of the flour mixture to the egg mixture. Whisk on low speed until just combined.

In a separate bowl, whisk together the sour cream, blood orange juice, and blood orange zest. Add one-third of the sour cream mixture to the egg mixture and whisk to combine.

Continue alternating additions of the flour and the sour cream mixtures, whisking until both are fully combined.

Transfer the batter to the prepared cake pan. Bake for 20 minutes, or until the cake just springs back when you touch it. Set aside to cool completely.

Make the blood orange filling:

In the bowl of a stand mixer fitted with the whisk attachment, combine the cream, crème fraîche, and confectioners' sugar and whisk until stiff peaks form. Stir a large spoonful of the cream mixture into the blood orange preserves to lighten them, then add the remaining cream mixture and fold until well combined.

Spoon the mixture into a 4-cup (1-l) bowl and freeze until set, about 2 hours, or overnight.

Make the lingonberry filling:

In the bowl of the stand mixer, still fitted with the whisk attachment, combine the cream, crème fraîche, and confectioners' sugar and whisk until stiff peaks form. Stir a large spoonful of the cream mixture into the lingonberry preserves to lighten them, then add the remaining cream mixture and fold until well combined.

To assemble:

Spoon the lingonberry filling into a 6-cup (1.2-l) bowl. Gently warm the bowl containing the frozen blood orange filling with a kitchen torch or blow dryer to release. Turn the half sphere of blood orange filling, the rounded side down, into the bowl lined with the lingonberry filling, and press so that the lingonberry filling and blood orange filling are level. Cover with plastic wrap and freeze for two hours.

Gently press the *Mandelkränzchen* layer on top of the filling. Trim to fit if needed.

With an offset spatula, smooth the ¼ cup (60 ml) lingonberry preserves over the *Mandelkränzchen* layer. Gently press the blood orange cake on top of the lingonberry-covered *Mandelkränzchen* layer, trimming to fit if needed, and freeze until set, at least 2 hours, or overnight.

Make the meringue topping:

In a heavy saucepan, combine the granulated sugar with ⅓ cup (80 ml) water and stir over low heat until the sugar has completely dissolved.

Increase the heat to medium-high, attach a candy thermometer to the side of the saucepan, and heat the sugar mixture to 240°F (116°C).

Meanwhile, in the bowl of a stand mixer fitted with the whisk attachment, combine the egg whites and salt. When the temperature reaches 230°F (110°C), start the mixer on high speed so that the egg whites are foamy by the time the sugar mixture comes to temperature.

With the mixer running on medium speed, very slowly pour the hot sugar mixture down the side of the bowl and into the egg whites. Once all of the sugar is added, increase the mixer speed to high and whisk until very stiff, white, glossy peaks form. Transfer the meringue to a large pastry bag fitted with a large star tip.

Invert the bowl containing the cakes and fillings over a platter and gently warm the bowl with a kitchen torch or blow dryer to release the cake, flat side down. At the top of the dome, pipe a rosette 1 inch (2.5 cm) wide. Continue piping rosettes so that they touch one another and cover the entire surface of the cake.

If you like, gently brown the meringue rosettes with a kitchen torch. Serve immediately.

Chapter 2

LIGHT
&
SCRUMPTIOUS

SPONGE CAKES

THE FIRST KNOWN SPONGE CAKE RECIPE APPEARS IN A BOOK TITLED

The English Huswife, Containing the Inward and Outward Virtues Which Ought to Be in a Complete Woman. Ahem.

You'll be happy to know that the book was published in 1615 and has scarcely any consequence in our modern lives. I'll take the sponge-cake recipe, though. It's believed to be the first cake made not with yeast but instead with eggs, providing the necessary rise to give cake a tender crumb yet allowing it to retain a beautifully sturdy structure.

In any sponge cake formula, it's the eggs that dictate the quantities of other ingredients. A yolk-heavy cake will have a denser texture and a white-heavy one will be lighter. The proper amount of sugar is also crucial, as too little sugar will throw the cake off kilter, spoiling the color and creating a tough crumb. And let's not forget flour. You'd think for something called a "sponge" that cake flour would be the only way to go in order to maintain a light, spongy effect. However, a decent amount of gluten is crucial in some recipes for sturdy structure in a sponge cake, keeping it from collapsing on itself once out of the oven, so the most common flour employed in sponge cakes is all-purpose. And the best part: butter. Not all sponge cakes have added butter, but when they do, ooh la la! Of course the cake won't be as light and airy, as the inclusion of butter results in a little density, but it will have great flavor.

CITRUSY ANGEL FOOD CAKE
WITH ORANGE MARMALADE

Makes 1 (10-inch / 25-cm) cake

WHY, OH WHY, WOULD I put angel food cake in the sponge cake section instead of the meringue section of this book? I could and probably should have put it in the meringue section because it's so damn full of whipped egg whites and sugar, but I was compelled to share my recipe here as a lesson in transition from one technique to the next. The angel food cake we all know and love is made with only the egg whites instead of the whole egg. First you make a stable meringue and then you gently add flour. If that's not a perfect bridge from meringue to sponge cake, then I don't know what is! And here the lovely layers of colors and flavors within a cake that's usually just plain white (but just plain tasty) make for a rousing introduction to sponges.

FOR THE CAKE:

1¼ cups (250 g) granulated sugar

½ cup (50 g) confectioners' sugar

2 tablespoons cornstarch

1 cup (140 g) cake flour, sifted

1 teaspoon salt

12 egg whites, at room temperature

⅓ cup (80 ml) fresh lemon juice

1 teaspoon lemon zest

1 teaspoon cream of tartar

1 drop yellow food coloring

1 drop lime-green food coloring

1 teaspoon lime extract (*not* oil) or powder

1 drop orange food coloring

1 teaspoon orange extract (*not* oil)

TO SERVE:

½ cup (120 ml) orange marmalade (I use Bonne Maman)

Make the cake:

Preheat the oven to 350°F (175°C).

In the bowl of a food processor fitted with the blade attachment, add the sugars and the cornstarch and pulse until very fine.

In a large bowl, add half of the sugar-cornstarch mixture (reserving the other half), the cake flour, and salt and stir to combine. Sift the mixture onto a large piece of parchment paper. Sift again back into the large bowl, then sift a third time back onto the parchment paper.

In the bowl of a stand mixer fitted with the whisk attachment, combine the egg whites, lemon juice, lemon zest, and cream of tartar. Whisk on high speed until the whites become white and frothy. Slowly add the reserved sugar-cornstarch mixture to the beating egg whites and continue whisking until medium peaks form.

Sift one-quarter of the sugar-flour mixture on top of the egg whites and use a large rubber spatula to gently fold it in. In quarter portions, continue sifting the remaining sugar-flour mixture on top and folding it into the batter, until all of the sugar-flour mixture is incorporated.

Divide the batter evenly among three very clean bowls. Fold the yellow food coloring into one, the lime-green food coloring and lime extract to the second, and the orange food coloring and orange extract into the third. It's all right if the colors in the batters are a little streaky, as this gives a softer look and also allows you to keep more aeration in the batter.

Gently spoon the batter into an ungreased angel food cake pan. Bake for 35 minutes, or until a wooden skewer inserted into the middle of the cake comes out dry. Invert the cake pan onto an empty wine bottle so that the cake is suspended in the air while it cools (this keeps the crumb of the cake from compressing).

To serve:

Angel food cake is best when torn instead of sliced, to keep the cake from getting smooshed. But if you want beautifully even slices, gently "saw" with a serrated knife.

Serve with a dollop of marmalade.

GREEN MOUNTAIN TIRAMISU

Makes 10 servings

TIRAMISU IS ITALIAN FOR "PICK-ME-UP." It's a lovely dessert that's ubiquitous on Italian menus, and it's a truly light confection, with its airy layers of ladyfingers and the addition of fluffy mascarpone and whipped cream laced with marsala wine and cocoa. It's a veritable cloud of sweetness that invites you to partake even if you have to unbutton your jeans to bully through it. When I get to make it at home, I make it with a Vermont twist, replacing the traditional marsala with maple sugar and rum for a little New England oomph.

Traditionally, even the best home baker goes straight for the store-bought ladyfingers. But I say *stop right there*! You can create such a glorious cake when you make your very own. You aren't confined to the conventional ladyfinger shape—I prefer to bake the batter on a half sheet pan in one single layer so that I have options for how to build the dessert: Do I want to make slices? Do I want to make individual rounds? Making your own sheet cake gives you the opportunity to create exactly the shape and size of tiramisu that will pick you up! This makes for a gorgeous presentation and a glorious mouthful of creamy delight.

FOR THE LADYFINGERS LAYER:

3 eggs, separated, at room temperature

2 drops fresh lemon juice

½ teaspoon salt

¼ cup (50 g) granulated sugar

2 tablespoons maple syrup

½ cup (70 g) bread flour

6 tablespoons (50 g) cornstarch

FOR THE FILLING:

½ cup (120 ml) dark rum, divided

1 teaspoon powdered gelatin

3 egg yolks

6 tablespoons (90 ml) maple syrup

1 cup (240 ml) heavy cream

1 cup (250 g) mascarpone

FOR THE ASSEMBLY:

1 cup (240 ml) strong coffee, at room temperature

¼ cup (20 g) Dutch-process cocoa powder (I use Cacao Barry Extra Brute)

Make the ladyfingers layer:

Preheat the oven to 425°F (220°C). Line a half sheet pan with parchment paper and spray with nonstick cooking spray.

In the bowl of a stand mixer fitted with the whisk attachment, combine the egg whites, lemon juice, and salt and whisk until foamy. With the mixer on high speed, slowly add the granulated sugar and continue whisking until the egg whites form stiff peaks but aren't dry. Transfer the mixture to a clean mixing bowl and set aside.

In the same bowl of the stand mixer (you don't need to clean it), combine the egg yolks and maple syrup and whisk on high speed until pale and thick. Sift the flour and cornstarch over the yolk mixture and use a large rubber spatula to gently fold them into the yolk mixture.

Add one-third of the egg whites to the yolk mixture and gently stir. Add the remaining whites and gently fold with the large rubber spatula until no white streaks remain.

Spread the batter in an even layer onto the prepared pan. Bake for 10 minutes, or until golden brown. Set aside to cool completely.

Make the filling:

Pour half of the rum into a microwave-safe bowl and sprinkle the gelatin over it in an even layer to bloom, about 3 minutes (it should look soggy throughout). Microwave the mixture at 50% power in 10-second intervals, swirling the bowl in between, until the gelatin has completely dissolved.

In the bowl of a stand mixer, combine the egg yolks, maple syrup, and remaining rum. Set the bowl over a saucepan of simmering water and whisk constantly over medium-low heat until the mixture thickens to the point that it coats the back of a spoon. Transfer the bowl back to the stand mixer fitted with the whisk attachment and whisk on high speed until the bowl is cool. Transfer the mixture to a clean mixing bowl, cover with plastic wrap, and refrigerate.

Meanwhile, in the same bowl of the stand mixer (you don't need to clean it), still fitted with the whisk attachment, combine the cream and mascarpone and whisk until stiff peaks form.

Remove the egg yolk mixture from the refrigerator and add a spoonful of it to the bowl containing the gelatin; stir until the two are completely combined. Pour the gelatin mixture back into the bowl with the yolk mixture and stir. Add one-third of the cream-mascarpone mixture to the egg yolk–gelatin mixture and gently stir to combine. Add the remaining cream mixture. Using a large rubber spatula, gently fold the cream into the yolk-gelatin mixture until well combined.

To assemble:

Using a sharp paring knife, release the ladyfinger layer from the sheet pan by gently cutting along the edges of the pan. Invert the sheet pan onto a cutting board the same size or slightly larger than the cake layer, so the cake now rests on the cutting board. Gently remove the parchment paper from the cake.

Using a very sharp serrated knife, cut the cake into 3 strips, each 3½ by 16 inches (9 by 40.5 cm).

Place one ladyfinger strip on a serving platter and brush lightly with the coffee (you don't want to soak the cake, just lightly moisten the top). Spread one-third of the filling over this layer. Sift 1 tablespoon cocoa powder over the filling. Cover with a second ladyfinger strip; brush with coffee. At this point, I let the partially assembled cake set in the freezer for 10 minutes.

Remove the cake from the freezer. Spread one-third of the filling over the layer and sift 1 tablespoon cocoa powder over the filling. Place the last ladyfinger strip over the filling and place the cake in the freezer for 10 more minutes to set.

Remove the cake from the freezer and brush the top layer with the remaining coffee, then spread it with the remaining filling and smooth the top. Dust with an even layer of the remaining cocoa powder. Serve immediately.

VICTORIA SPONGE CAKE

Makes 1 (8-inch / 20-cm) cake

THE VICTORIA SPONGE WAS QUEEN VICTORIA's favorite cake. It's simple in the extreme, a very plain vanilla cake, neither dense nor particularly fluffy. Its most common presentation is with two even layers of sponge sandwiching a hearty layer of sweetened whipped cream dotted with berries, the top gently dusted with confectioners' sugar. Simple indeed. But damned delicious. And I'll tell you something: By placing the strawberries right at the edge of the first layer, you create a stunning berry border usually exclusive to professional pastry shops. I've never seen any wedding cake half as beautiful as a stack of Victoria sponges, their naked sides showing the world their creamy filling and juicy berries. The Queen would approve.

FOR THE SPONGE CAKE:

2 cups (455 g) unsalted butter, at room temperature
2 cups (400 g) granulated sugar
7 eggs, at room temperature
1 teaspoon vanilla extract
¼ cup (60 ml) whole milk
2 cups (250 g) all-purpose flour
2 teaspoons baking powder
1 teaspoon salt

FOR THE FILLING:

2 cups (480 ml) heavy cream
⅓ cup (35 g) confectioners' sugar
1 teaspoon vanilla bean paste

FOR THE ASSEMBLY:

4 pints (1 kg) fresh strawberries
¼ cup (25 g) confectioners' sugar

Make the sponge cake:

Preheat the oven to 350°F (175°C). Prepare two 8-inch (20-cm) round cake pans by lining the bottom of each with a round of parchment paper and spraying with non-stick cooking spray.

In the bowl of a stand mixer fitted with the paddle attachment, beat the butter, granulated sugar, and cream until light and fluffy, about 8 minutes.

Using a large rubber spatula, scrape the sides and bottom of the bowl. Add 1 egg. Beat on high speed for 30 seconds. Scrape down the sides of the bowl again and add another egg. Continue in this manner until all the eggs are incorporated. Add the vanilla extract and milk. Beat for a few seconds.

In a bowl, sift together the flour, baking powder, and salt. With the mixer on medium-low speed, slowly add the flour mixture and mix until just incorporated. Using a large rubber offset spatula, scrape the bottom and sides of the bowl and gently fold the batter a few times to ensure that the flour is evenly distributed.

Divide the batter evenly among the prepared pans, smoothing the batter with a small offset spatula. Bake for 20 to 25 minutes, until the tops are golden brown and the cake springs back when touched. Allow to cool completely.

Make the filling:

In a mixing bowl, combine the cream, confectioners' sugar, and vanilla bean paste and whisk until stiff and smooth.

To assemble:

Set aside 3 or 4 of the best-looking strawberries and keep them whole. Find 20 strawberries that are of very similar height and hull them. Hull and halve the remaining strawberries.

Place one of the cake layers on a serving plate. Spread all of the filling over the layer and arrange the halved strawberries over the filling.

Place the second cake layer over the berries and cream, dust with confectioners' sugar, and strategically place the reserved whole berries on top of the dusted layer. Serve immediately.

A NOTE FROM THE SWEET TALKER: Sponge cakes utilize what's called the "foaming method" in baking parlance. This means that you whisk eggs, either separately or together, to the point that they are gorgeously aerated. The air whipped into the eggs provides the leavening in the cake instead of baking powder or soda. Some methods require that you beat the whites and yolks separately, which allows the whites to reach their greatest height; the whipped whites and yolks are then folded together later in the process. Other methods require the eggs to be whipped together whole, along with the sugar. This way the eggs will aerate beautifully but won't quite reach the volume that egg whites on their own will. There's also a method wherein the eggs are whipped with the sugar over a bain marie (a metal bowl placed over a saucepan half filled with gently simmering water) and then transferred to a mixer to beat until doubled in volume. Heating the eggs stabilizes the egg structure, ensuring that when you whip them, they maintain their increased volume in the oven. All of these are foaming methods, and practice will make you an expert in any of them. However, different cakes require different methods so don't switch them out willy-nilly and expect the same results.

WILD BLUEBERRY AND GUANABANA BAVARIAN CREAM LAYER CAKE

Makes 1 (8-inch / 20-cm) cake

THIS IS A WONDERFUL EXAMPLE of the simple delight that is sponge cake: a delicate vanilla sponge cradling creamy, fruity Bavarian cream and accented by tart guanabana curd. Guanabana, you ask? Why, yes! It's actually not as exotic as you might think and is available in cans of "nectar" in the international sections of most grocery stores. The taste is a cross between a strawberry and a pineapple, just a little more tart. And what makes this cream Bavarian? Must you yodel to it as you stir? Sadly, no. It's merely the addition of gelatin to a traditional pastry cream. The ripest berries in season are crucial, so you should feel free to swap out the blues I suggest for other varieties. Each element's flavor and color sing without overpowering one another, the sponge both playing host to the filling and providing structure to the beautiful layers.

FOR THE SPONGE CAKE:

7 eggs, at room temperature

1 cup (200 g) granulated sugar

½ teaspoon salt

2 cups (250 g) all-purpose flour

¼ cup (55 g) unsalted butter, melted

1 teaspoon vanilla extract

FOR THE GUANABANA CURD:

2 teaspoons powdered gelatin

1½ cups (360 ml) guanabana juice, divided (from one 12-ounce / 360-ml can; I use Goya brand)

1½ cups (300 g) granulated sugar

14 egg yolks

4 tablespoons unsalted butter

FOR THE BAVARIAN CREAM:

1 cup (240 ml) whole milk

2 cups (480 ml) heavy cream, divided

6 egg yolks

½ cup (100 g) granulated sugar

¼ cup (30 g) cornstarch

pinch salt

1 teaspoon orange extract

1 teaspoon powdered gelatin

3 cups (570 g) fresh wild blueberries, divided

FOR THE BUTTERCREAM:

1 cup (200 g) sugar

¼ cup (60 ml) guanabana juice

5 egg whites, at room temperature

pinch salt

1 pound (455 g) unsalted butter, at room temperature

1 to 2 drops orange gel food coloring

FOR THE ASSEMBLY:

1 cup (190 g) fresh wild blueberries

Make the sponge cake:

Preheat the oven to 350°F (175°C). Prepare two 8-inch (20-cm) round cake pans by lining the bottom of each with a round of parchment paper and spraying with nonstick cooking spray.

In the heatproof bowl of a stand mixer, combine the eggs, granulated sugar, and salt and gently whisk to break apart the eggs. Place the bowl over a saucepan of simmering water and whisk constantly until the sugar has completely melted and the mixture is warm to the touch.

Remove the bowl from the saucepan and, using a stand mixer fitted with the whisk attachment, whisk until the egg mixture is light and fluffy and the bowl is cool to the touch.

Sift the flour over the egg mixture and, using a large rubber spatula, gently fold the flour into the eggs. In a small bowl, stir together the melted butter and vanilla extract, pour the mixture over the batter, and gently fold it in until completely integrated.

Divide the batter between the two prepared pans and bake for 20 minutes, or until the cakes are golden brown and spring back when you gently touch them. Set aside to cool completely. Gently run a sharp paring knife around the edges of the cakes and turn them out onto a cooling rack.

Make the guanabana curd:

In a small bowl, sprinkle the gelatin on top of ¼ cup (60 ml) of the guanabana juice and let it sit until it has bloomed (the gelatin will become saturated and look soggy). Set aside.

In a heatproof metal bowl, combine the remaining guanabana juice, the granulated sugar, and egg yolks. Place the bowl over a saucepan of simmering water and cook, whisking constantly, until the mixture forms ribbons when you lift the whisk, about 15 minutes. Remove the bowl from the saucepan, immediately add the gelatin, and whisk until it is completely dissolved. Add the butter and whisk until it is fully incorporated.

Transfer the curd to a bowl and cover with plastic wrap, pressing the plastic directly onto the surface to prevent a skin from forming. Refrigerate until set, about 2 hours.

Make the Bavarian cream:

In a saucepan, combine the milk and 1 cup (240 ml) of the cream and bring to a simmer over medium heat.

Meanwhile, in the bowl of a stand mixer fitted with the whisk attachment, combine the egg yolks, granulated sugar, cornstarch, salt, and orange extract. Whisk on high speed until the mixture is pale and ribbons when you lift the whisk. With the mixer on medium speed, slowly pour the hot milk mixture down the side of the bowl and whisk until combined.

Scrape the mixture back into the saucepan and whisk over medium heat until the pastry cream thickens to the consistency of ketchup. Transfer the mixture to a clean mixing bowl and cover the top completely with plastic wrap, making sure the wrap adheres to the top of the pastry cream to keep a skin from forming. Set aside.

Place ¼ cup (60 ml) lukewarm water in a small microwave-safe bowl and sprinkle the gelatin evenly over the surface to bloom (the gelatin will become saturated and look soggy), about 3 minutes. Microwave the mixture at 50% power in 5-second intervals, swirling the bowl in between, until the gelatin has completely dissolved.

Bring the pastry cream to room temperature. Stir together a heaping tablespoon of the pastry cream and the gelatin, stirring to combine completely; note that the gelatin will seize and clump if the pastry cream isn't at room temperature. Stir in the remaining pastry cream. Cover the pastry cream–gelatin mixture with plastic wrap and place over a bowl of ice, stirring every few minutes, until the gelatin just begins to set and the mixture thickens slightly.

In the bowl of a stand mixer fitted with the whisk attachment, add the remaining 1 cup (240 ml) cream and whisk until soft peaks form.

Gently fold one-third of the pastry cream–gelatin mixture into the whipped cream. Add the remaining pastry cream–gelatin mixture and fold into the cream until no white streaks remain.

If the top of each cake has domed during baking, use a long and very sharp serrated knife to level it. Using a ruler (or just by eyeballing it), cut each cake horizontally into two even layers.

Place a single cake layer on a serving platter and top with ½ cup (65 g) of the guanabana curd. Using a small offset spatula, spread the curd thinly and evenly. Top evenly with 1 cup (190 g) of the blueberries. Transfer one-third of the Bavarian cream to the layer and spread very evenly over the curd and blueberries. Freeze for 10 minutes to stabilize. Repeat with the next two layers—cake, curd, blueberries, and Bavarian cream—freezing for 10 minutes between layers to stabilize.

Top with the last layer of cake and press very gently to adhere. Use a large offset spatula or a bench scraper to remove any filling that may have oozed onto the side of the cake. Wrap tightly with parchment paper (this may take a few pieces) and use tape to keep the parchment cocoon in place. Freeze for at least 2 hours or overnight, to set completely.

Make the buttercream:

In the bowl of a stand mixer, combine the sugar, guanabana juice, egg whites, and salt. Whisk the sugar–egg white mixture over a bain marie (a saucepan half filled with simmering water) until the sugar has completely melted and the temperature of the mixture has reached at least 160°F (72°C; it will likely go far over, but you want to ensure you reach 160°F / 72°C to kill any bacteria in the raw egg whites).

Transfer the bowl to the stand mixer fitted with the whisk attachment and whisk on high until the meringue has quadrupled in volume and the bowl is cool to the touch.

Add the butter, a few tablespoons at a time, until the mixture thickens and becomes a smooth, spreadable icing. You may not need all the butter.

To assemble:

Cover the cake with a smooth, even layer of the buttercream (see pages 68–69). Top decoratively with blueberries.

Allow the cake to thaw for at least 2 hours before serving.

A NOTE FROM THE SWEET TALKER: Some tips on eggs. First, I always use organic, free-range eggs. (Actually, I use my own hens' eggs, so I know for a fact that they are organic and free range.) I also know my hens' diet includes large doses of croissants and yummy cake crumbs, which make their egg yolks a rich, marigold orange. But despite the fact that each hen receives the same amount of food and their eggs all have glorious, sunshiny yolks, each hen ends up laying a different size of egg. Thankfully, I am in possession of some very useful information: the correct weight of a egg. In baking, large eggs are used (not medium, not extra large, not jumbo). My hens frankly don't care that I'd like a bit of uniformity, so I end up weighing the eggs each time. For a egg, the white should weigh just a little over 1 ounce (30 g), while the yolk is .6 ounce (18 g).

Here's the trick for separating eggs: They should be cold. Very cold. The chance of a yolk breaking during separation grows exponentially higher as an egg becomes warmer. However, when you use eggs in baking, you want them to be at room temperature. A room-temperature egg reaches full volume much faster than a cold egg. So, it's best to separate the cold eggs, then wait 30 minutes before using them so they have time to warm.

1　*Smooth the buttercream on the top . . .*

2　*. . . and sides of the cake to make a crumb coat.*

3　*Smooth the buttercream and refrigerate to set.*

4　*Apply a second layer of buttercream.*
Smooth with a clean, hot bench scraper.

bake it like you mean it

5

*Use an icing smoother
to level the top.*

THE MADAME BUTTERFLY

Makes 1 (3-by-12-inch / 7.5-by-30.5-cm) layer cake

OPERA CAKE IS ONE OF my all-time favorite intricate layer cakes. It's beautiful—oh, is it ever beautiful. When you slice into it, you are treated to a smorgasbord of textures, flavors, and colors. Well, maybe the colors aren't so vibrant in a traditional Opera cake, with its earth-tone palette of tan, latte, and dark-cocoa layers. My Madame Butterfly recipe, however, packs in all the flavor variety found in a traditional opera cake—exotic hints of almond mingling with bright mango and hints of green tea—and infuses it with an aria of gorgeous, vibrant colors.

FOR THE GREEN TEA SPONGE CAKE:

4 eggs, at room temperature

½ cup (100 g) granulated sugar

½ teaspoon salt

2 drops forest-green food coloring (optional)

1 cup (140 g) almond flour or meal

¼ cup (35 g) cake flour, sifted before measuring

2 tablespoons matcha powder (green tea powder, available at Asian markets or online)

2 tablespoons unsalted butter, melted and brought to room temperature

FOR THE MANGO BUTTERCREAM:

5 egg whites

pinch salt

1 cup (200 g) granulated sugar

1 pound (455 g) unsalted butter, slightly cooler than room temperature

¼ cup (60 ml) mango purée

1 or 2 drops orange food coloring (optional)

FOR THE WHITE CHOCOLATE GANACHE:

1 pound (455 g) white chocolate, finely chopped

1 cup (240 ml) heavy cream

2 tablespoons unsalted butter

1 teaspoon vanilla bean paste

FOR THE GREEN TEA SIMPLE SYRUP:

2 green tea bags

1 cup (200 g) granulated sugar

FOR THE ASSEMBLY:

2 (7-ounce / 200-g) packages almond paste (I use Odense)

1 cup (100 g) confectioners' sugar

2 tablespoons matcha powder

Make the green tea sponge cake:

Preheat the oven to 325°F (165°C). Line a half sheet pan with parchment paper and lightly spray with nonstick cooking spray.

In the heatproof bowl of a stand mixer, combine the eggs, granulated sugar, and salt. Whisk the egg mixture over a bain marie (a saucepan half filled with gently simmering water) until the sugar has completely melted.

Transfer the bowl to a stand mixer fitted with the whisk attachment and whisk on high speed until the eggs have tripled in volume and the bowl is cool to the touch. Add the forest-green food coloring at this point, if using.

In the bowl of a food processor, pulse together the almond flour, cake flour, and matcha powder. Pulse until very fine. Sift the mixture through a fine-mesh sieve two times.

Hold the sieve over the whipped eggs and sift the flour mixture over the eggs. Using a large rubber spatula, gently fold the flour mixture into the eggs until just combined.

Pour the butter over the batter and gently fold until completely incorporated.

Pour the batter into the prepared pan and smooth with a large offset spatula. Bake for 20 minutes, or until the cake springs back when gently touched and just begins to pull away from the sides of the pan. Allow to cool completely.

Make the mango buttercream:

In the bowl of a stand mixer fitted with the whisk attachment, combine the egg whites and salt and whisk until foamy.

Meanwhile, combine the granulated sugar and ⅓ cup (80 ml) water in a large heavy saucepan. Stir over medium heat until the sugar is completely melted. Attach a candy thermometer to the side of the saucepan and heat the mixture to 240°F (116°C).

With the mixer running, pour the sugar syrup down the side of the mixing bowl into the egg whites. Whisk on high speed until stiff white peaks form.

Decrease the mixer speed to medium and add small pieces of the butter one at a time. Add it slowly, as you may not need all of it. When the buttercream starts to look as if it's curdling (or as if something has gone terribly wrong), add just one more small pat of butter, increase the mixer speed to high, and whisk for a few minutes until the texture becomes smooth and creamy. With the mixer on low speed, add the mango purée and whisk until completely incorporated. If you like, you may add the orange food coloring, but the mango should give you plenty of vibrancy on its own.

Make the white chocolate ganache:

Place the white chocolate in a large bowl.

In a large saucepan, combine the cream, butter, and vanilla bean paste and bring just to a simmer.

Pour the hot cream mixture over the white chocolate, making sure the chocolate is completely covered. Allow to sit undisturbed for a few minutes. With a balloon whisk, gently stir clockwise until the ganache is smooth and emulsified. Allow to cool until just set but still spreadable.

Make the green tea simple syrup:

In a saucepan, bring 1 cup (240 ml) water to a simmer. Add the tea bags and simmer for 5 minutes. Remove the tea bags and carefully squeeze out any excess tea (it'll be hot). Add the granulated sugar and stir over medium heat until the sugar has completely dissolved. Set aside to cool.

To assemble:

Set aside a rectangular serving platter at least 4-by-12-inch (10-by-30.5-cm) in size. (If you don't have one, find a clean cardboard box and cut a 4-by-12-inch (10-by-30.5-cm) rectangle out of it; cover with aluminum foil.)

Break the almond paste into small pieces and knead them until they are malleable. Place the almond paste on a large piece of parchment paper and, using a rolling pin lightly dusted with flour, roll into a rough rectangle about 3½ by 12 inches (9 by 30.5 cm). Cover with a second piece of parchment so that the paste doesn't dry out.

Cut the sponge cake into three even strips; each piece should be approximately 3½ by 12½ inches (9 by 32 cm).

Carefully transfer one layer of cake to the prepared platter. With a pastry brush, brush a thin layer of simple syrup over the layer. Using a small offset spatula, spread 1 cup (200 g) of the ganache very evenly atop the layer and then spread 1½ cups (300 g) of buttercream very evenly over the ganache layer. Place the ganache/buttercreamed cake layer in the refrigerator to set until it is firm but not hard, no more than 10 minutes.

Place the second layer of cake atop the buttercream and press gently to ensure that it adheres to the buttercream and the cake is perfectly level. (I've even taken a spirit level to measure the cake layers, but you don't have to go that far.)

Brush simple syrup over the second layer, then use the offset spatula to spread 1 cup (250 g) of the ganache very evenly over the layer and then 1½ cups (300 g) buttercream atop the ganache. Return the cake to the refrigerator for a few minutes to set. Place the last layer of cake atop the buttercream and press gently to adhere and to make everything level (use the spirit level if you have to!).

Brush the last layer with simple syrup, then use the offset spatula to spread 1 cup (200 g) of the buttercream very evenly over the layer. Gently pull the parchment off of the almond paste rectangle and, keeping the bottom parchment adhered, carefully invert the almond paste layer over the assembled cake so that it completely covers the top layer. Remove the remaining parchment and, using a very sharp knife, carefully trim any almond paste that's hanging over.

Spread a very thin layer of the remaining ganache over the almond paste layer. (You may need to gently reheat the ganache to get it sufficiently spreadable.) Return the cake to the refrigerator for at least 2 hours or up to overnight. If refrigerating overnight, carefully cover the sides of the cake with plastic wrap to prevent drying. You want the buttercream and ganache to be completely set for slicing later—I've even gone so far as to freeze the cake until very firm to ensure beautiful slices.

Trim the ends of the cake so it measures approximately 12 inches (30.5 cm) in length (the ends tend to be a bit scraggly, and this is also a great way to get a preview of your masterpiece).

In a bowl, whisk together the confectioners' sugar and matcha powder. Use a ruler to measure the cake; make small notches every 3 inches (7.5 cm). Gently adhere a stencil to the cake and lightly sift the matcha mixture over the cake and stencil. Carefully blow away any excess powder atop the cake and gently remove the stencil.

To slice, run a very sharp knife under scalding hot water and dry. Cut cleanly through the first notch, then run your knife under scalding water and dry again for every remaining cut. Allow the cake to come to room temperature before serving.

A NOTE FROM THE SWEET TALKER: Stencils are an easy and elegant way to decorate the top of a cake. Nowadays cake stencils are quite easy to purchase, giving you an immediate decorative leg up. But if you want to create your own, you might try cutting out snowflakes or a simple heart shape from a piece of construction paper. Or if you just want to create a cool pattern on the top of the cake, simply cut strips of paper and evenly space them on top of the cake, then dust confectioners' sugar or cocoa over the top. Carefully remove the paper strips, and voilà—a stripey cake!

sponge cakes

MALAKOFFTORTE À LA RAYMO

Makes 1 (8-inch / 20-cm) cake

A *MALAKOFFTORTE*—A GLORIOUS COMBINATION OF light, airy ladyfinger-biscuit layers and a laced whipped-cream filling—is a cake built for the old-school European coffeehouse set. If there's anything more popular than a steaming cup of freshly brewed java at an Austrian café, it's the *Schlag*, or whipped cream, that's presented alongside every pastry on offer. Traditionally a *Malakofftorte* is made with rum; however, with a tip of the hat to the best coffee maker of my acquaintance—my husband, Raymond—I have made this delight with Kahlúa instead (you could substitute another coffee liqueur, if you like) and added a hint of chocolate along with the coffee and a healthy dose of whipped cream.

FOR THE LADYFINGERS:

2 eggs, separated, at room temperature

6 tablespoons (75 g) granulated sugar, divided

2 drops fresh lemon juice

¼ cup (30 g) cornstarch

1⅓ ounces (185 g) bread flour

¼ cup (20 g) Dutch-process cocoa powder

1 teaspoon freshly and very finely ground espresso beans

¼ cup (25 g) confectioners' sugar

FOR THE FILLING:

1 cup (240 ml) whole milk

3 cups (720 ml) heavy cream, divided

¼ cup (60 ml) cold strong coffee

¼ cup (60 ml) Kahlúa

6 egg yolks

½ cup (100 g) granulated sugar

¼ cup (30 g) cornstarch

pinch salt

FOR THE COFFEE SIMPLE SYRUP:

1 cup (240 ml) hot coffee

1 cup (200 g) granulated sugar

FOR THE ASSEMBLY:

¼ cup (20 g) cocoa powder

2 cups (480 ml) heavy cream

¼ cup (25 g) confectioners' sugar

1 teaspoon vanilla bean paste

Make the ladyfingers:

Preheat the oven to 400°F (205°C). Line three half sheet pans with parchment paper.

In the bowl of a stand mixer fitted with the whisk attachment, combine the egg yolks and 2 tablespoons of the granulated sugar and whip on high speed until light and thick. Transfer the yolk mixture to a mixing bowl and set aside.

In a clean bowl of the stand mixer, combine the egg whites, another 2 tablespoons of the granulated sugar, and the lemon juice. Whisk until foamy. In a separate bowl, stir together the cornstarch and remaining granulated sugar and slowly add the mixture to the egg whites, whisking until stiff peaks form.

Using a large rubber spatula, fold together the egg yolk and egg white mixtures. Then sift the flour, cocoa powder, and espresso over the mixture and fold into the batter until well combined. Transfer the batter to a large pastry bag with a large open tip.

On the first sheet pan, pipe 15 strips of batter, each 3 inches (7.5 cm) long. Sift the confectioners' sugar over the ladyfingers and bake for 8 to 10 minutes, until the ladyfingers are golden brown. Set aside. On the remaining two sheet pans, with an 8-inch (20-cm) round cake pan as a guide and using a Sharpie or magic marker, trace three circles onto each piece of parchment. Flip the parchment over so the circles are visible but won't transfer to the batter.

Victoria Sponge Cake

Malakofftorte à la Raymo

Using the same pastry bag and tip, pipe the batter to fill the circles, starting at the center of each and spiraling out to the edge of the circle, resulting in four (8-inch / 20-cm) round layers. Bake for 15 to 20 minutes, until the layers are golden brown. Set aside to cool completely.

Make the filling:

In a heavy saucepan, combine the milk, 1 cup (240 ml) of the cream, the coffee, and Kahlúa and bring to a simmer.

Meanwhile, in the bowl of a stand mixer fitted with the whisk attachment, combine the egg yolks, granulated sugar, cornstarch, and salt. Whisk on high speed until the mixture is thick and pale.

With the mixer running on medium speed, very slowly pour the simmering milk-cream mixture down the side of the bowl into the egg yolk mixture. Continue mixing until all the ingredients are well combined.

Transfer the mixture back to the saucepan and whisk over medium heat until the mixture thickens to the consistency of mayonnaise.

Transfer the pastry cream to a bowl and cover with plastic wrap, pressing the plastic directly onto the surface to prevent a skin from forming. Refrigerate until completely cool, about 2 hours.

Vigorously stir the pastry cream with a wooden spoon to smooth it out a bit (it sets to a very firm consistency).

In the bowl of a stand mixer fitted with the whisk attachment, whisk the remaining 2 cups (480 ml) cream until stiff peaks form.

Transfer one-third of the whipped cream to the pastry cream and stir. Using a large rubber spatula, gently fold the remaining whipped cream into the pastry cream.

Make the coffee simple syrup:

In a saucepan, combine the coffee and sugar and heat until the sugar is completely dissolved.

To assemble:

Place 1 ladyfinger round on a serving platter. Using a pastry brush, brush the layer evenly with simple syrup.

Transfer the filling to a large pastry bag fitted with a large open tip and pipe one-third of the filling over the ladyfinger layer, starting at the center and spiraling out to cover the entire layer.

Place the next ladyfinger layer on top of the filling and press gently to adhere. Brush the second layer with simple syrup and pipe a spiral of about one-third of the remaining filling onto the layer. Gently press the third ladyfinger round layer on top of the filling and press gently to adhere. Brush the third layer with simple syrup. If you have any remaining filling, spread it evenly on top with a small offset spatula.

Arrange your individual ladyfingers next to one another in a neat row, so that the tops are even with one another. Trim the bottoms just a little so they are also even and sift the cocoa powder evenly over the ladyfingers. Press the individual ladyfingers onto the sides of the cake, cut side down and flat side in, pressing gently so the ladyfingers adhere to the filling. Continue placing the ladyfingers around the cake until the sides are completely covered. Wrap the cake gently with plastic wrap and refrigerate until set, about 1 hour.

In the bowl of a stand mixer fitted with the whisk attachment, combine the cream, confectioners' sugar, and vanilla bean paste and whisk until stiff peaks form.

Transfer the whipped cream to a large pastry bag fit with a large star tip and pipe decorative designs on top of the cake. Serve immediately.

KARDINALSCHNITTEN
THE CARDINAL'S SLICES

Makes 10 servings

THIS IS A LOVELY, STRIPEY PASTRY. Like a *Malakofftorte*, it's filled with a luscious cream, but it is slightly more whimsical, with its jaunty lines of alternating meringue and ladyfingers. Traditionally the two batters are left plain, creating a white and off-white pattern, but lacing the ladyfingers with cocoa and the meringue with raspberry purée creates pink and brown stripes that not only taste wonderful but will drag a smile out of every person in the room. I promise.

FOR THE FRENCH MERINGUE:
½ cup (120 ml) egg whites
a few drops fresh lemon juice
¼ cup (60 ml) raspberry purée (see page 48)
½ teaspoon salt
1¼ cups (250 g) granulated sugar

FOR THE LADYFINGERS:
2 eggs, separated, at room temperature
6 tablespoons (75 g) granulated sugar
2 drops fresh lemon juice
¼ cup (30 g) cornstarch
5 tablespoons (45 g) bread flour
2 tablespoons Dutch-process cocoa powder

FOR THE FILLING:
1 cup (200 g) granulated sugar
5 egg whites
pinch salt
2 cups (480 ml) heavy cream
1 tablespoon vanilla bean paste
1 teaspoon powdered gelatin

FOR THE ASSEMBLY:
2 pints (500 g) fresh raspberries

Make the French meringue:

In the bowl of a stand mixer fitted with the whisk attachment, combine the egg whites, lemon juice, raspberry purée, and salt. Whisk on high speed until frothy. Slowly add the granulated sugar and continue whisking on high speed just until stiff peaks form—do not overwhip. Transfer the egg white mixture to a pastry bag fitted with a large open tip.

Make the ladyfingers:

In the bowl of a stand mixer fitted with the whisk attachment, combine the egg yolks and 2 tablespoons of the granulated sugar and whip on high speed until light and thick. Transfer the yolk mixture to a mixing bowl and set aside.

In a clean bowl of the stand mixer, combine the egg whites, 2 tablespoons of the sugar, and the lemon juice. Whisk until foamy. In a small bowl, stir together the cornstarch and the remaining sugar. Slowly add the cornstarch-sugar mixture to the egg whites and whisk until they hold stiff peaks.

Using a large rubber spatula, fold together the egg yolk and egg white mixtures. Sift the bread flour and the cocoa powder over the batter and fold in until well combined.

Make the stripes:

Preheat the oven to 275°F (135°C). Line two half sheet pans with parchment. On the first parchment, pipe 5 strips of meringue, 4 inches (10 cm) long, leaving a 1-inch (2.5-cm) gap between each stripe. Repeat in the same manner on the second parchment. Discard any

remaining meringue from the pastry bag (or you can pipe meringue kisses to bake later) and refill the bag with the ladyfinger batter. Pipe stripes of ladyfinger batter on the outside and in between the meringue stripes so that the meringue and ladyfinger batter touch.

Bake for 60 to 70 minutes, or until the cake is golden brown. Allow to cool completely.

Make the filling:

In a heavy saucepan, combine the granulated sugar and ¼ cup (60 ml) water. Heat over low heat, stirring until the sugar has completely melted. Increase the heat to medium-high and attach a candy thermometer. Heat the syrup to 240°F (116°C).

Place the egg whites and salt in the clean bowl of a stand mixer fitted with the whisk attachment. Whisk on high speed until foamy. When the syrup comes to temperature, decrease the mixer speed to medium and slowly pour the syrup down the side of the bowl into the whisking egg whites. Once all the sugar syrup is added, whisk on high speed until very stiff, glossy peaks form. Transfer the egg whites to a clean bowl.

Using the same bowl in which you whipped the egg whites (you needn't clean it), combine the cream and vanilla bean paste. Whisk on high speed until soft peaks form.

Using a large rubber spatula, fold the whipped cream into the egg whites.

In a small, microwave-safe bowl, add ⅓ cup (80 ml) water and sprinkle the gelatin in an even layer over the water. Allow the gelatin to bloom (it should become saturated and look soggy), about 3 minutes. Microwave the gelatin at 50% power in 10-second intervals, stirring in between, until the gelatin has completely dissolved.

Stir a large spoonful of the cream into the gelatin mixture to temper the gelatin. Quickly stir the tempered gelatin into the remaining cream.

To assemble:

Set aside 10 of the best-looking raspberries.

Transfer the filling to a large pastry bag fitted with a large open tip. Pipe all of the filling evenly over one strip. Gently press 1 pint (125 g) of raspberries into the cream. Remove the parchment from the reserved strip and gently press on top of the filling. Refrigerate the cake until the filling is set.

Dip a very sharp serrated knife into scalding water and dry completely. Cut the cake into approximately 2-inch (5-cm) slices. Scatter the remaining raspberries atop the slices before serving.

MINI BERRY LADYFINGER TARTS

Makes 8 individual tarts

THIS DESSERT IS SO DARNED PRETTY, it's just begging for a garden party. If you have activities planned prior to serving dessert, you may want to hide these tarts because otherwise they are going to be all anyone can talk about or look at or be dying to eat ASAP. By making your own ladyfingers, you can tailor the size of your "picket fence" to suit your own taste.

FOR THE LADYFINGERS:

4 eggs, separated

½ teaspoon salt

¾ cup (150 g) granulated sugar, divided

1 cup (140 g) cake flour, sifted

½ teaspoon vanilla extract

1 cup (100 g) confectioners' sugar, for dusting

1 cup (240 ml) ice cubes

FOR THE FILLING:

1 cup (240 ml) whole milk

2 cups (480 ml) heavy cream, divided

½ cup (100 g) granulated sugar, divided

6 egg yolks

pinch salt

5 tablespoons (40 g) cornstarch

¼ cup (60 ml) raspberry purée (see page 48)

FOR THE ASSEMBLY:

2 cups (250 g) fresh raspberries

2 cups (250 g) mixed whole fresh berries

1 spool decorative ribbon, 1 inch (2.5 cm) wide

Make the ladyfingers:

Preheat the oven to 350° (175°C). Line two half sheet pans with parchment paper.

In the bowl of a stand mixer fitted with the whisk attachment, beat the egg whites with the salt until foamy. Slowly add 3 tablespoons of the granulated sugar and beat until soft peaks form. Transfer the egg whites to a clean bowl.

In the same stand mixer bowl (you needn't clean it), combine the egg yolks and the remaining sugar. Whisk until the yolks become thick and pale and the mixture forms ribbons when the whisk is lifted.

Sift the flour over the egg yolk mixture and add one-quarter of the egg white mixture. Using a large rubber spatula, fold together gently. Add the remaining egg whites and fold into the batter.

Transfer the batter to a large pastry bag fitted with a large open tip. Pipe 8 circles, each 2 inches (5 cm) wide, on the first sheet pan; these will act as the base of your cakes. On the second sheet pan, pipe the remaining batter into strips 3 inches (7.5 cm) long. Using a fine-mesh sieve, dust the circles and strips with half of the confectioners' sugar; allow the sugar to dissolve into the batter completely. Dust again with the remaining confectioners' sugar and allow to sit undisturbed for 3 minutes.

Place a piece of parchment next to the sheet pans. Lift the parchment holding the ladyfinger batter and tilt it up a bit, so that the extra confectioners' sugar on the parchment falls onto your empty piece of parchment.

Open the oven doors and toss the ice cubes onto the bottom of the oven. Close the doors for 10 seconds. Place the ladyfingers in the now steaming oven and bake for 10 to 15 minutes, until the sugar beads on top and the ladyfingers are lightly golden brown. Allow to cool completely.

Make the filling:

In a large saucepan, combine the milk and 1 cup (240 ml) of the cream and bring to a simmer. Meanwhile, in the bowl of a stand mixer fitted with the whisk attachment, combine the granulated sugar, egg yolks, salt, cornstarch, and raspberry purée. Whisk on high speed until combined. Once the milk mixture has come to a simmer, slowly pour it down the side of the bowl into the whisking egg yolk mixture and continue whisking until well combined.

Transfer the mixture back to the saucepan. Over medium heat, whisk constantly until the mixture thickens to the consistency of mayonnaise. Transfer the mixture to a bowl and cover with plastic wrap, pressing the plastic directly onto the surface so that a skin doesn't form. Refrigerate until cool, about 2 hours.

Remove the filling from the refrigerator. It will have firmed up quite a bit; stir it with a wooden spoon until it loosens and is smooth.

In the bowl of a stand mixer fitted with the whisk attachment, whisk the remaining cream until stiff peaks form. Using a large rubber spatula, fold the whipped cream into the filling until combined. Transfer the raspberry filling into a pastry bag fitted with a large open tip.

To assemble:

Place 8 metal rings (see Sidebar, page 201) on a parchment-lined half sheet pan. Line each ring with ladyfingers, the sugar-dusted side facing out, by standing them up side by side until the ring is filled. Place a ladyfinger cake round into the bottom of the ring, trimming the round if it's too tight a fit with the standing ladyfingers. Repeat with each of the remaining rings.

Place 3 raspberries on the bottom layer of each ring. Pipe filling into each ring until it just reaches the top of the standing ladyfingers. Refrigerate until firm, at least 2 hours.

To serve, carefully remove the rings. (Heat the rings gently with a kitchen torch or blow dryer for easier removal if necessary.) Arrange the mixed berries atop the filling. For an especially adorable presentation, gently tie a ribbon around each tart.

A NOTE FROM THE SWEET TALKER: Confectioner's sugar, aka powdered sugar: You know the stuff, but what you might not know is that it's full of cornstarch. In many applications, this extra cornstarch doesn't really affect the recipe. But in some cases, it's best to make your own confectioners' sugar for maximum results. To make your own, simply add 1 cup (200 g) of granulated sugar at a time to your food processor or blender. Pulse until the sugar becomes a powder. Run the powder through a fine-mesh sieve to eliminate any residual granules, and then measure per the recipe. For recipes like individual ladyfingers, making confectioners' sugar from scratch (i.e., minus the cornstarch) is key for the sugar to bead properly on top of the ladyfingers. Plus, it's so easy!

RIGÓ JANCSI SLICES

Makes 1 (8-by-12-inch / 20-by-30.5-cm) cake

I'M GOING TO INDULGE IN some gossip here, of the 1890s type. We tend to think in our media-cluttered modern world that we are living in a new and ugly age of pseudo-celebrities and reality stars. Well, we are living through nothing original except for the fact that in earlier times, something good actually came out of the exploits of the rich and pampered—like yummy desserts.

Clara Ward was a wealthy and beautiful American heiress. She married a very poor and much older Belgian nobleman. But in the bargain, she became a princess and, for all their democratic values, Americans were pleased as punch by this marriage, and it made for great newspaper copy. As we all know, a rich, attractive American girl who gets too much media attention is bound to take a wrong turn somewhere and Clara, Princess of Chimay, made quite a hairpin. One evening, at a lovely meal with her royal husband, Clara laid eyes on the gypsy violinist providing the evening's entertainment. The next thing anyone knew, she'd taken off with the musician and was heading to his hometown of Budapest. Scandal! Gossip! Dessert! Hungarians, being the master bakers they are, named a cake after their hometown hero: Rigó Jancsi, gypsy violinist turned lothario! The glorious confection consists of two layers of chocolate sponge cake cradling a very dense chocolate mousse filling topped with a chocolate glaze. Not surprisingly, the marriage lasted just a few years, but the cake will live forever.

FOR THE SPONGE CAKE:

½ cup (60 g) all-purpose flour

½ cup (40 g) Dutch-process cocoa powder (I use Cacao Barry Extra Brute)

1 cup (200 g) granulated sugar

5 eggs, at room temperature

1 teaspoon salt

1 tablespoon vanilla bean paste

6 tablespoons (85 g) unsalted butter, melted

FOR THE FILLING:

1 cup (230 g) unsalted butter

8 eggs, separated, at room temperature

2 cups (480 ml) heavy cream

½ cup (100 g) granulated sugar, divided

¼ teaspoon salt

1 pound (455 g) bittersweet chocolate, finely chopped (I use Callebaut 60/40)

FOR THE CHOCOLATE GLAZE:

8 ounces (225 g) bittersweet chocolate, finely chopped (I use Callebaut 60/40)

⅓ cup (80 ml) heavy cream

2 tablespoons unsalted butter

1 tablespoon vanilla bean paste

FOR THE ASSEMBLY:

½ cup (120 ml) smooth apricot preserves

2 cups (480 ml) heavy cream

½ cup (50 g) confectioners' sugar

1 teaspoon vanilla bean paste

Make the sponge cake:

Preheat the oven to 350°F (175°C). Line a half sheet pan with parchment paper and spray with nonstick cooking spray.

Sift the flour, then measure out ½ cup (60 g) and place in a small bowl. Sift the cocoa powder, then measure out ½ cup (40 g) and add to the flour. Whisk the two, then sift them together.

In a heatproof metal bowl of a stand mixer fitted with the whisk attachment, combine the granulated sugar, eggs, and salt. Place the bowl over a bain marie (a saucepan half filled with gently simmering water) and whisk constantly until the sugar has completely melted. Return the bowl to the stand mixer and whisk on high speed until the mixture is pale and fluffy and the bowl is cool to the touch. Add the vanilla bean paste and whisk on high speed until completely incorporated.

Sift one-third of the flour–cocoa powder mixture over the egg mixture and, using a large rubber spatula, fold it into the batter until incorporated. Sift and fold in another third of the flour-cocoa mixture until incorporated; sift and fold in the remaining third. Fold until no streaks of egg remain.

Fold the butter into the batter until incorporated. Transfer the mixture to the prepared sheet pan, using a large offset spatula to even out the batter.

Bake for 20 to 25 minutes, until the cake springs back when you touch it and starts to pull away from the sides of the pan. Set aside to cool completely.

Make the filling:

Place a large metal bowl over a bain marie and add the butter. Allow to melt completely.

Add the egg yolks, cream, ¼ cup (50 g) of the granulated sugar, and the salt. Whisk until the mixture coats the back of a spoon. (If you are fearful of bacteria, I suggest you attach a candy thermometer to ensure that the mixture reaches 160°F / 72°C, the temperature at which bacteria are killed.)

Put the chocolate in a large heatproof bowl. Remove the egg yolk mixture from the heat and pour it over the chocolate, making sure the chocolate is completely covered; let sit undisturbed for a few minutes to allow the chocolate to melt. With a clean whisk, stir the mixture until the chocolate is completely melted. (If necessary, place the bowl over the bain marie again and stir until the chocolate is melted.) Set aside.

In a heatproof bowl of a stand mixer fitted with the whisk attachment, add the egg whites and remaining sugar. Place

the bowl over the bain marie and whisk until the sugar has completely melted (again, you can attach a candy thermometer to ensure that the mixture reaches 160°F / 72°C).

Return the bowl to the stand mixer and whisk on high speed just until the egg whites achieve soft peaks. (Do not overwhip to the point of dryness; the whites should be smooth and easy to incorporate into the chocolate mixture.)

Transfer one-quarter of the egg whites to the chocolate mixture and, using a large rubber spatula, gently stir the egg whites into the chocolate to lighten. Add the remaining egg whites and gently fold them into the chocolate until no white streaks remain.

Make the glaze:

Place the chocolate in a large metal bowl.

In a large saucepan, combine the cream, butter, and vanilla bean paste and simmer over low heat until the butter has completely melted. Pour the cream mixture over the chocolate, making sure the chocolate is completely covered. Allow to sit undisturbed for a few minutes, then whisk until the mixture has emulsified.

To assemble:

Run a sharp paring knife along the edge of the sponge cake to release it from the pan. Place a cutting board slightly larger than the sheet pan over the pan and invert the two together so that the cake falls onto the cutting board. Gently peel off the parchment paper. Trim the outer edges of the cake. Cut the cake in half lengthwise so you have 2 sponge layers, each approximately 8 by 12 inches (20 by 30.5 cm).

In a small saucepan, combine the apricot preserves with 3 tablespoons of water. Cook over low heat, stirring, until the preserves and water melt together and form a thick sauce.

Line an 8-by-12-inch (20-by-30.5-cm) casserole pan with plastic wrap, allowing the wrap to hang over the sides of the pan. Place a single layer of sponge cake inside the pan (it should be just large enough to cover the entire bottom of the pan). With a pastry brush, brush half of the apricot preserves in an even layer over the cake. Pour all of the chocolate filling over the preserves and use a small offset spatula to spread the filling into an even layer. Place the

second cake layer on top of the filling, pressing very gently to adhere the cake to the filling. Brush the remaining apricot preserves over the second layer and refrigerate for about 10 minutes, until the preserves set.

Make sure the chocolate glaze is still very fluid. If it has set, place the bowl over the bain marie and stir constantly until the mixture loosens and is smooth.

Pour the glaze over the top cake layer and use a large offset spatula to spread the glaze evenly. Refrigerate until set, at least 2 hours, or overnight.

In the bowl of a stand mixer fitted with the whisk attachment, combine the cream, confectioners' sugar, and vanilla bean paste and whisk until stiff peaks form. Transfer the whipped cream to a pastry bag fitted with a large star tip.

Remove the cake from the casserole dish, using the overhanging plastic wrap as "handles."

Pipe the whipped cream decoratively atop the cake and serve immediately.

A NOTE FROM THE SWEET TALKER: In pastry shops, we use fancy pastry frames to assemble cakes containing fillings that require a fair amount of "setting time" before serving. Why? Because if you assemble the cake on a surface with no "sides" to contain the filling while it's setting, it will simply seep out, leaving you with two layers of cake smooshed together and a puddle of filling around it. A pastry frame can be made to the exact size of a cake and contains high sides so you can build the cake inside the frame, creating a dam for the filling. You can refrigerate and freeze the cake in the frame until it's set and then cut into slices when the filling won't go anywhere. I find that it's a huge waste of money to buy pastry frames and cake molds if you aren't a pastry chef using the equipment every day. You probably have things at home that can function just as well! Casserole dishes work incredibly well as stand-ins for cake frames when you are building rectangular cakes, especially Austrian-Hungarian style *Schnitten*. For individual cakes, I save round tins of all sizes—tuna, cat food, tomato soup, and coffee cans. You name it—I save it (and of course clean it *really* well). Using a can opener, fully remove the top and bottom of the can, and you've just got yourself a cake mold!

CHOCOLATE-NUTELLA PAVÉ

Makes 1 (4-by-14-inch / 10-by-35.5-cm) cake

PAVÉ IS THE FRENCH WORD for paving stone or cobble-stone. It's also the moniker of a dessert, which might lead you to surmise that said dessert has the consistency of its namesake. Thankfully, you'd be terribly wrong. The dessert iteration takes its name from the shape of a cobblestone (rectangular or square), not its texture, and consists of spongy cake layered with scrumptious filling and smothered in icing. At my pastry shop in Montpelier, this version was an instant hit with everyone, both those seeking gluten-free treats and those simply yearning to plunge their taste buds into some luscious chocolate goodness. It's so good, in fact, you might just fraudulently imply to your fellow pastry lovers that this cake does indeed resemble a cobblestone in texture, just to keep more for yourself.

FOR THE CAKE:
8 ounces (225 g) bittersweet chocolate (at least 70%;
  I use Black and Green's Organic 72% baking chocolate;
  see page 12), finely chopped
2 tablespoons unsalted butter, softened
½ cup (120 ml) strong, piping-hot coffee
7 eggs, separated
½ teaspoon salt
1 cup (200 g) granulated sugar
2 tablespoons cornstarch
1 teaspoon vanilla bean paste

FOR THE FILLING:
¼ cup (55 g) unsalted butter
2 cups (480 ml) heavy cream, divided
½ cup (120 g) Nutella, or 5½ ounces (155 g) canned hazelnut
  praline paste (see Note)
4 eggs, separated, at room temperature
8 ounces (225 g) bittersweet chocolate (at least 60%),
  finely chopped
¼ cup (50 g) granulated sugar
¼ teaspoon salt

FOR THE GANACHE:
1 pound (455 g) bittersweet chocolate, finely chopped
2 cups (480 ml) heavy cream
4 tablespoons (55 g) unsalted butter
2 tablespoons corn syrup
¼ cup (60 ml) Frangelico or other hazelnut liqueur

FOR THE SIMPLE SYRUP:
1 cup (240 ml) hot coffee
1 cup (200 g) granulated sugar

FOR THE ASSEMBLY:
¼ cup (20 g) Dutch-process cocoa powder

NOTE: Use the hazelnut praline paste if you'd like a more hazelnut-forward taste; I use Love'n Bake. Praline pastes tend to separate in the can, with the oil on top and the paste on the bottom. The paste gets rather dry. This is normal. Stir together to recombine, or, if need be, put the entire contents in a food processor and pulse until smooth.

Make the cake:

Preheat the oven to 375°F (190°C). Line a half sheet pan with parchment.

In a heatproof metal bowl, combine the chocolate, butter, and coffee. Allow to sit undisturbed for 2 minutes, then stir. If the chocolate isn't completely melted, place the bowl over a bain marie (a saucepan half filled with simmering water) to melt completely. Set aside.

In the bowl of a stand mixer fitted with the whisk attachment, combine the egg whites and salt. Beat on high speed until white and foamy. In a small bowl, stir together the granulated sugar and cornstarch. Slowly add the sugar mixture to the whisking whites. Continue whisking until stiff, shiny peaks form, making sure not to overbeat to the point of dryness. Set aside.

In a bowl, whisk the egg yolks to break them apart a bit. (Make sure they are at room temperature or they can cause the chocolate to seize.) Once the chocolate has cooled slightly, add the yolks to the chocolate mixture, whisking constantly to ensure that the yolks' contact with the chocolate doesn't cause them to scramble.

Stir one-quarter of the egg whites into the chocolate mixture to lighten. (You can stir vigorously; this process, lightening, is about loosening up the chocolate so that it's light enough to gently add the remaining egg whites with ease.) Add the remaining egg whites, and this time, using a large rubber spatula, fold them gently into the mixture. Make sure no visible white streaks remain but be careful not to deflate the stiff peaks.

With an offset spatula, spread the batter into the prepared pan. Bake for 10 to 15 minutes, or until the cake springs back when you touch it and a cake tester inserted in the center comes out with moist crumbs (not with wet batter). The cake will puff and rise considerably in the oven but will fall when you take it out. This is perfectly normal! Allow to cool completely.

Make the filling:

In a large heatproof metal bowl, add the butter and place the bowl over a bain marie (a large saucepan half filled with gently simmering water). Once the butter is melted, add 1 cup (240 ml) of the cream and the Nutella or hazelnut paste. (If using the paste, add it with the butter so that it has time to melt.) Whisk together, then whisk in the egg yolks. Continue whisking until the mixture coats the back of a spoon.

Place the chocolate in a heatproof bowl. Remove the egg yolk mixture from the heat and immediately pour it over the chocolate, making sure the chocolate is completely

covered. Let sit undisturbed for a few minutes. Stir until the mixture is completely smooth and all the chocolate is melted and integrated into the custard. Set aside.

In the clean bowl of a stand mixer, combine the egg whites, granulated sugar, and salt. Place the bowl over a bain marie, whisking constantly, until the sugar has completely melted and the egg white mixture is hot to the touch.

Transfer the bowl to a stand mixer fitted with the whisk attachment and whisk on high speed until stiff, white peaks form. Do not overbeat to the point of dryness.

Using a large rubber spatula, transfer one-quarter of the egg whites into the chocolate custard and stir to combine. Add the remaining egg whites and gently fold the whites into the custard. Set aside.

Add the remaining cream to the same bowl in which you whisked the egg whites. Whisk until very stiff, but be careful not to overbeat.

Gently fold the whipped cream into the custard mixture until there are no white streaks remaining. Transfer the mousse to a bowl and cover with plastic wrap. Refrigerate until firm.

Make the ganache:

Place the chocolate in a large mixing bowl. In a large saucepan, combine the cream, butter, corn syrup, and Frangelico. Bring to a simmer. Pour the cream mixture over the chopped chocolate, making sure the chocolate is completely covered. Let sit undisturbed for 2 minutes. Gently whisk the mixture until it emulsifies and becomes smooth and shiny. Set aside.

Make the simple syrup:

In a saucepan, combine the coffee and granulated sugar. Stir over medium heat until the sugar has melted completely.

*Chocolate-
Nutella Pavé*

*Walnut Coffee-
Cream Torte*

To assemble:

Run a paring knife around the inner edges of the sheet pan to release the cooled cake. Place a clean kitchen towel on a work surface. Sift the cocoa powder in an even layer over the towel. Invert the sheet pan to release the cake onto the towel. Carefully remove the parchment. Trim the edges of the cake so that it measures approximately 11 by 16 inches (28 by 40.5 cm), then cut the cake along its long side into 3 even strips, each 3½ inches (9 cm) wide and 12 inches (30.5 cm) long. (I open a measuring tape along the long side of the cake, mark off every 3½ inches / 9 cm, then cut.) If you have a large cake spatula, this is the time to put it to use. This cake is very delicate—that's part of its charm. But if you don't have a large cake spatula, use a piece of cake board; gently slip it entirely under the first strip. Then gently transfer the first strip to a sturdy piece of cardboard covered with aluminum foil, measuring a few inches longer in width and length than the cake strips. Using a pastry brush, brush the first strip with simple syrup.

Place strips of parchment along the bottom perimeter of the first layer (under the edges, if possible, onto the foil-covered cardboard) to catch any stray bits of mousse or ganache. This will keep your serving surface clean.

Transfer the chocolate mousse filling to a pastry bag fitted with a large open tip (you'll have to refill the bag a few times). Pipe the mousse in long strips to cover the first strip of cake. (You can also spoon the mousse onto the cake and use a small offset spatula to spread it, but you'll find that piping makes a more even layer and is a tidier process.) Place the second layer of cake on top of the mousse and press very gently to adhere. Use a small offset spatula to scrape away any excess mousse that has escaped outside the sides of the cake. Place this layer in the freezer for 20 minutes to set.

Remove the cake from the freezer and brush the top layer with simple syrup. Pipe mousse in long strips to cover the top. Place the third layer of cake on top of the mousse and press gently to adhere. Scrape away any excess mousse and make sure the sides are completely smooth. This is the time to take a good look at your cake to make sure that it's straight and even. If you find that it's lopsided, gently push the cake so that it's nice and plumb. Place in the freezer to set until extremely stable, at least 20 minutes.

You may have excess mousse. If so, simply place the remainder in a bowl and give your family a couple spoons!

Check the consistency of the ganache. If it has set and become hard, remove the plastic wrap and place the bowl over a bain marie and stir until the ganache is smooth and pourable.

Using a ladle, pour the ganache over the top of the cake. Using a small offset spatula, gently smooth the ganache so that it covers the top of the cake in an even layer and starts to cascade down the sides of the cake. Use the spatula to smooth the ganache along all the sides in an even coating. Refrigerate the cake until the ganache has set, 1 to 2 hours.

Before serving, rip 12 strips of parchment in various lengths, each about ¼ to ½ inch (6 mm to 12 mm) thick Very gently stagger the strips approximately ½ inch (12 mm) apart on top of the cake so that the irregular strips resemble zebra stripes. Sift the cocoa powder over the cake; gently remove the strips to reveal beautiful stripes. Dip a very sharp serrated knife into scalding hot water, dry the knife, and slice. (Do this before each slice for best results.) Serve immediately.

OPTIONS!

Does this recipe overwhelm you? Well, you can break it down and simplify!

MOUSSE: Of course you could just make the mousse, spoon it into handsome glasses, chill it, and call it a day. There's no shame in that.

GANACHE LAYERS: If the mousse is what overwhelms you, you can fill the cake layers with slightly set ganache (allow to cool just enough that it's spreadable and holds its shape when you spoon it onto the cake).

TRIFLE: If it's the free-from stacking of the layers that gives you pause, why not make this into a trifle? Layer cake pieces into a glass trifle bowl and spoon mousse over the layers. Skip the ganache and add berries if you like. Top the trifle with whipped cream and berries, and you'll have a delicious dessert that will fulfill all your impress-the-guests needs.

ROULADE: Another unstacked but beautiful option is to leave the cake uncut on the kitchen towel and cover it with a thin layer of spreadable ganache. Top the ganache with a layer of chocolate mousse about ½ inch (12 mm) deep, and roll the cake, starting at the narrower end, into a spiral. Make sure to roll gently and not too tightly so that you don't squeeze the mousse out from inside the cake. Roulade cakes tend to crack as you roll them. One way to prevent this is to turn the cake out onto the dusted kitchen towel while it's still very hot and roll the cake into a spiral (rolling the kitchen towel into the spiral to prevent the cake from sticking to itself). Allow it to cool like this, then unroll the cake gently to fill.

WALNUT COFFEE-CREAM TORTE

Makes 1 (8-inch / 20-cm) square layer cake

THIS IS A GENTLE RIFF on a famous cake of my mother's that I will forever call "Helga Cake" in her honor. Her version contained pecans and was layered throughout with chocolate buttercream. This version uses walnuts, and the filling is a lovely coffee-infused buttercream iced with deep chocolate. The walnuts make for an incredibly moist sponge while the coffee buttercream is a delicious counterpoint to the dark chocolate outer shell and the nutty cake layers. I think Helga would approve.

FOR THE CAKE:

18 ounces (510 g) walnut pieces

1½ cups (300 g) granulated sugar

12 eggs, separated, at room temperature

4 whole eggs

1 tablespoon vanilla bean paste

1 tablespoon baking powder

1 teaspoon salt

FOR THE BUTTERCREAM FILLING:

6 egg yolks

1 cup (200 g) granulated sugar

½ cup (120 ml) coffee

1 tablespoon vanilla bean paste

1 pound (455 g) unsalted butter, cut into small pieces, at room temperature

FOR THE CHOCOLATE BUTTERCREAM:

8 ounces (225 g) bittersweet chocolate, finely chopped

6 egg yolks

1 teaspoon vanilla extract

⅓ cup (80 ml) strong coffee, very hot

¾ cup (170 g) unsalted butter, cut into small pieces, at room temperature

Pinch salt

FOR THE SIMPLE SYRUP:

1 cup (240 ml) coffee

1 cup (200 g) granulated sugar

FOR THE ASSEMBLY:

4½ ounces (125 g) very finely chopped walnuts

Make the cake:

Preheat the oven to 350°F (175°C). Prepare four 9-inch (23-cm) square cake pans by lining the bottom of each with parchment paper and spraying the bottom (not the sides) with nonstick cooking spray.

In the bowl of a food processor fitted with the blade attachment, combine the walnut pieces with ½ cup (100 g) of the granulated sugar and pulse until the mixture resembles coarse cornmeal.

Add the 12 egg yolks, 4 whole eggs, vanilla bean paste, and baking powder and blend until a smooth paste forms.

In the bowl of a stand mixer fitted with the whisk attachment, combine the 12 egg whites and salt and whisk until just foamy. Slowly add the remaining sugar and whisk on high speed until the whites are glossy and hold stiff peaks, being careful not to overwhip to the point of dryness.

Transfer the walnut paste to a mixing bowl and stir in one-third of the egg whites to lighten the batter. Using a large rubber spatula, gently fold the remaining egg whites into the batter until no white streaks remain. Smooth the batter evenly onto the prepared cake pans and bake for 20 minutes, or until the cake springs back when touched. Allow to cool completely.

Make the buttercream filling:

In the bowl of a stand mixer fitted with the whisk attachment, combine the egg yolks, granulated sugar, coffee, and vanilla bean paste. Place the mixing bowl over a bain marie (a saucepan half filled with gently simmering water) and whisk constantly until the sugar has completely melted and the mixture thickens slightly. (If you worry about bacteria in the eggs, attach a candy thermometer to ensure that the mixture reaches 160°F / 72°C, the temperature at which bacteria are killed.)

Transfer the bowl to the stand mixer and whisk on high speed until the egg mixture has tripled in volume and the bowl is cool to the touch. Add the butter, a few pieces at a time, and continue whisking until the filling is smooth and spreadable. When you first start adding the butter, the mixture will look as if it has broken, but continue to whisk on high and it will come together as a smooth filling.

Make the chocolate buttercream:

In the bowl of a food processor fitted with the blade attachment, add the chocolate, egg yolks, vanilla extract, and salt. While pulsing, add the coffee in a slow, steady stream. Add the butter, a few pieces at a time, and process until the buttercream is smooth and spreadable.

Make the simple syrup:

In a saucepan, combine the coffee and sugar and stir over low heat until the sugar has completely melted.

To assemble:

Place one of the cake layers on a serving platter. Using a pastry brush, brush an even layer of simple syrup over the layer. Place 1½ cups (300 g) filling onto the first layer and spread evenly with a small offset spatula. Place the second cake layer on top; press gently to adhere and brush with simple syrup. Place 1½ cups (300 g) filling on top and spread evenly. Top with the third cake layer; press gently to adhere and brush with simple syrup. Spread 1½ cups (300 g) of the filling on the third layer and spread evenly. Top with the remaining layer of cake. Brush with simple syrup. Use the remaining filling to apply a crumb coat of filling over the entire cake: Using a bench scraper or large offset spatula, smooth the filling over the top and sides of the cake in a very thin, even layer. Place in the refrigerator to set the outside layer, from 20 minutes up to 1 hour (the filling should feel a bit hard and no longer tacky).

Using a large offset spatula, cover the cake with the buttercream, starting at the top of the cake and working along the sides. To create a really smooth finish, work quickly and heat your spatula often by running it under scalding water and drying completely. (The heat of the spatula goes a long way in smoothing the icing, but be sure that the spatula is totally dry.)

Cut a 1/2-inch (12-mm) strip of parchment paper and wrap it around the middle of the sides of the cake, pressing gently to adhere. Cut 4 more 1/2-inch (12-mm) strips to create a box in the middle of the cake. Press the walnuts onto the sides and top of the cake and brush off any excess. Remove the parchment strips before serving.

BANANA CARAMEL SLICES

Makes 8 slices

BANANA. CARAMEL. CREAM. CHOCOLATE. These slices combine some of the most comforting dessert elements while retaining an elegance that will make for a gorgeous dinner-party presentation. Each slice reveals a subtle color progression from the light cocoa of the cake to the amber of the caramel cream to the lovely soft yellow of the banana, all topped with a rich black chocolate glaze and a caramelized slice of banana. Perfect.

FOR THE CARAMEL CREAM:
1 cup (200 g) granulated sugar, divided
1 squirt fresh lemon juice
2½ cups (600 ml) heavy cream, divided
2 cups (480 ml) half-and-half
6 egg yolks
¼ cup (30 g) cornstarch
pinch salt
1 tablespoon vanilla bean paste (or an equal measure of vanilla extract)

FOR THE SPONGE CAKE:
4 eggs
½ cup (100 g) granulated sugar
½ teaspoon salt
1 teaspoon vanilla bean paste
1 cup (140 g) cake flour
2 tablespoons Dutch-process cocoa powder
2 tablespoons unsalted butter, melted and cooled

FOR THE GLAZE:
8 ounces (225 g) bittersweet chocolate, finely chopped
½ cup (120 ml) heavy cream
2 tablespoons honey
2 tablespoons unsalted butter

FOR THE SIMPLE SYRUP:
½ cup (100 g) granulated sugar

FOR THE ASSEMBLY:
3 pounds (1.4 kg) bananas (6 large)
1 cup (200 g) granulated sugar

Make the caramel cream:

In a heavy saucepan, combine ½ cup (100 g) of the granulated sugar, ¼ cup (60 ml) water, and the lemon juice and stir constantly over medium heat until the sugar has completely melted. Stop stirring and continue cooking until the sugar turns a light amber. Remove from the heat and add ½ cup (120 ml) of the cream. The mixture will bubble furiously at first but will subside. Stir until well combined. Transfer to a heatproof bowl and set aside until cool, about 1 hour.

In a large saucepan, heat the half-and-half over low heat until it just simmers.

In the bowl of a stand mixer fitted with the whisk attachment, combine the egg yolks, the remaining sugar, the caramel sauce, cornstarch, salt, and vanilla bean paste. Whisk on high speed until the color lightens and the mixture has thickened.

With the mixer running on medium, slowly pour the hot half-and-half down the side of the bowl into the egg yolk mixture. Increase the mixer speed to high and mix until well combined.

Transfer the caramel cream to the saucepan and whisk over medium heat until the cream thickens to the consistency of mayonnaise.

Transfer the caramel cream to a large bowl and cover with plastic wrap, pressing the plastic directly onto the surface to prevent a skin from forming. Refrigerate until

completely cool, about 2 hours. The caramel cream will be finished in a future step.

Make the sponge cake:

Preheat the oven to 350°F (175°C). Line a half sheet pan with parchment paper and spray with nonstick cooking spray.

In the bowl of a stand mixer fitted with the whisk attachment, combine the eggs, granulated sugar, salt, and vanilla bean paste. Whisk constantly over a bain marie (a large saucepan half filled with gently simmering water). Attach a candy thermometer to the side of the saucepan and heat the mixture to 110°F (43°C). Return the bowl to the mixer and whisk on high speed until the bowl is cool to the touch and the mixture has tripled in volume and forms ribbons when you lift the whisk.

Remove the bowl from the stand mixer. Sift the cake flour twice, then sift the flour and the cocoa powder together onto the batter. Using a large rubber spatula, gently fold them into the batter. Add the butter and gently fold it into the batter.

Spread the batter evenly onto the prepared pan and immediately bake for 15 minutes, or until the cake begins to pull away from the sides of the pan and springs back when you touch it.

Make the glaze:

Place the chocolate in a heatproof bowl.

In a saucepan, combine the cream, honey, and butter. Bring to a simmer.

Pour the hot cream mixture over the chocolate, making sure the chocolate is completely covered. Let sit undisturbed for 2 minutes. Whisk until the chocolate is completely melted and the mixture is smooth. Set aside.

Make the simple syrup:

In a saucepan, combine the granulated sugar with ½ cup (120 ml) water and stir over medium heat until the sugar has completely melted. Set aside.

Finish the caramel cream:

Whip the remaining 2 cups (480 ml) cream until stiff peaks form.

Remove the caramel cream from the refrigerator. Whisk until the mixture loosens and is smooth. Using a large rubber spatula, spoon one-third of the whipped cream into the caramel cream and stir to lighten. Gently fold in the remaining whipped cream.

A NOTE FROM THE SWEET TALKER: FOLDING. What makes folding so different from simply stirring? Quite a lot, actually. When you fold ingredients into one another, you use a large "paddle" to mix the ingredients, usually a large, flat rubber spatula. When you fold, instead of whirring the spatula in circles, round and round like a whirlpool, you want to behave like a gentle rower, slicing through the batter with your spatula "oar," scraping along the bottom, and coming back up again. In doing this, you incorporate the ingredients without deflating the aeration in the batter.

Transfer the caramel cream to a large pastry bag fitted with a large open tip (it may not all fit—don't force it to!).

To assemble:

Trim the edges of the cake. Cut the cake lengthwise into 3 long, even strips, each measuring about 3½ by 16 inches (9 by 40.5 cm).

Transfer 1 strip to a cake platter and, using a pastry brush, brush with an even layer of simple syrup.

Cut 4 of the bananas in half. Slice each half lengthwise. Lay the banana slices along the entire bottom strip of cake.

Pipe approximately half of the caramel cream atop the bananas and place the partially assembled cake in the freezer to set, about 20 minutes. Refrigerate the remaining caramel cream.

Place a second strip of cake atop the cream and press gently to adhere. Using a pastry brush, brush with an even layer of simple syrup. Pipe the remaining caramel cream atop the layer. Freeze until set, about 20 minutes.

Place the final strip of cake atop the cream and press gently to adhere. Freeze until set, about 20 minutes.

Meanwhile, brûlée the bananas: Cut the remaining 2 bananas in half, then slice each half lengthwise. Place the banana slices on a parchment-lined sheet pan, rounded side down. Sprinkle the granulated sugar in an even layer over the bananas. Using a kitchen torch, gently run the flame back and forth evenly over the sugar until it begins to brown and caramelize. Allow to cool and set aside. Remove the cake from the freezer. Stir the glaze to make sure its consistency is still pourable. (If it has hardened, place the bowl containing the glaze over a bain marie and stir until it loosens and is smooth.) Spoon the glaze over the top of the cake and allow it to run in an even layer down the sides. Use a small offset spatula to smooth the glaze over the top and around the sides of the cake.

Allow the glaze to set, about 15 minutes. Place the brûléed bananas atop the cake. Serve immediately.

DOBOS TORTE

Makes 1 (8-inch / 20-cm) cake

THE DOBOS IS ARGUABLY THE MOST FAMOUS of all Hungarian tortes. I feel a traditional café experience isn't complete if I don't see a Dobos on display. It's immediately recognizable, with its seven—and always seven—layers of vanilla sponge cake. And it's always filled with chocolate cream and topped with caramel-coated, jauntily placed wedges of cake layer. You could combine the elements differently, assemble the cake in just a few layers, slather on the buttercream, and serve the caramel on the side. But then it wouldn't be an official Dobos, and somehow it just wouldn't taste the same.

FOR THE SPONGE LAYERS:

6 eggs, separated, at room temperature

1 cup (200 g) granulated sugar, divided

½ teaspoon salt

1 teaspoon vanilla bean paste

1½ cups (210 g) cake flour, sifted

2 tablespoons unsalted butter, melted

FOR THE BUTTERCREAM:

12 ounces (340 g) bittersweet chocolate, finely chopped

8 egg yolks

1 tablespoon vanilla extract

½ cup (120 ml) strong coffee, very hot

1 cup (230 g) unsalted butter, cut into small pieces, at room temperature

FOR THE CARAMEL:

1 cup (200 g) granulated sugar

2 tablespoons corn syrup

¼ teaspoon fresh lemon juice

pinch salt

2 tablespoons unsalted butter

FOR THE SIMPLE SYRUP:

1 cup (200 g) granulated sugar

¼ cup (60 ml) rum

Make the sponge layers:

Preheat the oven to 350°F (175°C). Prepare four 8-inch (20-cm) round cake pans by lining the bottom of each with a round of parchment paper and spraying with non-stick cooking spray (if you have only two pans, work in batches once the batter is ready).

In a heatproof metal bowl of a stand mixer fitted with the whisk attachment, add the egg yolks and ½ cup (100 g) of the granulated sugar. Place the bowl over a bain marie (a saucepan half filled with gently simmering water) and whisk constantly until the sugar has completely melted and the mixture thickens. Return the bowl to the stand mixer and whisk on high speed until the mixture has tripled in volume and the bowl is cool to the touch. Transfer the egg yolk mixture to another bowl and clean the mixing bowl and whisk attachment.

In the clean stand mixer bowl, add the egg whites and salt and whisk on high speed until just foamy. Slowly add the remaining sugar and the vanilla bean paste and whisk until soft peaks form.

Add one-third of the egg white mixture to the egg yolk mixture and gently stir. Add the remaining egg whites and, using a large rubber spatula, gently fold into the egg yolk mixture.

Sift the flour over the batter and gently fold in with the large rubber spatula. Add the butter and continue folding until combined.

Divide the batter evenly among the four prepared pans and bake for 15 to 20 minutes, until the cake springs back when touched and is golden brown. Set aside to cool completely.

Make the buttercream:

In the bowl of a food processor fitted with the blade attachment, add the chocolate, egg yolks, and vanilla extract and pulse a few times just to combine. While pulsing, add the coffee in a slow, steady stream. Add the butter, a few pieces at a time, and process until the buttercream is smooth and spreadable. Reserve about 1 cup (200 g) buttercream for decoration by placing it into a large pastry bag fitted with a large star tip and setting it aside.

Make the caramel:

In a heavy saucepan, combine the granulated sugar, corn syrup, lemon juice, and salt and stir over low heat until the sugar has completely melted. Raise the heat to medium-high, stop stirring, and continue cooking until the sugar is light amber. Remove from the heat and stir in the butter. Keep the caramel warm and spreadable by placing over another saucepan of barely simmering water.

Make the simple syrup:

In a small saucepan, combine the granulated sugar, ¾ cup (180 ml) water, and the rum and stir over low heat until the sugar has completely melted. Let cool slightly.

To assemble:

Release the cakes from the pans by gently running a paring knife along the edges of the pan and inverting onto a wire rack. Carefully split each cake layer in half horizontally so you have 8 very thin, even layers.

Place a wire rack over a parchment-lined half sheet pan. Select the best-looking layer for the cake-top decoration and place it on the rack. Spread all of the caramel in an even layer on top of the cake. Allow to set slightly, about 3 minutes, then cut the layer into 12 even wedges. Allow to set completely.

Place one of the remaining 7 layers on a cake platter. Brush the layer with simple syrup, then spread a very thin layer of buttercream, no more than ⅛ inch (3 mm) thick, onto the cake. Top with another cake layer, brush the layer with simple syrup, and spread a thin layer of buttercream on top. Continue this process until the remaining layers are assembled. Use the remaining buttercream (not including the amount you've set aside) to cover the top and sides of the cake in a smooth, even layer.

Using a sharp knife, mark the cake into 12 even portions. Pipe 12 small mounds of the reserved buttercream into the middle of each marked slice. Lean a caramel-covered cake wedge (pointed toward the center) on each mound of buttercream, tilted at a 45-degree angle and propped up on one side with the buttercream mound, so that when all the wedges are placed on the cake it appears to be a fan of caramel. Serve immediately.

A NOTE FROM THE SWEET TALKER: CAKE LAYERS. A gorgeous cake doesn't get that way without a little surgery. Even layers make all the difference in creating a uniform interior and a smooth, level exterior. You'll have noticed, though, that cakes tend to dome when you bake them. Or one cake is larger than the rest, so you've got a wonky layer structure on your hands (and differing baking times). The solution: Weigh your batter. Place your cake pan on a scale, zero out its weight, and pour in the batter (write down the weight). Repeat with the remaining pans, then steal batter from a heavier pan for a lighter one until you've got even measures. Also, invest in a very long, sharp serrated knife. Saw the domes of your layers off. Take a ruler, measure all along the perimeter of the cake, marking as you go with toothpicks, and use the toothpicks as a guide to saw off the dome.

STRAWBERRY–MEYER LEMON CHIFFON CAKE
WITH HONEY-THYME BAVARIAN CREAM

Makes 1 (8-inch / 20-cm) cake

IF GENOISE IS THE WORKHORSE of European sponge cakes, chiffon is the workhorse of many an American bakery. The addition of oil instead of butter makes this cake richer and also allows the cake to be frozen without negative impact on its quality. So you can imagine that this is a beloved recipe in the wedding-cake world, where cakes often stand six feet tall and require days of intricate work: You can work on one tier at a time while the others stay fresh in the freezer. This recipe pays tribute to the most popular of chiffons, the lemon variety. But instead of the standard lemon, Meyer lemons are my choice. Meyer lemons are slightly sweeter than your typical lemon and have a hint of herbaceousness. Pairing the lemon cake with a touch of thyme and honey sets off the undertones already present in the citrus and makes for an uncommonly refreshing cake.

FOR THE CAKES:
⅓ cup (80 ml) canola oil
4 eggs, separated
1 tablespoon Meyer lemon zest
½ cup (120 ml) fresh Meyer lemon juice
1½ cups (210 g) cake flour, sifted
1 cup (200 g) granulated sugar, divided
2 teaspoons baking powder
1 teaspoon salt

FOR THE BAVARIAN CREAM:
2 pints (500 g) fresh strawberries
3 tablespoons granulated sugar
1 teaspoon powdered gelatin
3 tablespoons fresh Meyer lemon juice
2 cups (480 ml) heavy cream
½ cup (115 g) mascarpone
2 tablespoons honey
1 teaspoon fresh thyme, minced

FOR THE BUTTERCREAM:
5 egg whites
1½ cups (300 g) granulated sugar, divided
¾ cup (180 ml) fresh Meyer lemon juice, divided
1 pound (455 g) unsalted butter, slightly cooler than room temperature, cut into small cubes

Make the cakes:

Preheat the oven to 375°F (190°C). Butter the bottoms—but not the sides—of three 8-inch (20-cm) round cake pans (traditional stainless-steel pans, if possible). Line each with a round of parchment paper. (This method prevents the delicate cake from falling, as the sides of the cakes will stick to the pans and keep everything upright. We're also going to cool the cakes upside down inside the pans, and if you grease the sides, those puppies are going to slide right out. I also forewarn you that this will be the one and only time your nonstick cake pans work—when you least want them to—so use traditional stainless steel if you can.)

In a large mixing bowl, combine the oil, egg yolks, lemon zest, and lemon juice and stir just to combine the ingredients.

Sift the flour, one-third of the granulated sugar, the baking powder, and salt over the egg yolk mixture and, using a large balloon whisk, whisk all the ingredients until well combined, about 2 minutes.

In the bowl of a stand mixer fitted with the whisk attachment, add the egg whites and whisk until white and foamy. Slowly add the remaining sugar and whisk until stiff, glossy white peaks form.

Gently stir one-third of the meringue into the egg yolk–flour mixture. Using a large rubber spatula, fold the remaining meringue into the batter.

Divide the batter evenly among the three prepared pans, using a small offset spatula to even and smooth the tops. Bake for 20 minutes, or until the cake springs back when touched.

Invert the pans on a cooling rack but don't unmold until the cakes are completely cool.

Make the Bavarian cream:

Reserve about 10 perfect strawberries to finish the cake. Hull and halve the remaining strawberries. In a bowl, toss the strawberry halves with the sugar to macerate. (The sugar compels the juices of the strawberries to flow. The acid in the fruit causes the sugar to dissolve. Win-win!)

In a small microwave-safe bowl, sprinkle the gelatin over the lemon juice in a very even layer. Allow to bloom until all the gelatin granules are saturated and look soggy.

In the bowl of a stand mixer fitted with the whisk attachment, combine the cream, mascarpone, honey, and thyme. Whisk until stiff peaks form.

Microwave the gelatin mixture at 50% power in 5-second intervals, swirling the bowl in between, until the gelatin has completely dissolved. Allow the mixture to cool for 1 minute. Make sure your additional cake elements are ready because once you add the gelatin to the cream mixture, you must use it immediately.

Stir a heaping spoonful of the whipped-cream mixture into the gelatin mixture and stir to temper.

Working quickly, fold the tempered gelatin into the Bavarian cream. Use immediately.

To assemble the layers:

Run a sharp paring knife along the edges of the cake pans to release the cakes. Place one layer on a cake platter.

With a pastry brush, brush an even layer of the juice from the macerated strawberries on the cake layer. Cover the cake with half of the strawberries, cut side down.

Spread half of the Bavarian cream over the strawberry-lined cake layer.

Place a second layer of cake over the Bavarian cream. Press very gently to adhere. Brush the layer with the remaining macerating juices and line the cake layer with the remaining strawberries. Spread the remaining Bavarian cream over the cake and top with the remaining layer.

Place the cake in the freezer to set, at least 2 hours but preferably overnight.

Make the buttercream:

Place the egg whites and 1 cup (200 g) of the granulated sugar in the bowl of a stand mixer fitted with the whisk attachment.

In a heavy saucepan, combine the remaining ½ cup (100 g) sugar and ½ cup (120 ml) of the lemon juice with ⅓ cup (80 ml) of water. Stir constantly over medium heat until the sugar is completely melted. Attach a candy thermometer to the side of the saucepan. Stop stirring. As the temperature of the syrup reaches around 225°F (107°C) start whisking the egg whites so they are foamy before you add the syrup in the next step; then continue heating the syrup until it reaches 240°F (116°C).

Once the syrup has reached 240°F (116°C), reduce the mixer speed to medium and slowly pour the syrup down the side of the bowl into the whisking egg whites. Once all the syrup is added, increase the mixer speed to high and whisk until the egg whites form stiff, shiny white peaks and the bowl is cool to the touch.

With the mixer on medium speed, add the butter, a few cubes at a time. When the buttercream starts to look like it's curdling, add just one more cube of butter and continue whisking for a few minutes until the texture becomes smooth and creamy. Add the remaining ¼ cup (60 ml) lemon juice and whisk until incorporated.

To assemble:

Remove the cake from the freezer and ice it with the buttercream until completely smooth. Artfully place the reserved strawberries on the top of the cake.

Place the cake in the refrigerator for at least 2 hours to allow the filling to defrost, then allow the cake to sit at room temperature for about 20 minutes (to soften the buttercream) before serving.

CHARLOTTE ROYALE

Makes 1 (10-inch / 25-cm) dome cake

THE MOST COMMON CHARLOTTE IS one that's lined with ladyfingers, the sweet biscuits standing at attention around the perimeter of the pastry like little cake soldiers. But the Charlotte has another identity: the Royale. Ooh-la-la! Although the standard Charlotte is indeed a beauty, the Royale takes cake glory to another dimension. Instead of ladyfingers lining the outside, rolled sponge cake (layered with a rich almond filling) is sliced into swirls and used to line a bowl, creating a confectionary kaleidoscope. The interior is filled with mousse. This particular Charlotte combines chocolate, almond, and marionberry, creating a sensory feast fit for royalty.

FOR THE CAKE:
2 (7-ounce / 200-g) tubes almond paste
9 eggs, separated, at room temperature
½ teaspoon salt
¼ teaspoon cream of tartar
¾ cup (150 g) granulated sugar
1 tablespoon vanilla extract
¾ cup (65 g) Dutch-process cocoa powder (I use Cacao Barry Extra Brute)
1 cup (100 g) confectioners' sugar for dusting

FOR THE COFFEE SIMPLE SYRUP:
coffee simple syrup (½ cup / 120 ml coffee and ½ cup / 100 g sugar heated together until the sugar is dissolved)

FOR THE MOUSSE:
1 tablespoon powdered gelatin
8 ounces (225 g) white chocolate (I use Cacao Barry), chopped
3 cups (720 ml) heavy cream, divided
¼ cup (60 ml) marionberry juice concentrate
4 egg whites, at room temperature
¼ cup (50 g) granulated sugar
1 teaspoon almond extract
½ teaspoon salt
2 cups (310 g) whole fresh marionberries

FOR THE CAKE BASE:
¼ cup (55 g) unsalted butter
4 ounces (115 g) bittersweet chocolate
1 tablespoon strong coffee
¼ cup (50 g) granulated sugar
¼ cup (20 g) Dutch-process cocoa powder
¼ teaspoon salt
2 eggs
1 teaspoon vanilla extract

FOR THE GANACHE:
4 ounces (115 g) bittersweet chocolate, finely chopped
¼ cup (60 ml) heavy cream
1 tablespoon unsalted butter

Make the cake:

Preheat the oven to 350°F (175°C). Line a half sheet pan with parchment paper and spray with nonstick spray.

Roll the almond paste between two sheets of parchment paper into a 9-by-14-inch (23-by-35.5-cm) rectangle. Set aside.

In the bowl of a stand mixer fitted with the whisk attachment, add the egg whites, salt, and cream of tartar and whisk just until foamy. Slowly add ½ cup (100 g) of the granulated sugar and whisk on high speed until stiff peaks form. (Be careful not to overwhip to the point of dryness or clumping.)

Transfer the egg whites to a large, clean bowl.

In the same stand mixer bowl (you needn't clean it), add the egg yolks, the remaining granulated sugar, and the vanilla extract and whisk on high speed until the mixture is pale yellow and forms ribbons when you lift the whisk.

Stir one-third of the egg whites into the yolk mixture. Using a large rubber spatula, gently fold in the remaining egg whites. Sift the cocoa powder over the egg mixture and fold into the batter until just combined. Using a large offset spatula, spread the batter evenly into the prepared pan. Bake for 25 minutes, or until the cake springs back lightly when touched.

Sprinkle the confectioners' sugar onto a clean kitchen towel in an even layer. Run a very sharp paring knife along the side of the pan to release the cake. Invert the cake onto the towel and remove the parchment.

While the cake is still very warm, place the rectangle of almond paste onto the cake. Using the kitchen towel to help you, roll the cake into a jelly roll and wrap the towel tightly around the cake to keep it in place. Allow to cool completely.

To assemble the jelly-roll rounds:

Line a 10-inch (25-cm) metal mixing bowl with plastic wrap so that the plastic hangs over the side. Cut the jelly roll into rounds ⅓ inch (8 mm) thick. Dip the bottom of each round quickly into the coffee simple syrup and use the rounds to line the bowl. Start at the middle, and place them packed tightly together soaked side down. Set aside.

Make the mousse:

In a small bowl, sprinkle the gelatin in an even layer over ¼ cup (60 ml) warm water. Allow to bloom for a few minutes, until the gelatin is saturated and appears soggy.

Place the white chocolate and 1 cup (240 ml) of the cream in a heatproof metal bowl. Place the bowl over a bain marie (a saucepan half filled with gently simmering water). Stir constantly until the white chocolate is completely melted. (White chocolate burns quite easily, so it's important that you stir constantly to keep it from scalding.)

Stir the gelatin mixture into the white chocolate mixture until well combined. Stir in the marionberry concentrate. Set aside to cool.

In the bowl of a stand mixer, combine the egg whites, granulated sugar, almond extract, and salt. Place the bowl over a bain marie and whisk constantly until the sugar has completely dissolved and the egg whites feel warm to the touch. (If you wish, you can attach a candy thermometer to ensure that the egg whites reach 160°F / 72°C, the temperature at which bacteria are killed.) Immediately transfer the bowl to a stand mixer fitted with the wire whisk and whisk on high speed until the egg whites have tripled in volume and the bowl is cool to the touch.

Transfer the whites to a large, clean mixing bowl.

Pour the remaining cream into the same stand mixer bowl (you needn't clean it). Whisk the cream until stiff peaks form, being careful not to overbeat.

Using a large rubber spatula, gently fold the egg whites into the whipped cream.

Stir the white chocolate mixture to loosen, then add one-third of the whipped-cream mixture to the white chocolate to temper and further loosen it. Fold the remaining whipped cream mixture into the white chocolate–marionberry mixture.

Pour the mousse into the cake-lined bowl and smooth with a small offset spatula. Place in the freezer to firm for 20 minutes and then gently place the fresh marionberries along the perimeter of the mousse, pressing gently so that the berries are flush with the mousse. Freeze overnight to set.

Make the cake base:

Preheat the oven to 325°F (165°C). Line the bottom of a 10-inch (25-cm) cake pan with a round of parchment paper and spray with nonstick spray.

In a heatproof bowl, combine the butter, chocolate, and coffee. Place the bowl over a bain marie (a large saucepan half filled with gently simmering water) and stir until melted and completely smooth.

In the bowl of a stand mixer fitted with the whisk attachment, whisk together the granulated sugar, cocoa powder, and salt. Add the eggs, one at a time, and continue whisking until smooth. Add the vanilla extract. Scrape down the sides of the bowl. With the mixer running on low speed, carefully pour the chocolate mixture down the side of the bowl into the egg mixture and mix until completely smooth.

Transfer the batter to the prepared pan. Bake for 15 to 20 minutes, until the cake is slightly firm to the touch and bubbles a bit in the center. Cool completely.

Make the ganache:

Place the chocolate in a medium-size mixing bowl.

Bring the cream and butter to a simmer in a small saucepan and pour over the chocolate. Allow to sit undisturbed for 2 minutes, then whisk until smooth. Allow to cool but make sure the ganache is still spreadable.

To assemble:

Run a sharp paring knife along the edge of the cake base to release it from the pan. Transfer the cake layer to a serving platter.

Remove the cake from the freezer and spread the ganache over the mousse layer. Trim any cake spirals that are sticking out beyond the mousse to create a clean edge. Place the cake layer on top of the ganache and press lightly to adhere.

Gently heat the bowl with a kitchen torch or a blow dryer to release the cake. Pull gently on the overhanging plastic wrap to release the cake onto the platter. Remove the plastic wrap. Trim any overhang from the cake base.

Allow the cake to rest for at least 2 hours in the refrigerator to allow the mousse to thaw to a servable temperature, then serve immediately.

CHOCOLATE PYRAMID

Makes 8 servings

WHAT IF YOU COULD MAKE an extraordinary chocolate cake—I mean one of the best darned fudgy chocolate cakes you've ever tasted? And what if you layered it with glorious chocolate frosting? And what if the whole package looked like a triangle instead of a boring old circle or square? If this fantasy interests you, you've come to the right place. This cake is delicious and will have everyone talking about your madly brilliant layering skills.

FOR THE CAKE:
6 eggs, separated
¾ cup (150 g) granulated sugar
½ teaspoon salt
1 scant cup (130 g) cake flour
1 cup (85 g) Dutch-process cocoa powder

FOR THE BUTTERCREAM:
⅔ cup (130 g) granulated sugar
2 eggs, at room temperature
1 teaspoon vanilla bean paste
pinch salt
1 cup (230 g) unsalted butter, cut into small cubes,
    at room temperature
8 ounces (225 g) bittersweet chocolate, finely chopped,
    melted, and cooled slightly

FOR THE SIMPLE SYRUP:
1 cup (200 g) granulated sugar

FOR THE GLAZE:
4 ounces (115 g) bittersweet chocolate
¼ cup (60 ml) heavy cream
1 tablespoon unsalted butter

FOR THE ASSEMBLY:
½ cup (40 g) Dutch process cocoa powder (I use Cacao
    Barry Extra Brute)

For the cake:

Preheat the oven to 400°F (205°C). Line a half sheet pan with parchment paper. Do not spray with nonstick spray.

In the bowl of a stand mixer fitted with the whisk attachment, combine the egg yolks and one-quarter of the granulated sugar and beat until the mixture thickens but isn't stiff. Switch to the paddle attachment. Add the almond paste, a small bit at a time to avoid lumps. Transfer this mixture to a mixing bowl and clean the stand mixer bowl and whisk attachment thoroughly.

In the clean bowl of your stand mixer, combine the egg whites and salt and whisk until the mixture is white and foamy. With the mixer running, slowly add the remaining sugar and whisk until stiff peaks form. (Be careful not to whip to the point of dryness or chunks.) Using a large rubber spatula, fold one-third of the egg white mixture into the egg yolk mixture to lighten. Add the remaining whites and gently fold until the two are incorporated.

In a bowl, whisk together the flour and cocoa powder. Sift the flour mixture over the egg mixture and fold together with a large rubber spatula. Spread the batter onto the prepared pan in a very even layer. Bake for 10 minutes, or just until the cake springs back when touched.

Make the buttercream:

In a heavy saucepan, combine the granulated sugar with ¼ cup (60 ml) water and stir constantly over medium heat until the sugar has completely dissolved. Stop stirring.

Attach a candy thermometer to the side of the saucepan and cook until the sugar syrup reaches 240°F (116°C).

Meanwhile, in the bowl of a stand mixer fitted with the whisk attachment, combine the eggs, vanilla bean paste, and salt. Whisk until the eggs are broken. When the sugar has reached temperature, continue whisking the egg mixture on medium speed and slowly pour the sugar syrup in a slow stream down the side of the mixing bowl. Once all the sugar is added, increase the speed to high and whip until the bowl is cool to the touch.

Reduce the mixer speed to medium-low and add the butter, a few cubes at a time, until it has all been incorporated. Transfer a large spoonful of this mixture to the melted chocolate and stir vigorously until incorporated. With the mixer running on medium speed, add the chocolate to the remaining buttercream mixture.

Make the simple syrup:

In a saucepan, combine the granulated sugar with 1 cup (240 ml) water and stir over medium heat until the sugar has completely dissolved. Let cool slightly.

Assemble the layers:

Once the cake has cooled, use a pastry brush to gently brush off the top "skin" of the cake. Trim the edges of the cake, then divide the cake into 4 even strips, each approximately (or slightly less than) 4 by 12 inches (10 by 30.5 cm).

Transfer a cake layer to a serving platter. Using a pastry brush, brush a layer of simple syrup over the entire cake surface. Spread a thin layer of buttercream over the sponge layer, spreading it as evenly as possible, about ¼

inch (6 mm) thick. Top the buttercream with the second cake layer, pressing gently to adhere. Brush with simple syrup and spread with buttercream. Continue layering with cake, simple syrup, and buttercream until the fourth layer is applied. Cut the cake in half lengthwise. Spread an even layer of buttercream on top of one half and place the second cake half on top so you are left with 8 cake layers. Wrap the cake in plastic wrap and freeze until very firm, about 1 hour.

Trim any uneven sides off the cake. Dip a long, very sharp serrated knife in scalding water and dry off. Cut the strip in half diagonally, forming two long triangles (see photo 1).

Flip the triangles so that the uncut sides are facing each other (see photo 2).

Spread a thin layer of buttercream along one of the uncut sides (see photo 3), then press the two uncut sides together, with the buttercream acting as glue (see photo 4). You've now created a triangle. Cover the cake with plastic wrap and refrigerate for 1 hour.

Make the glaze:

Place the chocolate in a medium mixing bowl. Bring the cream and butter to a simmer in a small saucepan over medium heat, then pour the cream mixture over the chocolate. Allow it to sit undisturbed for 2 minutes, then whisk until smooth.

Place the cake on a cooling rack. Spread the glaze over the cake with a small offset spatula. Sift the cocoa powder evenly over the cake to coat the glaze.

BECAUSE YOU'RE MINE CAKE

Makes 1 (10-inch / 25-cm) cake

THIS CAKE REQUIRES FOUR SEPARATE elements. A vanilla cake that acts as base and top. Ganache for sealant and decoration. Chocolate roulade for the vertical layers. Buttercream for the roulade filling and to hold it all together. It's a simple black-and-white cake, but when you cut into it, the layers stand vertically. I took one look at a slice and thought of the man in black, the most stand-up husband and guy in music. And the name of the cake presented itself: "Because you're mine, I walk the line."

FOR THE VANILLA CAKE:
½ cup (115 g) unsalted butter, at room temperature
1 cup (200 g) granulated sugar
2 eggs
1 teaspoon vanilla bean paste
1½ cups (185 g) all-purpose flour
1½ teaspoons baking powder
½ teaspoons salt
¾ cup (180 ml) buttermilk

FOR THE CHOCOLATE ROULADE:
24 egg yolks
1 cup (200 g) granulated sugar
1 teaspoon vanilla extract
1 teaspoon coffee extract (optional)
8 egg whites
1 teaspoon salt
1 cup (140 g) bread flour
½ cup (40 g) Dutch-process cocoa powder
   (I use Callebaut Extra Brute)

FOR THE BUTTERCREAM:
15 egg whites
3 cups (600 g) granulated sugar
pinch salt
1 teaspoon vanilla bean paste
3 pounds (1.4 kg) unsalted butter

FOR THE GANACHE:
8 ounces (225 g) bittersweet chocolate, finely chopped
½ cup (120 ml) heavy cream
2 tablespoons unsalted butter

Make the vanilla cake:

Preheat the oven to 350°F (175°C). Spray a 10-inch (25-cm) cake pan or ring with nonstick baking spray and line the bottom with parchment.

In the bowl of a stand mixer fitted with the whisk attachment, combine the butter and granulated sugar and whisk until light and fluffy. Add the eggs, one at a time, waiting until each egg is incorporated before adding the next. Add the vanilla bean paste.

In a bowl, whisk together the flour, baking powder, and salt. Add one-third of the flour to the egg-sugar mixture and mix just until combined; then add half of the buttermilk and combine. Continue alternating additions of flour and buttermilk until all are just incorporated. Do not overmix.

Transfer the batter to the prepared pan. Bake for 20 minutes, or until the cake is golden brown and springs back lightly when touched.

Allow to cool completely. Remove the cake from the pan and carefully split it in half horizontally, to form two equal layers. Set aside.

Make the chocolate roulade:

Preheat the oven to 400°F (205°C). Line two half sheet or jelly-roll pans with parchment and spray with nonstick spray.

In the bowl of a stand mixer fitted with the whisk attachment, combine the egg yolks, half of the granulated sugar, the vanilla extract, and the coffee extract (if using) and whisk until the mixture lightens to a pale yellow. Transfer this mixture to a mixing bowl and clean the stand mixer bowl and whisk attachment thoroughly.

In the clean bowl of the stand mixer, whisk together the egg whites and salt until foamy. Slowly add the remaining sugar. Whip until stiff peaks form.

In a bowl, whisk together the flour and cocoa powder.

Stir one-third of the egg whites into the yolk mixture to lighten. Using a large rubber spatula, gently fold in the remaining whites. Sift the flour-cocoa mixture over the eggs and gently fold until evenly incorporated (turn the bowl as you go to get everywhere the flour may hide).

Divide the batter evenly between the prepared pans and smooth the layers. Bake for 7 to 10 minutes, until the cakes spring back when you touch them. Let them cool completely, then cover with plastic wrap and let rest overnight.

Make the buttercream:

Combine the egg whites, granulated sugar, vanilla, and salt in the bowl of a stand mixer. Place over a bain marie (a large saucepan half full of simmering water) and stir until the sugar has completely melted. Insert a candy thermometer to ensure that the mixture rises about 160°F (72°C), the temperature at which bacteria are killed. Transfer the bowl to a stand mixer fitted with the whisk attachment and whisk on high speed until the mixture has quadrupled in volume and the bowl is cool to the touch.

Add the butter, a few tablespoons at a time, until the mixture thickens and becomes a smooth icing.

Make the ganache:

Place the chocolate in a heatproof bowl.

In a saucepan, combine the cream and butter and bring to a simmer.

Pour the hot cream over the chocolate, making sure the chocolate is completely covered. Allow to sit undisturbed for 2 minutes. Then whisk until the chocolate is completely melted and the mixture is smooth.

To assemble:

Leaving the cakes in the pan, cut each chocolate cake into long strips, 4 inches (10 cm) wide; you'll get 3 strips from each pan, 6 altogether. (I notch the top and the bottom of the cake every 3 inches (7.5 cm) and then use a ruler to keep the strips even.)

Divide half the buttercream evenly between the two cakes, reserving the rest to cover the cake, and spread a very thin, even layer over the surface of each cake.

Roll the first strip, buttercream side in, into a tight roll. Move the strip over to the start of the next strip, and continue rolling, with the end of the first roll touching the beginning of the second. Keep adding strips to make a big fat spiral of cake! You may have more cake than you need. Stop when your spiral is 10 inches (25 cm) in diameter.

Spread a thin layer of buttercream over one of the vanilla cake layers, just enough to cover the top. Place your giant spiral cake on top of the buttercream. Smear a thin layer of buttercream over the top of the spiral and top with the remaining layer of yellow cake. If you have a 10-inch (25-cm) cake ring, secure it around the cake to protect it while it sets. Otherwise, wrap it in plastic wrap. Place the cake in the freezer to set for 1 hour.

Remove the cake ring or plastic wrap and cover the entire cake with a thin layer of buttercream. Place in the refrigerator to set for 20 minutes.

With the remaining buttercream, coat the cake in a smooth, even layer. Refrigerate until firm, about 20 minutes.

Place the remaining ganache in a pastry bag fitted with a medium open tip. Place a piece of parchment on a sheet

pan and pipe hearts onto the parchment paper. Freeze the hearts until set.

When the ganache hearts have hardened, remove them with a small offset spatula and apply to the top and sides of the cake. If you're having trouble getting them to stick, add a little softened ganache to the back of the hearts as glue.

CUCKOO FOR COCOA

The quality of chocolate (and cocoa powder) you choose to work with in pastry makes all the difference in the world. Not just in taste, mind you. Of course taste is terribly important, but so is the outcome of the final product. Fine-quality chocolates of the semi- and bitter-sweet varieties will often show percentages on the packaging to indicate the cocoa-liquor content of a particular bar. Unsweetened chocolate contains 100%. Bittersweet chocolate must contain at least 35% and may contain up to 99%; less than 12% may be milk solids and the rest is sugar. That's a huge range! Don't be fooled into thinking that a top-of-the-charts percentage is necessarily a reflection of quality, though. The quality of the cocoa beans and the processing used to render the beans into liquor determine quality. I stick with my favorites—Callebaut/Cacao Barry and Valrhona—to ensure the best flavor and quality in my desserts.

The higher the cocoa liquor percentage, the less sweet the chocolate will be. Milk chocolate has less than 10% cocoa content and more than 12% milk solids. White chocolate is, technically speaking, not a chocolate at all because it doesn't contain any cocoa liquor. (I know. Makes no sense.)

The higher the cocoa-liquor content, the firmer the chocolate will be. Here's the best test you'll ever take: Open a bar of Hershey's milk chocolate and a bar of 70% chocolate. Break off a piece of both. You'll notice the milk chocolate is incredibly soft, whereas the bittersweet is snaps and breaks. (Might as well eat the chocolate at this point; shame to waste it.) When you're making a chocolate mousse, this higher percentage will play a large role in how the mousse sets up (becomes firm). Most mousse recipes, outside of dark chocolate ones, call for gelatin to set the stuff. With a dark chocolate mousse, the cocoa liquor acts as the firming agent. So, you can see where things can go terribly wrong if you indiscriminately switch chocolates in a recipe—both in its taste and in its physical structure.

LOVE IS PATIENT PUZZLE CAKE

Makes 8 to 10 servings

FOR THIS PUZZLE OF A CAKE, you'll need layers and layers of chiffon cake. You may think to yourself that there's possibly too much cake involved. And I'd agree with you—if you were already adept at making this. As it is, you'll thank me that you have extra with which to play. (See pages 166–167 for an idea on what to do with any extra.)

Keep in mind that for a single cake, you're going to need 3 layers of pomegranate chiffon and 3 layers of key lime chiffon. Each layer will be ½ inch (12 mm) thick. Keep repeating this to yourself: 3 layers pomegranate and 3 layers key lime chiffon, ½ inch thick. Before you start, make sure you have the following handy: (1) cardboard cake rounds or something similar to hold all your layers; (2) toothpicks; (3) a large, very sharp serrated knife; (4) a revolving cake stand; (5) two 10-inch (25-cm) cake rounds; and (6) patience.

FOR THE POMEGRANATE CHIFFON CAKES:

8 eggs, separated, at room temperature
⅔ cup (160 ml) vegetable or canola oil
1 cup (240 ml) pomegranate juice
1 drop red food coloring (optional)
3 cups (420 g) cake flour
1½ cups (300 g) granulated sugar
1 tablespoon plus 1 teaspoon baking powder
1 teaspoon salt

FOR THE KEY LIME CHIFFON CAKES:

8 eggs, separated, at room temperature
⅔ cup (160 ml) vegetable or canola oil
½ cup (120 ml) key lime juice, mixed with ½ cup (120 ml) water
3 cups (420 g) cake flour
1½ cups (300 g) granulated sugar
1 tablespoon plus 1 teaspoon baking powder
1 teaspoon salt

FOR THE BUTTERCREAM:

3 cups (600 g) granulated sugar
1 squirt fresh lemon juice
15 egg whites
pinch salt
2 pounds (910 g) unsalted butter, a little cooler than room temperature

FOR THE ASSEMBLY:

1 cup (200 g) granulated sugar

Make the pomegranate chiffon cakes:

Preheat the oven to 375°F (190°C). Prepare two 10-inch (25-cm) round cake pans by lining the bottom of each with a round of parchment paper that has been sprayed with nonstick baking spray. Do not spray the sides of the pans with nonstick spray. (Here, you don't want the cake to pull from the sides because the sticking helps keep the cake from collapsing before it cools and keeps the size of the cakes uniform.) Or use bottomless cake rings: Place parchment on a half sheet pan, spray the parchment, then plop the rings down onto the parchment so that none of the spray touches the sides.

In a stand mixer fitted with the whisk attachment, combine the egg yolks and oil and whisk until combined. Slowly add the pomegranate juice and food coloring, if using, and whisk until just combined.

In a bowl, sift together the flour, ½ cup (100 g) of the granulated sugar, the baking powder, and salt. Slowly add the flour mixture to the egg yolk mixture and whisk for 40 seconds until smooth. Transfer the mixture to a mixing bowl and set aside. Clean and dry the bowl and the whisk of the stand mixer thoroughly.

In the clean stand mixer bowl, whisk the egg whites until foamy. Slowly add the remaining sugar and whisk on high speed until stiff, white peaks form. (Make sure not to over-whip to the point of dryness or chunks.)

Using a large rubber spatula, gently fold the egg white mixture into the egg yolk mixture until fully combined.

Divide the batter evenly between the 2 prepared pans. Bake for 25 minutes, until the cake springs back when you touch it. Allow the cakes to cool completely. Then run a very thin, sharp knife run around the edge of each cake to release it from the pan. (If you release the cakes too soon, they may collapse. Patience!)

Make the key lime chiffon cakes:

Make 2 key-lime chiffon cakes by following the previous instructions for the pomegranate cakes, substituting the key lime chiffon ingredients (adding the key lime juice mixture to the egg yolks instead of the pomegranate juice).

Make the buttercream:

In a heavy saucepan, combine the granulated sugar, 1 cup (240 ml) water, and the lemon juice. Stir until the sugar is completely saturated so that it looks like wet sand and no dry spots can be seen. Place over medium-low heat and stir with a wooden spoon until the sugar has completely dissolved. With a pastry brush dipped in water, brush the sides of the pan to remove any sugar crystals clinging to the sides. Stop stirring, increase the heat to high, attach a candy thermometer to the side of the saucepan, and heat the mixture to 234°F (112°C).

Meanwhile, in a clean bowl of the stand mixer fitted with a cleaned whisk attachment, combine the egg whites and salt and whisk until they are foamy. When the sugar syrup has come to temperature, with the mixer on medium-high speed, very slowly and carefully pour the hot syrup down the side of the bowl and into the whisking egg whites. Once you've added all the syrup, increase the mixer speed to high and whisk until stiff peaks form and the bowl is cool to the touch. (This is important—if the meringue is warm, the butter will melt and the buttercream won't form a fluffy, smooth frosting. If this has happened, put the bowl in the freezer for a minute and then start mixing again.)

Slowly add bits of butter, about 2 tablespoons at a time. (There's a chance you won't need all of it.) When the buttercream starts to look like it's curdling, add just one more bit of butter and continue whisking for a few minutes until the texture becomes smooth and creamy. Keep at room temperature until needed.

To assemble:

In a microwave-safe bowl, combine the sugar with 1 cup (240 ml) water. Microwave at 50% power in 5-second intervals, swirling the bowl in between, until the sugar has completely dissolved into the water.

We want 3 layers of pomegranate and 3 layers of key lime chiffon—right now you have 2 layers of each kind. So once the layers are fully cooled and released from the pans, place them in the freezer for 5 to 10 minutes to firm them for easier slicing.

Place the first round of cake on a cake stand. Trim the top of the cake to make it perfectly level. Then, using a ruler, measure and mark the cake every ½ inch (12 mm) with a toothpick from the top down.

Take a long, very sharp serrated knife and place it horizontally on the edge of the cake at the level of the top toothpick. The trick is to keep the knife perfectly level, using the toothpick as a guide. Put one hand on top of the cake and slowly spin the cake on the cake stand, keeping the knife level. Let the spinning motion do the work: Don't saw, just maintain light, steady pressure on the knife, so that it slices cleanly through the cake, making an even layer.

Set the first cut layer aside on a cardboard round. Repeat the process to create 2 more layers from the first cake

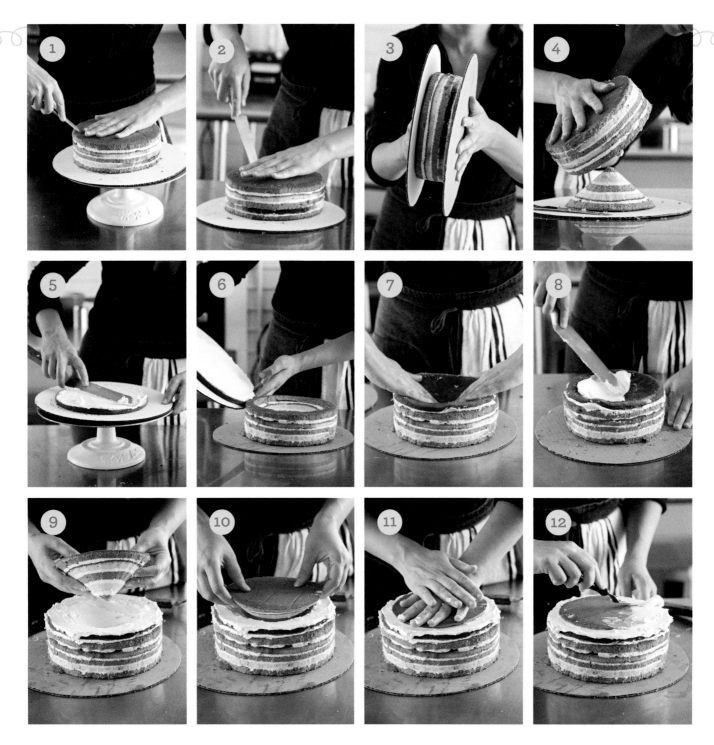

bake it like you mean it

round, so you end up with 3 layers total. Do this with the remaining 3 cake rounds, for a grand total of 12 layers of cake.

Chances are, not all of the layers are perfect. If they are, then you could theoretically make 2 separate cakes (and have 2 layers left over!). But I've got a feeling you're looking at the mess before you and you're thanking St. Valentine that you've got the extra. Choose the best-looking and most even layers of cake: 3 of pomegranate and 3 of key lime. Brush the top of each layer with simple syrup and set one layer of key lime aside on a cake round and cover with plastic wrap.

Place a pomegranate layer on a cardboard cake round and spread about 1 cup of buttercream evenly over the top, about ⅛ inch (3 mm) thick. Place a key lime cake layer on top of the buttercream layer and press gently to adhere. Add another ⅛-inch (3-mm) layer of buttercream to the top. Repeat the process with another pomegranate and then another key lime cake layer, then another pomegranate. You now have a 5-layer cake sitting in front of you. Phew. The easy part is over. Place this cake in the refrigerator until the buttercream has completely set, about 1 hour.

Take a deep breath. Now take another. Find a 9-inch (23-cm) round cake pan or pot lid. (You need a guide, that's all.) Set it aside. Get a really sharp, thin knife. It can be serrated or not. Dip the knife in scalding-hot water and dry it. Take the cake out of the refrigerator and center your 9-inch (23-cm) circle guide on top of the cake. Using your knife, trace around the edge of the circle to create a very shallow guideline. Again, this is just a marker, not a deep cut.

Remove your circle guide. Place your knife at an angle of about 45 degrees and cut into the layers, along the outline you made in the cake (see photos 1 and 2). You want to take out a cone-shaped chunk from the middle of the cake. You may feel the knife hit the cardboard round at the bottom—that's okay. Just keep the knife steady and even as you cut at an angle into the cake. When you've gotten all the way around, take another cardboard round and place it on top of the cake. Invert the cake and lift it from the sides

so that the cone you've cut comes out (see photos 3 and 4). Set the cone of cake aside.

Invert the original cake, now with a crater in the center, back to its original position. Coat the third and last layer of key lime cake with a ⅛-inch (3-mm) layer of buttercream (see photo 5), then place it on the cratered cake so the coated side sits on top of the rim (see photo 6). Press very gently on the center of the cake so that you fill the crater with the piece of key lime cake. It may crack a little—that's OK. Keep pressing along the top until you've created an indentation at the middle of the cake that mimics your original crater (see photo 7). (It's scary to be shoving a cake into place, but that's what you need to do.)

Spread a ⅛-inch (3-mm) layer of buttercream into the crater and along the rim (see photo 8). Now grab the cone of cake you set aside and insert it into your newly formed crater. Press gently (see photos 9, 10, and 11). Apply a very thin layer (a crumb coat) of buttercream on the top and sides of the cake (see photo 12) and refrigerate until set.

Preheat the oven to 225°F (107°C).

Take a look around. It's a mess. But chances are you'll have a few cake bits lying around, even some whole layers. Take the pomegranate bits, cut off any browned areas, and place on a sheet pan. Place in the oven for about 20 minutes, until dry. Cool the cake pieces completely, then pulverize them in a food processor to create fine crumbs.

Spread the remaining buttercream on the cake in a smooth, finished layer.

Fold a piece of parchment paper in half and cut out varied sizes of half hearts (so they will be full hearts when you unfold them). Apply the heart stencils to the top and sides of the cake. Pat the cake crumbs evenly onto the areas of exposed buttercream on the top and sides of the cake. Brush any crumbs from the tops of the stencils so that the crumbs don't later tumble into the heart shapes. Gently remove the stencils. Breathe a sigh of relief, and serve.

Chapter 3

RICH & DECADENT

BUTTER and POUND CAKES

WE'RE STARTING OUR NEXT BAKING ADVENTURE WITH VARIATIONS ON

the classic pound cake because there's something so damned beautiful about a recipe that is insanely simple yet mind-blowingly delicious. The name of the cake will tell you everything you need to know—there's no way to keep this recipe a secret. A classic pound cake will always contain one pound each of flour, sugar, butter, and eggs. Period. That's it. No leavening. No fancy stuff. What results, with the proper technique, is a dense but moist loaf of decadence.

Of course bakers, being the creative animals we are, have fiddled with the ratios and added ingredients over the years. And of course there are variations depending on region and country. The traditional English pound cake is just butter, flour, sugar, and eggs, while Americans tend to add sour cream and even a touch of baking powder. The changes made to the traditional method are often due to the fact that if you don't execute the classic recipe correctly, the resulting loaf will be thick and dry. Adding sour cream and leavening gives you a better chance at great results.

Another splendid thing about pound-cake batters is that although the most traditional are baked in plain old loaf pans, the cakes lend themselves wonderfully to being molded into intricate Bundt pans, like the Austrian *Gugelhupf*, allowing a simple cake to appear regal and exquisitely adorned with little effort on your part.

CLASSIC POUND CAKE

Makes 2 loaves

SWEET, DENSE, AND BUTTERY. A classic pound cake, as simple as it first appears, has a profound ability to demand your full attention. You start with a single slice and find yourself hacking away until you've just about finished the entire loaf. Thank goodness this recipe makes two whole loaves—no one has to know you've polished off the first!

2 cups (400 g) granulated sugar
1 pound (455 g) unsalted butter, slightly cooler than
    room temperature
1 teaspoon vanilla bean paste
9 eggs, at room temperature
1 pound (455 g) all-purpose flour
2 teaspoons sea salt

Preheat the oven to 350°F (175°C). Spray 2 (9-by-5-inch / 23-by-12-cm) loaf pans with nonstick baking spray (which includes flour to keep the cake from sticking to the form).

In the bowl of a stand mixer fitted with the paddle attachment, cream together the granulated sugar and butter until light and fluffy. This can take up to 10 minutes. Properly creaming the butter and sugar together is essential to a perfect pound cake (see Sidebar, at right).

Add the vanilla bean paste, then the eggs, one at a time. After each addition, beat for 30 seconds to 1 minute and scrape down the sides and bottom of the bowl.

In a large bowl, whisk together the flour and salt. With the mixer on medium-low speed, add ¾ cup (90 g) of the flour mixture at a time, scraping the sides and bottom of the bowl between additions.

Divide the batter between the two prepared pans. Bake for 1 hour, or until the top of the cake is golden brown and a tester inserted in the center comes out clean. Allow to cool completely.

A NOTE FROM THE SWEET TALKER: You've read it in countless recipes: "Cream together sugar and butter." But what does "creaming" really mean? You know that it means to mix together, but really, it's so much more than that. To cream well, you need to beat the sugar and butter until the mixture is light and fluffy; at this point you've incorporated so much air into the fat that it helps the cake to rise properly. The sugar acts as a delivery agent, essentially punching holes in the fat to allow air bubbles to form. Make sure the butter is just cooler than room temperature, certainly not any warmer; otherwise the milk solids will separate and the mixture won't achieve that perfect fluffiness you're striving for and you'll end up with a flat, dense cake.

Classic Pound Cake

Lemon-Poppy Gugelhupf

Vermont Sandtorte Cakelets

VERMONT SANDTORTE CAKELETS

Makes 12 mini Bundt cakes

SANDTORTE IS THE VIENNESE ANSWER to traditional English pound cake. *Sand* translated from the German means—wait for it—"sand." This has no relation to the finished product; it's simply pastry lingo Viennese chefs utilize to describe a cake recipe that starts with creaming butter and sugar together (the two do look like wet sand at the beginning of the process). In this case, we'll be creaming together maple sugar and butter for the same effect. And the additional step of dipping in a yummy mixture of sugar and cinnamon gives the cake the appearance of having a shiny, sandy topping.

FOR THE CAKES:
1 cup (230 g) unsalted European butter, at room temperature
1 cup (220 g) maple sugar, divided
5 eggs, separated
1 teaspoon vanilla bean paste
1½ (210 g) cups cake flour
¼ teaspoon nutmeg
½ teaspoon salt

FOR THE ASSEMBLY:
½ cup (115 g) unsalted butter, melted
1 cup (200 g) granulated sugar
½ teaspoon cinnamon

Preheat the oven to 325°F (165°C). Spray a 12-cavity mini Bundt pan with nonstick baking spray. (I use a Nordicware Sweetheart Rose muffin pan.)

In the bowl of a stand mixer fitted with the paddle attachment, cream together the butter and ½ cup (110 g) of the maple sugar until light and fluffy, 8 to 10 minutes.

Scrape down the sides and bottom of the bowl and add 1 egg yolk. Beat on high speed for 30 seconds. Scrape down the sides and bottom of the bowl and add the next egg yolk. Repeat until all the egg yolks are incorporated. Add the vanilla bean paste, mix to combine, and transfer the mixture to a large bowl.

Sift the cake flour and nutmeg together onto a large piece of parchment paper. Resift two more times, leaving the sifted mixture on the parchment.

In a clean bowl of a stand mixer fitted with the whisk attachment, combine the egg whites and salt and whisk just until foamy but not stiff. With the mixer on high speed, slowly add the remaining maple sugar and whisk just until stiff, glossy peaks form. (Be careful not to overbeat to the point of dryness.)

Using a large rubber spatula, fold the egg white mixture into the egg yolk mixture. Sift the flour mixture over the egg mixture and fold it gently into the batter.

Divide the batter evenly among the individual mini Bundt cavities. Bake for 25 to 30 minutes, just until the tops are golden brown and a cake tester inserted in the center comes away clean.

To assemble:

Place the melted butter in a bowl that's wide enough to hold a mini cake. In a separate bowl of the same size, combine the sugar and cinnamon.

Dip the top of each mini cake in the butter mixture, then immediately dip in the sugar-cinnamon mixture.

Serve immediately, or cover with plastic wrap and store at room temperature for up to 2 days.

LEMON-POPPY GUGELHUPF

Makes 1 (9-inch) cake

POPPY SEEDS ARE HARVESTED FROM the opium poppy. Let's just get that bit of information out of the way. And yes, there are other types of poppies, but the only type used for culinary purposes is the opium poppy. For the illicit stuff, the pod is harvested before the seeds have fully developed and ripened. For culinary purposes, the pod is harvested once the pod has completely dried. I've eaten many a poppy seed–laden confection in my lifetime and cannot claim to have felt any adverse affects other than being uncomfortably full from overstuffing my pie hole. So there's no need to worry that your motor skills will be compromised if you eat a lovely piece of lemon-poppy *Gugelhupf* on your morning commute.

1 cup (200 g) granulated sugar

1 cup (230 g) unsalted butter, at room temperature

4 eggs, at room temperature

1 tablespoon lemon zest

2 cups (250 g) all-purpose flour

2 teaspoons baking powder

1 teaspoon salt

½ cup (70 g) black poppy seeds, ground (see Note)

½ cup (120 ml) buttermilk

1 tablespoon vanilla bean paste

1 teaspoon lemon extract

Confectioners' sugar, for dusting

NOTE: I prefer to use Dutch poppy seeds for all my poppy seed baking. They are superior in quality, shape, and taste and have a splendid dark, almost blue color. You can find poppy seeds in the bulk section of grocery stores.

Preheat the oven to 325°F (165°C). Spray a 9-inch (23-cm) *Gugelhupf* mold with nonstick baking spray and place the mold on a half sheet pan lined with parchment paper. If you can't find a traditional *Gugelhupf* mold, a 9-inch (23-cm) Bundt pan will do well.

In the bowl of a stand mixer fitted with the paddle attachment, combine the granulated sugar and butter and beat on high speed until light and fluffy, about 8 minutes. Scrape down the sides and bottom of the bowl. Add the eggs, one at a time, mixing on high speed for 1 minute and scraping down the bowl after each addition. Add the lemon zest and mix to incorporate.

In a bowl, whisk together the flour, baking powder, salt, and poppy seeds. In another bowl, whisk together the buttermilk, vanilla bean paste, and lemon extract. Add half of the flour mixture to the egg mixture and beat on low speed for 30 seconds. Add half of the buttermilk mixture to the eggs and mix on low speed for 30 seconds. Add the remaining flour and mix again for 30 seconds. Add the remaining buttermilk and mix until all the ingredients are fully incorporated.

Pour the batter into the prepared pan and gently tap the pan against your work surface a few times to get rid of any air pockets.

Bake for 1 hour, or until the cake is golden brown and a cake tester inserted in the center comes out clean. While the cake is still warm, invert the mold onto a serving platter to remove the cake. Allow to cool completely. Sift confectioners' sugar over the cake and serve.

A NOTE FROM THE SWEET TALKER: *Gugelhupf* is the name of both a cake and the form in which it's made. There are two types of *Gugelhupf* cake, one that's a pound cake and one that's based on a yeasted dough. Both are baked in a *Gugelhupf* mold, which is a tall and super fancy Bundt mold.

Mini Chocolate
Orange Pounds

Aztec Chocolate Crème
Fraîche Pound Cake

AZTEC CHOCOLATE CRÈME FRAÎCHE POUND CAKE

Makes 1 pound cake

CHOCOLATE ON CHOCOLATE WITH MORE CHOCOLATE, plus a hint of spice—nothing wrong with that, not at all! But add crème fraîche, a creamy and ever so slightly tangy soft French version of sour cream, and you add just the right amount of zip to the zing of this deliriously fudgy pound cake. It's covered in a chocolate glaze that gives it a sheen and a dramatic quality worthy of the Aztecs for whom it's named.

FOR THE CAKE:

4 ounces (115 g) bittersweet chocolate, finely chopped
½ cup (120 ml) coffee, very hot
¾ cup (170 g) unsalted butter
1¼ cups (250 g) granulated sugar
3 eggs
1 tablespoon vanilla bean paste
1 teaspoon lime oil
1¼ cups (155 g) all-purpose flour
½ cup (40 g) Dutch-process cocoa powder, sifted
1 teaspoon salt
1½ teaspoons baking powder
1 teaspoon cinnamon
½ teaspoon cayenne pepper
¾ cup (180 ml) crème fraîche

FOR THE GLAZE:

8 ounces (225 g) bittersweet chocolate, finely chopped
½ teaspoon lime oil
¼ cup (60 ml) heavy cream
2 tablespoons unsalted butter
1 tablespoon corn syrup

FOR THE ASSEMBLY:

½ cup (40 g) Dutch-process cocoa powder (I use Cacao Barry Extra Brute)

Make the cake:

Preheat the oven to 350°F (175°C). Liberally spray a large nonstick Bundt pan with nonstick baking spray. (I use a Chicago Metallic Ribbon Bundt mold with a 10-cup / 2.4-L capacity.)

In a small bowl, combine the chocolate and coffee. Allow to sit undisturbed for a few minutes to allow the chocolate to melt, then stir to combine. Set aside.

In the bowl of a stand mixer fitted with the paddle attachment, cream the butter and granulated sugar together until light and fluffy. Add the eggs, one at a time, beating between additions until each egg is completely incorporated. Add the vanilla bean paste and lime oil.

In a bowl, whisk together the flour, cocoa powder, salt, baking powder, cinnamon, and cayenne.

Add the crème fraîche to the chocolate mixture and stir to combine.

Add one-third of the flour mixture to the butter-sugar mixture and mix on low speed, then add half of the crème fraîche–chocolate mixture and stir to combine. Continue alternating additions until all the ingredients are incorporated and well combined. Spoon the batter into the prepared mold and level the batter with the back of a spoon. Bake for 1 hour and 20 minutes, or until a wooden skewer inserted in the center comes out clean. Allow the cake to cool for about 20 minutes. Unmold onto a cooling rack set over a parchment-lined sheet pan.

To finish:

Sift the cocoa powder evenly over the cake to coat.

DUTCH-PROCESS VERSUS NATURAL COCOA POWDER

Some recipes specify Dutch-process or natural cocoa powder but don't give you the reasoning behind the instruction. Let's discuss what the two varieties are in the first place: Natural cocoa is a powder made by crushing roasted cocoa beans into a fine powder. It's a light rust color. Nestlé's cocoa powder is a natural cocoa powder. Dutch-process, or alkalized, cocoa has been washed with a solution to neutralize its acidity and is a deep, rich, *chocolaty* brown. I wouldn't blame you if your first instinct was to lean toward the natural variety, assuming that it would possess a more robust chocolate flavor. But in this case, that's simply not true. Alkalizing removes just a small portion of the larger cocoa flavor spectrum, specifically its most bitter components, leaving the true chocolate flavor to surge ahead and really sing. A common warning in recipes calling for both baking soda and cocoa powder is that you must use *natural* cocoa because the lack of acidity in Dutch-process cocoa doesn't react properly with baking soda; that is, the balance of acidity is off and you won't get a rise. I've found this to be hogwash. Great-quality Dutch-process cocoa powders (such as Callebaut and Valrhona) aren't so harshly alkalized that they won't cause baking soda to lose its efficacy when the two are combined. There are some Dutch-process brands that *will* react adversely with baking soda, but those overly processed cocoas are of poor quality and offer very little in the way of taste or texture, even under the best of recipe circumstances.

MINI CHOCOLATE ORANGE POUNDS

Makes 6 half-sphere cakes

YOU'VE HAD A CHOCOLATE ORANGE, RIGHT? It comes in a box, wrapped in sparkly foil. When you peel off the outer protective layer, there it is: a chocolate orange. Without a shred of doubt, what sits before you is an orange, segmented as an orange should be. But instead of a nubby citrus peel, bright and pastel, the sphere before you is smooth, rich brown, and decidedly choc-olate—then when you slice through, an orange orb greets you like a smile. This pound cake emulates the taste of that wonderful treat—baked in a half-moon pan, with an orange hiding in the center and all coated with a shiny glaze—the glory of the chocolate orange in the form of a decadent pound cake.

FOR THE FILLING:

1 (8-ounce / 225-g) package cream cheese, at room temperature

1 teaspoon orange extract

¼ cup (25 g) confectioners' sugar

1 drop orange food coloring

FOR THE CAKE:

1 cup (200 g) granulated sugar

½ cup (115 g) unsalted butter, at room temperature

½ teaspoon orange extract

3 eggs

1 cup (125 g) all-purpose flour

¾ cup (65 g) Dutch-process cocoa powder (I use Cacao Barry Extra Brute)

½ teaspoon baking powder

1 teaspoon salt

FOR THE GLAZE:

¼ cup (60 ml) coffee, cold

1 teaspoon powdered gelatin

¼ cup (60 ml) heavy cream

¼ cup (20 g) Dutch-process cocoa powder

½ cup (100 g) granulated sugar

½ teaspoon orange extract

1 ounce (30 g) bittersweet chocolate, finely chopped

FOR THE ASSEMBLY:

6 strips curled orange peel

Make the filling:

In the bowl of a stand mixer fitted with the paddle attach-ment, combine all the ingredients and mix until smooth. Transfer the mixture to an airtight plastic container and cover with plastic wrap. Freeze until firm, about 30 minutes.

Make the cake:

Preheat the oven to 325°F (165°C). Prepare a 6-cavity half-sphere silicone mold by spraying it liberally with nonstick baking spray. (I use a Freshware 6-cavity mold, with each cavity measuring 2.8 inches / 7.4 cm in diameter.)

In the bowl of a stand mixer fitted with the paddle attach-ment, combine the granulated sugar and butter and beat until light and fluffy, about 10 minutes. Add the orange extract and mix to combine. Scrape down the sides and bottom of the bowl.

Add the eggs, one at a time, mixing on high speed for 1 minute and scraping down the bowl after each addition.

In a mixing bowl, whisk together the flour, cocoa powder, baking powder, and salt. Add the flour mixture to the bat-ter, 1 cup at a time, mixing on low speed after each addi-tion, until the flour is completely incorporated.

Divide the batter evenly among the cavities of the pre-pared pan.

Remove the filling from the freezer. Using a melon baller or tablespoon-size cookie scoop, make 6 perfectly round balls from the orange cream cheese filling. Press 1 orange round into the middle of the batter in each cavity.

Bake for 25 minutes, or until the cakes spring back when touched. Allow to cool completely and then turn over to release from the molds onto a cooling rack placed over a parchment-lined sheet pan. Space the cakes a few inches apart.

Make the glaze:

Place the coffee in a large microwave-safe bowl. Sprinkle the gelatin over the coffee in an even layer. Allow the gelatin to bloom until it is saturated and looks soggy, about 3 minutes. Microwave at 50% power in 5-second intervals, swirling in between, until the gelatin is completely melted.

In a small saucepan, combine the cream, cocoa powder, granulated sugar, and orange extract. Bring to a simmer over medium heat.

In a bowl, combine the chocolate and gelatin and pour the hot cream mixture over them, making sure the chocolate is completely covered. Allow to sit undisturbed for 2 minutes, then stir to melt the chocolate and combine the ingredients.

Pour the glaze through a fine-mesh sieve into a clean bowl and allow to thicken, about 5 minutes. Use immediately.

To assemble:

With a large soup ladle, pour the glaze slowly over each of the cakes, making sure to move the ladle back and forth so that every exposed inch of the cake is covered in glaze. Allow to set at room temperature, about 20 minutes.

Place an orange peel atop each cake. Serve immediately.

MARBLE POUND CAKE

Makes 1 large Bundt cake

IT'S SO BEAUTIFUL, THIS MARVEL of intermingled chocolate and vanilla. If you take the time to swirl and twirl the batters, you'll be rewarded with slice upon slice of black-and-white beauty. It's a lovely stand-alone cake when baked in a simple loaf pan.

FOR THE CAKE:

2 ounces (55 g) bittersweet chocolate (at least 60%), finely chopped

2 tablespoons Dutch-process cocoa powder (I use Cacao Barry Extra Brute)

¼ cup (60 ml) coffee, very hot

1 cup (230 g) unsalted butter, at room temperature

2 cups (400 g) granulated sugar

6 eggs, at room temperature

½ cup (125 g) crème fraîche

1 tablespoon vanilla bean paste

2 cups (250 g) all-purpose flour

2 teaspoons baking powder

1 teaspoon salt

FOR THE ASSEMBLY:

¼ cup (55 g) unsalted butter, melted

¼ cup (50 g) granulated sugar

Make the cake:

Preheat the oven to 350°F (175°C). Generously spray a non-stick Bundt pan (with a 10-cup / 2.4-L capacity) with baking spray. (I use a Nordicware Procast Bavarian Bundt pan.) Place the prepared pan on a sheet pan lined with parchment paper.

Place the chocolate in a small, microwave-safe mixing bowl. Add the cocoa powder and stir. Pour the coffee over the chocolate mixture. Allow to sit undisturbed for a few minutes. Stir until the chocolate has completely melted. If it hasn't, microwave the chocolate at 50% power in 30-second intervals until completely melted. Set aside.

In the bowl of a stand mixer fitted with the paddle attachment, combine the butter and sugar. Beat on high speed until light and fluffy, 8 to 10 minutes.

Scrape the sides and bottom of the bowl with a large rubber spatula. Add 1 egg to the butter-sugar mixture. Beat for 30 seconds, scrape the bowl, and add another egg. Continue beating, scraping, and adding until all 6 eggs are incorporated.

In a bowl, stir together the crème fraîche and vanilla bean paste. Add to the egg mixture and beat until incorporated.

In another bowl, whisk together the flour, baking powder, and salt. Add the flour mixture to the egg mixture, ½ cup (60 g) at a time, mixing for 30 seconds after each addition.

Remove the bowl from the stand mixer. Using a large rubber spatula, scrape the sides and bottom of the bowl and stir in any stray dry ingredients. Pour half of the batter into a second mixing bowl. Stir the chocolate mixture into one of the bowls of batter.

Spread half of the plain batter into the Bundt pan. Spoon all of the chocolate batter on top of the first layer of plain batter. Spread evenly. Spoon the remaining half of plain batter on top of the chocolate. Run a knife through the batter in a swirling motion to marble the cake.

Bake for 1 hour, or until a tester inserted in the center comes out clean.

To assemble:

While the cake is still warm, invert the pan onto a serving platter to release the cake. Immediately brush the butter over the outside of the cake and sprinkle with the granulated sugar.

CHESTNUT SLICES

Makes 8 servings

THERE ARE NOT ENOUGH CHESTNUTS IN LIFE. There's always a little singing about them during the holidays, tales of them roasting on an open fire. But it's terribly rare to actually see the little buggers, let alone eat one. But if you look, you'll find them. As a matter of fact, I've seen them in summertime, in jars in our local grocery store. I bought them straightaway and started to play. With such richness and flavor, there's every reason to partake of them all year round, not just when Jack Frost is nipping at your nose.

FOR THE FILLING:
8 ounces (225 g) bittersweet chocolate, finely chopped
2 (8-ounce / 225-g) packages Neufchâtel cheese

FOR THE CAKE:
1 (15.3-ounce / 430-g) can chestnut purée (I use Roland)
2 tablespoons Frangelico
½ cup (100 g) granulated sugar
1 cup (230 g) unsalted butter, softened
1½ cups (330 g) light brown sugar, firmly packed
1 tablespoon vanilla bean paste
6 eggs, at room temperature
3 cups (420 g) cake flour
1 teaspoon salt
1 tablespoon baking powder
1 cup (240 ml) heavy cream, at room temperature

FOR THE CHESTNUT FLORENTINE:
2 ounces (55 g) chestnuts (from a can of peeled chestnuts)
¼ teaspoon salt
1 tablespoon cake flour
2 tablespoons heavy cream
3 tablespoons granulated sugar
½ tablespoon unsalted butter

FOR THE ASSEMBLY:
¼ cup (20 g) Dutch-process cocoa powder

Make the filling:

Place the chocolate in a heatproof bowl and place the bowl over a bain marie (a large saucepan half filled with gently simmering water). Stir until the chocolate has completely melted.

In the bowl of a stand mixer fitted with the paddle attachment, add the Neufchâtel and mix on medium speed until smooth. Slowly add the chocolate and continue mixing until smooth.

Transfer the mixture into a large pastry bag. Set aside.

Make the cake:

Preheat the oven to 325°F (165°C). Line the bottom of a 16-by-4-by-4-inch (40.5-by-10-by-10-cm) Pullman loaf pan with parchment paper. Spray the entire pan with nonstick baking spray.

In the bowl of a food processor fitted with the blade attachment, blend together the chestnut purée, Frangelico, and granulated sugar until a smooth paste forms.

In the bowl of a stand mixer fitted with the paddle attachment, cream together the butter and brown sugar until pale and fluffy. Add the chestnut mixture and mix until fully incorporated.

Add the vanilla bean paste and then the eggs, one at a time, scraping down the bottom and sides of the bowl after each addition.

In a bowl, whisk together the flour, salt, and baking powder. Add one-third of the flour mixture to the egg mixture and mix on low speed until just incorporated. Then add half of the cream and mix again. Repeat additions until all the flour and cream are incorporated and well combined.

Transfer half of the batter to the prepared loaf pan. Cut the closed end of the pastry bag and pipe the filling in the middle of the batter, leaving a 1-inch (2.5-cm) gap on either side so that the filling does not touch the edges of the pan. Layer the remaining batter atop the filling. Bake for 60 to 80 minutes, until the top of the cake is golden brown and the cake feels firm. Allow to cool completely.

Make the chestnut Florentine:

Preheat the oven to 250°F (120°C). Line a half sheet pan with parchment paper.

Chop the chestnuts until very fine (each piece should be half the size of a corn kernel). Spread the pieces evenly on the parchment and bake for 10 minutes, or until the chestnuts just start to brown. Set aside to cool completely.

Raise the temperature of the oven to 325°F (165°C). Trace 8 (2-inch / 5-cm) circles on a piece of parchment, spacing them a few inches apart. Flip the parchment over onto a half sheet pan, so the circles are visible but will not transfer to the mixture during baking.

In the bowl of a food processor fitted with the blade attachment, add the chestnuts, salt, and flour and pulse to combine.

Meanwhile, in a saucepan, combine the cream, granulated sugar, and butter and bring to a boil. Add the chestnut mixture to the cream mixture and stir. Remove from the heat.

Spread the mixture onto the circle templates as evenly as possible. Bake for 10 to 15 minutes, until golden brown.

While the Florentines are still warm, using a small offset spatula, quickly transfer a Florentine round from the sheet pan to a work surface. Gently roll the Florentine around the handle of a wooden spoon to form a tube. Continue with the remaining Florentines. Allow to cool completely.

To assemble:

Remove the cake from the pan. Using a long, very sharp serrated knife, trim the top of the cake flat if it has domed.

Sift the cocoa powder over the cake and slice into 8 even pieces. Place a Florentine atop each slice and serve immediately, or cover with plastic wrap and store for up to 5 days in the refrigerator.

GERMAN CHOCOLATE CAKE

Makes 1 (8-inch / 20-cm) cake

GERMAN CHOCOLATE CAKE ISN'T GERMAN. Let me just get that out there right away. Nothing would rile me more than someone coming into my pastry shop and saying, "That's strange; you'd think a German baker would have German chocolate cake." I could be baking away in the back, industrial mixers whining, the oven buzzer shrieking, the convection ovens whirring away, and through all this din, that one question—"Why no German chocolate cake?"—could weasel its way into my ear canal and get me yelling in response, "Because it's not German!"

Why on earth should I be so offended by this assumption, when the cake is called, after all, *German* chocolate cake? If you aren't a German and you aren't a pastry chef, why would you know that this is inherently erroneous? Although the cake is actually named after the American Sam German who manufactured a baker's chocolate and is composed in large part of pecan and coconut (ingredients neither native to nor common in German cuisine), it doesn't follow that a civilian would guess at the cake's Texas roots. It took me making the cake myself, to my own specifications, to get over it. Now it's a cake I love to cut into, just to see the glorious intermingling of chewy pecan and coconut with luscious layers of dark chocolate. German or not, this is a cake to keep on the menu.

FOR THE CAKE:

1 cup (240 ml) refined organic coconut oil (see Note)
½ cup (115 g) unsalted butter
6 ounces (170 g) unsweetened chocolate, such as German's baking chocolate, finely chopped
4 eggs, at room temperature
1½ cups (300 g) cups granulated sugar
1 teaspoon vanilla bean paste
1 teaspoon kosher salt
1 cup (125 g) all-purpose flour

½ cup (40 g) Dutch-process cocoa powder
½ teaspoon baking powder

FOR THE FILLING:

1¼ cups (125 g) pecans
1½ cups (330 g) dark brown sugar, packed
1 cup (240 ml) evaporated milk
5 egg yolks, lightly beaten
¾ cup (170 g) unsalted butter, cut into pieces
½ teaspoon salt
1½ cups (125 g) sweetened flaked coconut
1 teaspoon vanilla bean paste

FOR THE GLAZE:

1 pound (455 g) bittersweet chocolate, finely chopped
½ cup (120 ml) coconut milk
2 tablespoons coconut oil, unrefined

FOR THE ASSEMBLY:

2 cups (150 g) sweetened, desiccated coconut

NOTE: Coconut oil comes in jars and is solid. The refined style is meant for high heat and baking and doesn't have a strong coconut flavor. To measure properly, I remove the lid and place the jar in a saucepan half filled with water and simmer over low heat to melt the oil, then pour it into a measuring cup.

Make the cake:

Preheat the oven to 350°F (175°C). Prepare three 8-inch (20-cm) round cake pans by lining the bottom of each with a round of parchment paper and spraying with non-stick baking spray.

In a saucepan, combine the coconut oil and butter. Stir over medium heat until the butter has melted completely. Remove from the heat and add the chocolate. Stir until the chocolate is completely melted.

In the bowl of a stand mixer fitted with the paddle attachment, add the eggs, sugar, vanilla bean paste, and salt and mix on low speed. With the mixer running, slowly pour the hot chocolate mixture down the side of the bowl into the egg mixture.

In a small bowl, stir together the flour, cocoa powder, and baking powder; gradually add to the egg-chocolate mixture until combined.

Divide the batter evenly among the three prepared pans. Bake for 20 to 25 minutes, until the cakes begin to pull away from edges of the pans. Allow the cakes to cool completely.

Make the filling:

Preheat the oven to 350°F (175°C). Place the pecans on a half sheet pan and bake for 8 to 10 minutes, until lightly browned and fragrant. Remove from the oven, let cool, then coarsely chop.

In a medium saucepan, combine the brown sugar, evaporated milk, egg yolks, butter, and salt. Cook over medium heat, stirring constantly. When the mixture begins to boil and thicken, remove from the heat. Stir in the pecans, flaked coconut, and vanilla bean paste. Let cool to a spreadable consistency.

Make the glaze:

Place the chocolate in a heatproof bowl.

In a saucepan, combine the coconut milk and coconut oil and bring to a simmer.

Pour the hot coconut milk mixture over the chocolate, making sure the chocolate is completely covered. Allow to sit for 2 minutes. Whisk until the chocolate is completely melted and the mixture is smooth.

To assemble:

Preheat the oven to 325°F (165°C).

Spread the desiccated coconut in an even layer on a parchment-lined sheet pan and toast until the coconut is just golden, about 5 minutes. Allow to cool completely.

Using a long, very sharp serrated knife, trim the tops of the cake layers if they have domed. Place one layer on a cake platter and arrange parchment strips under the perimeter of the cake to protect the platter from errant glaze.

Spread half of the filling on top of the cake in an even layer all the way to the edge. Place a second layer of cake on top and press gently to adhere. Spread evenly with the remaining filling. Place the third layer on top and press gently to adhere.

Pour the glaze in an even layer over the cake, allowing it to flow down the sides. Using a large offset spatula, spread the glaze smoothly over the top and along the sides.

Place the cake in the refrigerator to set, about 30 minutes.

Gently press the desiccated coconut onto the sides of the cake so it adheres to the exposed glaze. Gently press a small circle of coconut onto the glaze on the top of the cake. Serve immediately.

TRUFFLE CARAMEL FIG CAKE

Makes 1 (8-inch / 20-cm) cake

FIGS AND CARAMEL AND TRUFFLES are a glorious combination: The earthiness of truffles intermingles with the sweet buttered opulence of caramel and the succulent tartness of figs to create a quiet and stupefying sophistication. And the elegance of the figs layered inside the cake creates a visual treat. If you are still stumped as to whether I mean truffle as in mushroom or truffle as in chocolate confection, let me assure you: I am referring to the fungus. But give this unique cake a chance, and you'll experience its surprising harmony for yourself.

FOR THE CAKE:
24 fresh Mission figs
1 cup (230 g) unsalted butter
2 cups (400 g) granulated sugar
5 eggs, at room temperature
3 cups (375 g) all-purpose flour
1 teaspoon salt
1 tablespoon baking powder
1½ cups (360 ml) buttermilk
2 tablespoons truffle oil
2 tablespoons canola oil

FOR THE FILLING:
2 cups (440 g) dark brown sugar, firmly packed
½ teaspoon salt
1 cup (240 ml) evaporated milk
½ cup (115 g) unsalted butter, slightly cooler than room
   temperature
¼ cup (60 ml) light corn syrup
4 cups (400 g) confectioners' sugar
1 tablespoon vanilla bean paste

FOR THE ASSEMBLY:
¼ cup (50 g) granulated sugar

Make the cake:

Preheat the oven to 350°F (175°C). Prepare three 8-inch (20-cm) round cake pans by lining the bottom of each with a round of parchment paper and spraying with non-stick baking spray.

De-stem the figs and chop 7 of them into small pieces (reserve 12 of the remaining figs for the interior, and the 5 best-looking for décor).

In the bowl of a stand mixer fitted with the paddle attachment, combine the butter and granulated sugar and cream them together until light and fluffy, 3 to 4 minutes. Add the eggs, one at a time, scraping the bottom and sides of the bowl after each addition.

In a bowl, whisk together the flour, salt, and baking powder.

In a separate bowl, whisk together the buttermilk, truffle oil, and canola oil.

Add one-third of the flour mixture to the butter-egg mixture and mix until just combined. Add half of the buttermilk mixture and mix until just combined. Repeat additions until all the ingredients are incorporated. Stir in the chopped figs.

Divide the batter among the three prepared pans and bake for 30 minutes, or until the cake springs back when touched. Set aside to cool completely.

Make the filling:

In a saucepan, combine the brown sugar, salt, evaporated milk, butter, and corn syrup. Stir over medium heat until the butter and brown sugar have completely melted.

Continue stirring until the mixture thickens, 3 to 4 minutes.

Transfer the mixture to the bowl of a stand mixer fitted with the paddle attachment. Add the confectioners' sugar and vanilla bean paste and beat until the mixture is smooth and the bowl is cool to the touch.

To assemble:

Preheat the oven to 300°F (150°C). Using a long, very sharp serrated knife, trim the tops of the cake layers if they have domed. Break the trimmed cake bits into small pieces and place them on a parchment-lined sheet pan. Bake for 10 minutes to dry out the pieces. Allow to cool completely.

Place the pieces in a food processor and pulse until the mixture resembles fine cornmeal.

Place a layer of cake on a serving platter.

Cut the 12 reserved figs in half. Place half of them, face down, evenly along the edge of the cake layer. Set aside 1½ cups (300 g) of the filling. Spread half of the remaining filling onto the cake layer. Place a second layer of cake on the frosting and press gently to adhere. Cover with the remaining cut figs, and spread the second half of the remaining filling over this layer. Top with the last cake layer and press gently to adhere.

Spread a thin, even layer of the reserved filling over the top and along the sides of the cake, making sure there's enough filling for the cake crumbs to adhere to. Gently press the cake crumbs onto the top and sides of the cake.

Slice the reserved figs in half. Sprinkle the cut sides with an even layer of granulated sugar (about 1 teaspoon each). Using a kitchen torch, gently run the flame back and forth over the sugar until it is caramelized, being careful not to burn it. Arrange the figs, caramelized side up, on top of the cake for décor. Serve immediately.

STRAWBERRY-RHUBARB DREAM CAKE

Makes 1 (8-inch / 20-cm) round layer cake

EVERY SUMMER, MY MOTHER WOULD come tearing into the house with cartons of fresh strawberries, so luxuriously juicy that the cartons would be stained with red. She'd get busy making buttery cake layers and sweet cream. She'd macerate the berries and drench the cake with the juices. It was the perfect summer cake, made with love by the best of mothers. I add fresh rhubarb to the cake batter; it doubles the summer fun and adds a pop of bright green to the batter that bursts forth like a spring bud when you slice through the cake. My mother would have adored the addition of this tart little herbaceous stem.

FOR THE CAKE:

1 cup (230 g) unsalted butter

2 cups (400 g) granulated sugar

5 eggs, at room temperature

1 tablespoon vanilla bean paste

3 cups (375 g) all-purpose flour

1 tablespoon baking powder

1 teaspoon salt

1¼ cups (300 ml) buttermilk

2 cups (240 g) diced rhubarb

½ cup (55 g) pistachios, finely chopped

FOR THE FILLING:

3 pints (750 g) fresh strawberries, 10 perfect berries set aside, the remainder hulled and halved

zest of 1 lemon

¼ cup (50 g) granulated sugar

3 cups (720 ml) heavy cream

1 cup (230 g) mascarpone

¼ cup (25 g) confectioners' sugar

1 teaspoon vanilla bean paste

FOR THE BUTTERCREAM:

5 egg whites

1 teaspoon vanilla bean paste

1 cup (200 g) granulated sugar

1 pound (455 g) unsalted butter, cut into small pieces, slightly cooler than room temperature

TO FINISH:

1 cup (125 g) chopped pistachios

Make the cake:

Preheat the oven to 350°F (175°C). Spray three 8-inch (20-cm) round cake pans with nonstick baking spray and line the bottoms with parchment paper.

In the bowl of a stand mixer fitted with the paddle attachment, cream together the butter and granulated sugar until light and fluffy, 3 to 4 minutes. Add the eggs, one at a time, scraping the bowl after each addition. Add the vanilla bean paste and combine.

In a bowl, whisk together the flour, baking powder, and salt. With the mixer running on low speed, add one-third of the flour mixture to the butter-sugar mixture. Then add half of the buttermilk. Repeat additions until all the ingredients are incorporated. Fold the rhubarb and pistachios into the batter.

Divide the batter among the three prepared pans and bake for 30 minutes, or until the top of the cake is golden brown and the cake springs back when touched. Set aside to cool completely.

Make the filling:

In a large bowl, stir together the halved strawberries, the lemon zest, and granulated sugar. Allow to sit until the strawberries' juices have started running and the sugar has completely melted, about 10 minutes.

In the bowl of a stand mixer fitted with the whisk attachment, add the cream, mascarpone, confectioners' sugar, and vanilla bean paste and whisk until stiff peaks form.

Assemble the cake layers:

Place one cake layer on a serving platter. Using a pastry brush, brush an even layer of strawberry juice over the first layer. Place an even layer of cut strawberries, cut side down, onto the cake. Spread half of the cream filling on top of the strawberries. Freeze for 10 to 15 minutes to set.

Place the second layer of cake over the filling and press gently to adhere. Brush evenly with strawberry juice and layer with strawberries. Spread the remaining filling over the strawberries. Freeze for 10 to 15 minutes to set.

Place the last layer of cake over the filling and press gently to adhere. Using a large offset spatula or a bench scraper, remove any filling that's oozed from the layers. Line the outside of the cake with parchment to stabilize it, using two pieces and taping them together to make a tight fit. Freeze overnight.

Make the buttercream:

Place the egg whites and vanilla bean paste in the bowl of a stand mixer fitted with the whisk attachment.

In a large saucepan, combine the granulated sugar with 1 cup (240 ml) water. Stir constantly over medium heat until the sugar has completely melted. Attach a candy thermometer to the side of the saucepan. Stop stirring. As the temperature of the syrup reaches around 225°F (107°C), start whisking the egg whites so they are foamy before you add the syrup in the next step; then continue heating the syrup until it reaches 240°F (116°C).

When the syrup has reached 240°F (116°C), slowly pour it down the side of the bowl into the whisking egg whites. Increase the mixer speed to high and whip until the egg whites hold stiff peaks and the bowl is cool to the touch.

With the mixer on medium speed, add the butter, a few pieces at a time. When the buttercream starts to look like it's curdling, add a few more pieces of butter and continue whisking until the mixture becomes smooth and creamy.

Coat the cake with buttercream as instructed on pages 68–69. Refrigerate for 2 hours to allow the cake to defrost and serve immediately, garnished with the reserved whole strawberries and the pistachios.

THE VERY BEST ALMOND PEAR BEE STING

Makes 8 mini Bundt cakes

THIS IS MY FAVORITE CAKE. It's moist and flavorful. The combination of honey and almond is lovely. You can use this recipe in a number of applications: cake layers, mini pound-cake loaves, Bundt cakes. That's true of most cake batters, but you'll love this one so much that you'll be inclined to try it every which way. But leaving it simple—poaching a few pears, layering them in the batter, and baking the cake in an intricate Bundt form—allows this gem to shine.

FOR THE PEARS:

2 cups (480 ml) dry white wine

¼ cup (55 g) light brown sugar, firmly packed

2 Bosc pears, cored and sliced

FOR THE CAKE:

1 (7-ounce / 200-g) tube almond paste

1 cup (200 g) granulated sugar

1 cup (230 g) unsalted butter

¼ cup (60 ml) honey

1 teaspoon almond extract

1 teaspoon vanilla extract

6 eggs

1 cup (140 g) cake flour

½ teaspoon baking powder

½ teaspoon salt

FOR THE GLAZE:

1 cup (100 g) confectioners' sugar

2 tablespoons (30 ml) whole milk

1 teaspoon vanilla bean paste

Make the pears:

In a saucepan, combine the wine and brown sugar and bring to a simmer. Add the pear slices and poach until just tender. Using a slotted spoon, transfer the pears to a bowl and set them aside to cool.

Make the cake:

Preheat the oven to 325°F (165°C). Spray two 4-cavity Bundt pans with nonstick baking spray.

In the bowl of a stand mixer fitted with the paddle attachment, combine the almond paste and granulated sugar. Mix on medium speed until the almond paste has broken up and has become somewhat smooth. Add the butter, honey, and almond and vanilla extracts and beat together on high speed until light and fluffy. Scrape down the bottom and sides of the bowl. Add the eggs, one at a time, scraping the bowl after each addition.

In a bowl, sift together the flour, baking powder, and salt. Slowly add the flour mixture to the batter and mix until just combined.

In one of the prepared pans, fill each Bundt cavity one-quarter full. Place approximately 3 pear slices on top of each. Top each with more batter, until about two-thirds full.

Bake for 45 minutes, or until the cakes are golden brown and spring back when you touch them. While the cakes are still very warm, unmold them by inverting the pan onto a cooling rack set over a parchment-lined sheet pan.

Wipe down the insides of the Bundt molds with a paper towel and respray with nonstick baking spray. Repeat the layering and baking process with the remaining batter and pear slices in the second prepared pan.

Make the glaze:

In a small bowl, whisk together the confectioners' sugar, milk, and vanilla bean paste until very smooth. While the Bundts are still warm, spoon the glaze over each of the little cakes to coat.

HELGASTEINE

Makes 24

SINCE I WAS THE LITTLEST OF LITTLE GIRLS, *Domino-steine* have been a Christmas staple in our home. Resembling petit fours more than cookies, these scrumptious cubes sing with flavor. From the marzipan that coats them, to the lovely jam nestling inside, to the delicate spiced cake layered in between, it's a marvel of baking genius. My mother, Helga, coveted these bites of holiday cheer above all else, and I make them each year in her beloved memory.

FOR THE CAKE:
2 (7-ounce / 200-g) packages almond paste (see Note)
1 cup (230 g) unsalted butter, softened
¼ cup (60 ml) honey
1 cup (200 g) granulated sugar
6 eggs, at room temperature
1 teaspoon ginger
1 teaspoon cinnamon
½ teaspoon nutmeg
pinch ground cloves
pinch white pepper
1 cup (125 g) all-purpose flour
½ teaspoon salt
½ teaspoon baking powder
1 tablespoon black currant purée (see page 48)
1 tablespoon Dutch-process cocoa powder

FOR THE SIMPLE SYRUP:
1 cup (200 g) granulated sugar

FOR THE ASSEMBLY:
1 (15-ounce / 430-g) jar seedless currant (or raspberry) preserves
2 (7-ounce / 200-g) packages almond paste, rolled into a thin sheet about ⅛ inch (3 mm) thick (approximately the size of the finished stacked layers)
½ batch chocolate glaze (see page 83), warm

NOTE: Packaged almond paste is often dry; I know it is against store policy, but I surreptitiously squeeze the box to make sure the stuff is fresh and malleable before I buy it.

Make the cake:

Preheat the oven to 325°F (165°C). Line a half sheet pan with parchment paper and spray with nonstick baking spray.

In the bowl of a stand mixer fitted with the paddle attachment, combine the almond paste, butter, honey, and granulated sugar and beat until smooth. Add the eggs, one at a time, beating after each addition. Add the ginger, cinnamon, nutmeg, cloves, and white pepper and mix to incorporate.

In a bowl, whisk together the flour, salt, and baking powder. Fold the flour mixture into the egg mixture until just incorporated.

Divide the batter evenly among three bowls. Leave the first bowl plain; mix the black currant purée into the second bowl; and mix the cocoa powder into the third bowl.

Transfer the batters onto the prepared pan in three sections, spreading them evenly so that each batter takes up one-third of the pan. (If you want it to be neater, you can pipe each batter from a pastry bag fitted with a large open tip.) The batters will touch while baking but we'll trim those edges. Your objective is to have three individual blocks of cake: one plain, one currant, and one cocoa.

Bake for 20 minutes, or until the cake springs back when you touch it and begins to slightly brown. Allow to cool completely.

Helgasteine

Celebration Cake

Make the simple syrup:

In a small saucepan over medium heat, combine the granulated sugar with 1 cup (240 ml) water. Cook, stirring, until the sugar has dissolved completely. Set aside and allow to cool.

To assemble:

Using a sharp knife, separate the plain, currant, and cocoa cakes, trimming so the cakes have clean edges and are equal in size. Place the cocoa layer on a cake board.

Using a pastry brush, gently brush a thin layer of simple syrup over the cocoa layer. Using a small offset spatula, cover the layer with one-third of the preserves. Top with the plain layer and press gently to adhere. Brush the plain layer with simple syrup, then spread another third of the preserves on top. Top with the currant layer and press gently to adhere. Brush with simple syrup and spread a very thin layer of the preserves (only a few tablespoons, less than on the other layers) over the surface to act as an adhesive.

Double check that the rolled-out almond paste is large enough to cover the top of the assembled layers. If it's too large, trim it. Place it carefully on top of the currant layer. Cover the almond paste with a thin layer of ganache about ⅛ inch (3 mm) thick.

Place in the freezer for about 30 minutes. Dip a sharp knife in a glass of very hot water and dry. Score the cake into 2-inch (5-cm) squares (I grab a ruler for this job—I can't be trusted to eyeball anything with accuracy), cleaning the knife in the hot water often and making sure to dry it completely. Then dip the knife in the hot water again, dry it off, and cut the squares, dipping and drying the knife after every cut to keep the squares looking neat and clean.

PUMPKIN TOFFEE COFFEE CAKE

Makes 1 Bundt ring or cake

PUMPKIN IS TOO OFTEN relegated to Thanksgiving. That's an awful shame. It's a wondrous orange orb, that pumpkin. It's naturally sweet and mellow. It makes a smooth and luxurious purée. It brings moisture and decadence to the most humble of pastries. And it's healthy, bringing vitamins A, E, and C along for the ride. Add the crunch of butter toffee, and that's one gorgeous gourd.

FOR THE TOFFEE (SEE NOTE):

1 cup (230 g) unsalted butter

1 cup (200 g) granulated sugar

1 teaspoon salt

½ cup (65 g) all-purpose flour

¼ cup (50 g) granulated sugar

2 tablespoons unsalted butter, cold

FOR THE CAKE:

1 cup (230 g) unsalted butter, at room temperature

1 cup (220 g) light brown sugar, firmly packed

½ cup (120 ml) honey

½ cup (120 ml) maple syrup

3 eggs, at room temperature

2 cups (480 ml) pumpkin purée

1 teaspoon vanilla bean paste

2½ cups (310 g) all-purpose flour

2 teaspoons baking powder

1 teaspoon salt

2 teaspoons cinnamon

1 teaspoon nutmeg

½ teaspoon ground cloves

½ teaspoon ground ginger

FOR THE GLAZE:

1 cup (100 g) confectioners' sugar

1 teaspoon vanilla extract

2 tablespoons whole milk

NOTE: You can also substitute store-bought toffee bars for this step. Use 6 (1.4-ounce / 40-g) toffee bars; break them up and process them as indicated in the instructions.

Make the toffee:

Line a half sheet pan with parchment paper and spray with nonstick baking spray.

In a large saucepan, melt the butter over medium heat. Add the granulated sugar and salt. Attach a candy thermometer to the side of the saucepan and stir continuously until the temperature reaches 300°F (150°C).

Immediately pour the mixture onto the prepared pan and tilt the pan to allow the toffee to spread into a thin, even layer (it needn't be any specific shape; you're going to be breaking it apart in the end).

Allow the toffee to cool until completely set, about 30 minutes.

Break the toffee into small pieces and place in the bowl of a food processor fitted with the blade attachment. Pulse until the pieces are small. Add the flour, sugar, and butter and pulse until fine (be careful not to overprocess to the point that the mixture becomes a paste). Set aside.

Make the cake:

Preheat the oven to 350°F (175°C). Spray a Bundt pan or ring mold with a generous, even coating of nonstick baking spray. (I use a Nordicware Platinum Autumn Wreath pan.) Set the pan or mold on a parchment-lined sheet pan.

In the bowl of a stand mixer fitted with the paddle attachment, cream together the butter and brown

sugar until light and fluffy, about 5 minutes. Add the honey and maple syrup and continue creaming until well incorporated.

Add the eggs, one at a time, scraping the bottom and sides of the bowl after each addition and making sure each egg is completely integrated before adding the next. Add the pumpkin purée and vanilla bean paste and mix until all the ingredients are well combined.

In a bowl, whisk together the flour, baking powder, salt, cinnamon, nutmeg, cloves, and ginger. Add the dry mixture to the batter, mixing only until the ingredients are just incorporated.

Pour a little less than half of the batter into the pan or mold and smooth the top. Sprinkle half of the toffee mixture in an even layer over the batter and top with the remaining batter. Bake for 1 hour, or until the cake springs back when touched. Allow to cool in the pan, then invert onto a serving platter.

Make the glaze:

In a small bowl, whisk together the confectioners' sugar, vanilla extract, and 1 tablespoon of the milk. Stir until smooth. Add more milk if needed to produce a glaze that pours easily but still has some body, like thick maple syrup.

Drizzle the glaze over the top of the pumpkin cake and immediately sprinkle with the remaining toffee crumble.

QUINCE AND DULCE DE LECHE MINI CAKES

Makes 30 cannelles

QUINCE IS A SEXY FRUIT. If you don't believe me, just look to history. It was the quince that ancient Greek brides would consume just before entering the nuptial chamber "in order that the first greeting may not be disagreeable nor unpleasant." So said Plutarch. Which raises the question, what did the gentlemen do to freshen their breath? Quince was also Aphrodite's signature fruit and was brought as an offering to her at weddings to guarantee . . . I'll let you fill in the blanks.

Which makes it seem highly improbable that the fruit would be a staple on Puritan farms in New England, but it's documented that it was customary for orchards and gardens in the colonial Northeast to always have a quince tree planted at the lower corner—perhaps to ensure the fecundity of the garden rather than the human inhabitants.

I enjoy quince not because of its sultry reputation but simply because it's delicious. Belonging to the apple family, it's a tarter version of that fruit, and somehow headier. In paste form it's sweet and almost citrusy. It's also packed with pectin, which makes it wonderful in jams and also lends a gorgeous texture to baked goods. And there's something about quince that pairs gloriously with manchego cheese—just enter any Spanish tapas bar and ask. This petite offering combines companionable elements: bright, moist quince cake, rich and creamy dulce de leche, and a bite of sharp manchego. It's the perfect end to any meal.

FOR THE CAKE:
½ cup (115 g) unsalted butter, at room temperature
1½ cups (330 g) light brown sugar, firmly packed
4 eggs, at room temperature
½ cup (120 ml) quince jam
¼ cup (60 ml) heavy cream
1 teaspoon vanilla bean paste
1 tablespoon lemon zest
1½ cups (210 g) cake flour
½ teaspoon baking powder
½ teaspoon salt
½ teaspoon cinnamon

FOR THE DULCE DE LECHE:
1 (14-ounce / 400-g) can sweetened condensed milk

FOR THE ASSEMBLY:
1 ounce (30 g) manchego cheese, in small chunks

Make the cake:

Preheat the oven to 325°F (165°C). Spray two 15-cavity silicone cannelle molds with nonstick baking spray. Place them on a half sheet pan lined with parchment paper.

In the bowl of a stand mixer fitted with the paddle attachment, combine the butter and brown sugar. Cream on high speed until light and fluffy.

Add the eggs, one at a time, scraping the bowl after each addition. Add the quince jam, cream, and vanilla bean paste. Mix until just combined. Add the lemon zest.

In a bowl, whisk together the flour, baking powder, salt, and cinnamon. With the mixer running on low speed, add the flour mixture to the egg mixture and mix until just combined.

Pour the batter into the prepared molds, filling them two-thirds of the way. Bake for 10 minutes or until the little cakes spring back when touched. Allow to cool in the molds. Once cool, trim the bottoms of any of the cakes that have domed.

Make the dulce de leche:

Puncture two holes in the top of the can of condensed milk. Place the can in a tall saucepan and fill the saucepan with water so that it reaches two-thirds of the way up the side of the can.

Simmer for 2 hours, checking often so that the water level never drops below halfway down the side of the can. Allow the dulce de leche to cool a bit before handling the metal can.

Carefully remove the hot can from the water and allow to cool completely.

To assemble:

Remove the cakes from the molds. Place a dollop of dulce de leche in the small cavity at the top of each cake. Place a small chunk of manchego on top of the dulce de leche. Serve immediately.

> **A NOTE FROM THE SWEET TALKER:** NONSTICK. What a fabulous idea—a baking surface that doesn't hold pieces of your cakes or muffins hostage, one that allows them to slip away with nary a dent in the lovely contours promised by that fancy (and expensive) Bundt mold you've been dying to use. But what's that you say? The cake stuck? All those lovely crevices that promised intricate fretwork on your cake refused to release your tender morsels? Your nonstick . . . stuck? Whether it's treated metal or silicon, nonstick sticks. Even without nooks and crannies, a nonstick mold will still mangle your pastries if you don't properly prepare the pan. After many disasters and much experimentation, I've found that a hearty, even coating of nonstick baking spray is the superior method for smooth release of baked goods. A baking spray contains both oil and flour. You can grease a mold with traditional nonstick spray or butter and then coat evenly and lightly with flour, but you'll find that the results will be spotty, and often this method leaves a floury film over the outside of your pastry if your aren't terribly careful. And although my mantra is often "Spray the hell out if it," you'll find that if you overspray a mold, the excess oils can penetrate the batter and leave pockmarks on the surface. Bottom line: Prepare your nonstick molds with as much care as you would a traditional mold to ensure baking sanity.

DRUNKEN FIGGY PUDDING LOG CAKE

Makes 20 servings

BÛCHES DE NOËL ARE A HOLIDAY STAPLE, and quite frankly, I've grown quite tired of them. They are meant to replicate a Yule log. The dessert is meant to look like a hearty piece of wood, right? But it tends to resemble a refried bean–slathered burrito rather than a delectable, woodsy confection (that's why they always put a decorative mushroom on top, to let you know you're not ordering meat-filled, spicy Tex-Mex fare). I've done something to remedy this. I made a cake that actually looks like logs, and in case my message isn't clear, I've topped the cake with an edible ax. It's rich, sumptuous, and full of flavor (as well as a fair bit of rum). Together, let's put the "log" back in Yule log.

FOR THE CAKE:
¾ cup (180 ml) coffee, very hot
¼ cup (60 ml) Captain Morgan Spiced Rum
1½ cups (225 g) chopped dried figs
1 cup (230 g) unsalted butter, at room temperature
3 cups (660 g) dark brown sugar, firmly packed
7 eggs, at room temperature
1 teaspoon vanilla bean paste
½ cup (120 ml) buttermilk
3 cups (375 g) all-purpose flour
2 teaspoons baking powder
1 teaspoon salt

FOR THE FROSTING:
6 (8-ounce / 225-g) packages cream cheese, at room temperature
6 cups (600 g) confectioners' sugar
1 cup (200 ml) maple sugar
1½ cups (345 g) unsalted butter, at room temperature

FOR THE ASSEMBLY:
8 ounces (225 g) bittersweet chocolate, finely chopped

FOR THE AX COOKIE:
1 cup (125 g) all-purpose flour

½ teaspoon baking soda
1 tablespoon ground ginger
1 tablespoon cinnamon
1 teaspoon white pepper
1 teaspoon salt
½ teaspoon nutmeg
½ teaspoon ground cloves
⅓ cup (80 g) unsalted butter
½ cup (110 g) dark brown sugar, firmly packed
2 tablespoons organic barley malt syrup
1 egg
1 teaspoon vanilla bean paste
1 teaspoon grated fresh ginger (peel a nub of ginger root and use a Microplane to grate)
½ teaspoon orange zest
1 egg white
½ cup (100 g) granulated sugar

Make the cake:

Preheat the oven to 350°F (175°C). Line a half sheet pan with parchment paper and spray with nonstick baking spray.

In a bowl, combine the coffee and rum. Add the figs to the bowl to soak.

In the bowl of a stand mixer fitted with the paddle attachment, cream together the butter and brown sugar until light and fluffy, about 8 minutes. Add the eggs, one at a time, scraping the bowl after each addition. Add the vanilla bean paste and whisk until well incorporated.

Remove the figs from the coffee-rum mixture and set aside; reserve the liquid.

In a bowl, combine the reserved liquid with the buttermilk and stir to combine.

In another bowl, whisk together the flour, baking powder, and salt. Add one-third of the flour mixture to the egg-sugar mixture, then one-third of the buttermilk mixture, stirring just to combine after each addition. Repeat until all the ingredients are just incorporated. Fold in the figs.

Pour the batter into the prepared pan. Bake until golden brown, about 30 minutes. The cake should spring back when you touch it.

Make the frosting:

In a stand mixer fitted with the paddle attachment, combine all the ingredients and beat until smooth.

To assemble:

Cut three 6-inch (15-cm) rounds of cardboard and place a 6-inch (15-cm) round of parchment on top of each.

Cut 6 rounds from the cake, each 6 inches (15 cm) in diameter. Place a cake layer on each of the parchment-lined cardboard rounds. Top the 3 rounds with ⅓ cup (65 g) frosting each, then top with another cake layer and press gently to adhere, so you have 3 double-tiered cakes. Freeze until set, about 30 minutes.

Using a small offset spatula, frost the tops of the cakes smoothly and frost the sides roughly, to resemble bark. Place in the refrigerator to set, about 30 minutes.

Meanwhile, gently melt the chocolate over a saucepan of simmering water or in the microwave. Transfer the chocolate to a pastry bag fitted with a small open tip. Pipe several thin concentric circles on the top of each cake to resemble tree rings.

Stack the 3 cakes in a zigzag configuration. If you're afraid that the layers are unstable, secure them with a few long wooden skewers: Poke the pointy end down and through

the three cakes and tap gently with a hammer to force the skewer all the way through the three cakes and into their cardboard rounds (but remember where the skewers are so you can remove them before serving).

Make the ax:

Preheat the oven to 350°F (175°C). Line a half sheet pan with parchment paper.

On a separate piece of parchment, draw (to the best of your ability) an ax that's about 12 inches (30.5 cm) in length. Cut the ax from the parchment. Set aside.

In a large bowl, whisk together the flour, baking soda, ground ginger, cinnamon, white pepper, salt, nutmeg, and cloves. Set aside.

In the bowl of a stand mixer fitted with the paddle attachment, cream together the butter, brown sugar, and barley malt syrup until light and fluffy. Add the egg and continue to beat until completely incorporated. Add the vanilla bean paste. Slowly add the flour mixture, fresh ginger, and orange zest. Mix until just combined. Turn the dough out onto a sheet of plastic wrap, cover, and refrigerate for 20 minutes.

On a lightly floured work surface, roll the dough out to a ¼-inch (6-mm) thickness. Place the ax template, drawn side up, on the dough and use a sharp paring knife to carefully cut into the dough along the outline. Set the ax aside and continue cutting axes from the dough (it's great to have extras in case of breakage). Transfer all the cut-out axes to the prepared sheet pan. Brush the ax-head portions of the cookies with egg wash and sprinkle with granulated sugar. Place the sheet pan in the freezer for 10 minutes.

Bake the cookies for 10 to 15 minutes, until they are just beginning to brown around the edges. Allow to cool completely. Right before serving, carefully embed an ax head in the cake.

THE CELEBRATION CAKE

Makes 1 (10-inch / 25-cm) cake

THIS MULTILAYER CAKE WAS THE result of leftovers. At Gesine Confectionary, I would bake cake on huge sheet pans and stamp out the layers with cake rings. This way I could make various sizes from one big swath of cake. I could stamp out teeny-tiny rounds for petit fours. I could make them just a little bigger for palm-size mini layer cakes, or a little bigger yet to make a cake just for two. You get the idea! Sometimes I had leftover cake pieces to play with, and that's just what I did when I once found myself with a few layers each of vanilla bean cake and chocolate fudge cake. The vanilla cake, with its light and fluffy yet moist crumb, was scream-ing to be conjoined with the dense, fudgy succulence of the chocolate layers. I happened to have some luscious raspberry purée, freshly made, calling out to join the sweet party, and the Celebration Cake came into being. I knew that the flavors would meld together beautifully. What I wasn't ready for was slicing through the choco-late ganache top and beholding a stunning visual dis-play: creamy white against the darkest cocoa, mingling with a sweet splash of pink. A treat for all the senses.

FOR THE VANILLA LAYERS:

1 cup (230 g) unsalted butter, at room temperature

2 cups (400 g) granulated sugar

5 eggs, at room temperature

1 tablespoon vanilla bean paste

3 cups (375 g) all-purpose flour

1 tablespoon baking powder

1 teaspoon salt

1¼ cups (300 ml) buttermilk

FOR THE FLOURLESS CHOCOLATE LAYERS:

¾ cup (150 g) granulated sugar

½ cup (40 g) Dutch-process cocoa powder

½ teaspoon salt

6 eggs

8 ounces (225 g) bittersweet chocolate, finely chopped

1 cup (230 g) unsalted butter

1 teaspoon vanilla bean paste

FOR THE GANACHE:

½ cup (120 ml) heavy cream

2 tablespoons unsalted butter

2 tablespoons corn syrup

8 ounces (225 g) bittersweet chocolate, finely chopped

FOR THE RASPBERRY BUTTERCREAM:

5 egg whites, at room temperature

1 cup (200 g) granulated sugar

1 pound (455 g) unsalted butter, softened

¼ cup (60 ml) smooth raspberry preserves

FOR THE ASSEMBLY:

1 cup (240 ml) smooth raspberry preserves

1 pint (250 g) fresh raspberries

Make the vanilla layers:

Preheat the oven to 350° (175°C). Prepare three 10-inch (25-cm) round cake pans by lining the bottom of each with a round of parchment paper and spraying with non-stick baking spray.

In the bowl of a stand mixer fitted with the paddle attach-ment, cream together the butter and granulated sugar until light and fluffy. Scrape down the sides and bottom of the bowl. Add the eggs, one at a time, scraping the bowl after each addition and making sure that each egg is completely incorporated before adding the next. Add the vanilla bean paste and mix.

In a bowl, whisk together the flour, baking powder, and salt.

Add one-third of the flour mixture to the egg-butter mixture and mix until just incorporated. Add half of the

buttermilk and mix until just incorporated. Continue alternating additions of flour and buttermilk until both are fully incorporated.

Divide the batter evenly among the three prepared pans. Bake for 45 minutes, or until the tops of the cakes are golden brown and spring back when touched. Set aside to cool completely.

Make the flourless chocolate layers:

Preheat the oven to 325° (165°C). Prepare three 10-inch (25-cm) round cake pans by lining the bottom of each with a round of parchment paper and spraying with non-stick baking spray.

In the bowl of a stand mixer fitted with the whisk attachment, add the granulated sugar, cocoa powder, and salt and whisk together until well integrated. Add the eggs, one at a time, and mix until a smooth paste forms.

In a heatproof bowl, combine the chocolate and butter and place over a bain marie (a large saucepan half filled with gently simmering water). Stir with a large rubber spatula until the chocolate is completely melted.

With the mixer running on low speed, slowly pour the chocolate-butter mixture into the egg mixture, scraping all the chocolate into the bowl. Add the vanilla bean paste. Whisk until fully combined.

Divide the batter among the three prepared pans. Bake for 15 to 20 minutes, until the cake just begins to pull away from the sides of the pan and feels firm but not hard in the center. Set aside to cool completely.

Make the ganache:

In a saucepan, combine the cream, butter, and corn syrup. Bring to a simmer.

Place the chocolate in a heatproof bowl and pour the hot cream mixture over the chocolate, making sure the chocolate is completely covered. Allow to sit undisturbed for 2 minutes. Stir clockwise until the ganache is shiny and emulsified. Cover with plastic wrap and allow the ganache to cool just to a spreadable consistency.

Make the raspberry buttercream:

In the bowl of a stand mixer fitted with the whisk attachment, add the egg whites. Beat until just frothy.

Meanwhile, in a saucepan, combine the granulated sugar with ⅓ cup (80 ml) water. Stir over medium heat until the sugar is completely melted. Attach a candy thermometer to the side of the saucepan and bring the syrup to 240°F (116°C).

With the mixer running on medium speed, slowly pour the hot syrup down the side of the bowl into the egg whites. Increase the speed to high and whip until stiff peaks form and the bowl is cool to the touch.

Add the butter, a few pieces at a time (you may not need it all). When the buttercream starts to look like it's curdling, add just one more piece of butter and continue whisking for a few minutes until the texture becomes smooth and creamy. Add the raspberry preserves and whisk until integrated.

To assemble:

Place a vanilla layer on a serving platter. Spread 3 table-spoons preserves evenly over the layer. Refrigerate for 10 minutes to set. Spread a very thin layer of ganache, about ⅛ inch (3 mm) thick, along the top of the pre-serves. Top with a layer of chocolate cake and press gently to adhere. Spread a ¼-inch (6-mm) layer of rasp-berry buttercream on top of the chocolate layer. Continue alternating in that order—vanilla cake, raspberry preserves, ganache, chocolate cake, and raspberry buttercream—until you have topped the cake with the last chocolate layer. Spread an even layer of the remaining raspberry buttercream across the top.

Allow the buttercream top to set, uncovered, in the refrig-erator for 30 minutes, and then cover the cake tightly with plastic wrap. Let the cake rest in the refrigerator for about 2 hours.

If the remaining ganache has hardened, place it over a bain marie until it is very loose. Spread a thin, even layer over the sides of the cake and transfer the remaining ganache to a large pastry bag fitted with a large star tip. Pipe the ganache in a filigree pattern along the perimeter of the top of the cake. Allow the cake to set at room tem-perature for about 20 minutes.

THE LOVERS, THE DREAMERS, AND YOU CAKE

Makes 8 servings

I HAVE A SOFT SPOT for Kermit the Frog. It's not just any amphibian who would wrangle a banjo onto a lily pad, serenading any and all swamp creatures within earshot. It's not just any amphibian who would hold fast to a porcine hellion, to a swine both vain and unpredictably violent, with unwavering love and support. Miss Piggy is one lucky oinker. It's not just any amphibian who made it look so easy to be green, when we all know it isn't. And it's not just any amphibian who can sing of rainbows and dreams with an utter lack of cynicism and turn us all into believers.

So for Kermit, I have designed a rainbow layer cake built for the lovers, the dreamers, and you.

FOR THE CAKE:

1 pound (455 g) unsalted butter, at room temperature

4 cups (800 g) granulated sugar

10 eggs

2 teaspoons lemon extract

6 cups (750 g) all-purpose flour

2 tablespoons baking powder

2 teaspoons salt

2½ cups (600 ml) nonfat buttermilk

2 to 3 drops each of red, orange, yellow, green, blue, and purple food coloring

FOR THE FROSTING:

4 cups (400 g) confectioners' sugar

2 (8-ounce / 225-g) packages cream cheese, at room temperature

½ cup (115 g) unsalted butter, at room temperature

1 teaspoon vanilla extract

Make the cake:

Preheat the oven to 350°F (175°C). Line two half sheet pans with parchment. Using a ruler, measure along the shorter sides of the half sheet pans and mark the parchment paper in thirds, so the pans are split 3 ways lengthwise. Flip the parchment paper over so the marks are visible but do not transfer to the cakes during baking.

In the bowl of a stand mixer fitted with the whisk attachment, combine the butter and granulated sugar and whisk until light and fluffy. Slowly add the eggs, one at a time. Beat for 1 minute after each addition to incorporate. Add the lemon extract and stir to incorporate.

In a bowl, sift together the flour, baking powder, and salt. With the mixer running, add approximately one-quarter of the buttermilk to the butter mixture, then one-third of the flour mixture. Continue alternating additions of buttermilk and flour until both are incorporated. Don't overmix.

Divide the batter evenly among 6 bowls, approximately 2½ cups (600 g) of batter in each bowl. Mix and match drops of the food colorings in each bowl to come up with the following colors: red, orange, yellow, green, blue, and purple. Two drops of food coloring should be enough for each bowl.

Transfer the red batter to a pastry bag fitted with a large open tip. Pipe the batter onto one-third of the sheet pan. (You'll use all the red batter.) Clean the tip and bag (unless you are using disposable bags), then fill the clean bag with the orange batter. Pipe the orange batter onto the middle third of the sheet pan. Clean the tip and bag again, then fill the clean bag with the yellow batter and pipe it onto the last third of the sheet pan. On the second sheet pan, repeat the process with the green, blue, and purple batter (in that order).

Bake the cakes for 25 to 30 minutes, until the tops of the cakes spring back lightly when touched. Allow the cakes to cool completely.

Make the frosting:

In the bowl of a stand mixer fitted with the whisk attachment, combine all the ingredients and whisk until smooth. Refrigerate for 1 hour to set.

To assemble:

Trim each colored panel of cake to a strip approximately 5 inches wide by 16 inches long (12 by 40.5 cm). Trim the ends of the cakes as well. Transfer the red layer to a clean sheet pan lined with parchment paper. Apply a very thin, even layer of frosting over the red layer. Carefully place the orange layer on top of the frosted red layer and press gently to adhere. Repeat the frosting and layering process with the yellow, green, blue, and purple cake strips (in that order). Cover the assembled cake with plastic wrap and freeze for 30 minutes to stabilize it.

Using a very sharp serrated knife, trim the sides and ends of the cake. The sides need to be perfectly level, so be slow and steady. Apply a very thin coat of frosting on all sides of the cake and freeze again for 30 minutes.

Carefully transfer the cake to a serving platter, turning it over on its side so the layers are now vertical. Apply a thin layer of frosting to the newly exposed side of the cake and freeze for 10 minutes, or until the frosting has set. (You can leave the cake with the layers lying horizontally, if you prefer.)

Apply a finishing coat of frosting over the entire cake.

Preheat the oven to 225°F (107°C). Take some of the extra pieces of trimmed cake (I like to use the red), place them on a sheet pan, and bake until the pieces have dried (but not browned), about 10 minutes. Cool the pieces completely, then pulse in the food processor to fine crumbs.

Fold a piece of parchment paper in half and cut out varied sizes of half hearts (so they will be full hearts when you unfold them). Apply the heart stencils to the top of the cake. Pat the cake crumbs onto the exposed frosting along the sides and top of the cake. Make sure to brush the crumbs from the tops of the stencils so that the crumbs don't later tumble into the heart shapes. Gently remove the stencils to reveal the pristine hearts.

You can simply slice the cake and serve it as is. But if you'd like to create heart-shaped slices, cut a normal slice and use a heart-shaped cake ring or cookie cutter to stamp out a heart shape.

INTERIOR HEART

THIS IS ONE CAKE THAT is literally "full of heart." But you can make it full of flowers or shamrocks, if you'd like. Just follow the baking instructions and stamp out adorable shapes with a cookie cutter, to be revealed with every slice.

FOR THE CAKE
1 pound (455 g) unsalted butter, at room temperature
4 cups (800 g) granulated sugar
10 eggs, at room temperature
1 teaspoon vanilla extract
6 cups (750 g) all-purpose flour
1½ teaspoons salt
2 tablespoons baking powder
2½ cups (600 ml) nonfat buttermilk
3 or 4 drops red food coloring

FOR THE BUTTERCREAM
10 egg whites
2 cups (400 g) granulated sugar
pinch salt
1½ pounds (685 g) unsalted butter

Make the cake:

Preheat the oven to 350°F (175°C). Line a half sheet pan with parchment and spray with nonstick cooking spray. Spray a large tube or angel food baking mold with nonstick baking spray. Set aside.

In the bowl of a stand mixer fitted with the whisk attachment, cream the butter and granulated sugar until light and fluffy, 5 to 10 minutes. Scrape the sides and bottom of the bowl a few times. Add the eggs, one at a time, beating for 30 seconds between each addition. Add the vanilla.

In a large bowl, stir together the flour, salt, and baking powder. With the mixer on low, alternate additions of the flour mixture and the buttermilk. Using a large rubber spatula, scrape the bottom and sides of the bowl to ensure the batter is well mixed.

Transfer a little less than half of the batter to a large mixing bowl. Add the food coloring to the bowl and stir to distribute the color.

Spread the red batter in an even layer in the prepared half sheet pan and bake until the cake is just barely done and feels firm when touched but doesn't spring back, 10 to 15 minutes. Allow to cool completely.

Put half of the un-dyed batter in the bottom of the tube pan (see photo 1, page 164). Using a 3-inch (7.5 cm) heart-shaped cookie cutter, stamp out 14 or 15 heart shapes from the red cake (see photo 2, page 164). Place the hearts in the tube pan, rounded side down into the batter and point sticking up (see photo 3, page 164). Don't press the hearts all the way down into the batter, just enough that the batter keeps them upright. Place them as close together as you can while still keeping the hearts properly angled in the round.

Fill a large pastry bag with the remaining un-dyed batter and pipe it into the tube pan, making sure to fill any hard- to-reach areas and covering the hearts completely (see photo 4, page 164). Bake for 45 to 50 minutes or until the cake is golden brown and springs back when gently touched. Allow to cool completely in the pan.

For the buttercream:

In the bowl of a stand mixer, combine the egg whites, granulated sugar, and salt. Constantly whisk the egg white mixture over a bain marie (a large saucepan half full of simmering water) until the sugar has completely dissolved and feels warm to the touch (attach a thermometer and make sure the mixture reaches 160°F / 72°C if you are nervous about uncooked eggs).

Transfer the bowl to a stand mixer fitted with the whisk attachment and whisk on high until the mixture quadruples in volume and the bowl is cool to the touch.

Add the butter, a few tablespoons at a time, until the buttercream thickens. The icing may look as if it's starting to separate and appear chunky; this is perfectly normal. Just walk away for a few minutes while the mixer does its work, and you'll come back to beautiful buttercream.

To assemble:

Run a long, thin knife along the edge of the baking pan to release the cake. Place a cake platter on top of the tube pan, face down, and flip the pan over. Gently left the pan off so the cake remains on the platter.

Coat the cake with a smooth layer of buttercream. Serve immediately, or store in the refrigerator for up to 3 days.

CHECKERBOARD

[Using vanilla and raspberry cakes with buttercream from prior recipes.]

THIS CAKE CAN BE MADE with a special pan available online or at cake shops. This would certainly make it much easier, but also more expensive. If you don't want to spend money on a piece of equipment you may only use once, this tutorial will allow you to checkerboard most any cake. I suggest using the recipe for the interior heart on page 163. Divide the batter evenly between 2 bowls. Add ¼ cup (60 ml) raspberry purée and 2 drops of red food coloring to one bowl and 1 teaspoon of lemon extract to the other. Line two half sheet pans with parchment paper. Spread the raspberry batter on one and the lemon batter on the other. Bake at 350°F (175°C) for 30 minutes or until the cake springs back when touched. Use a 6-inch, 4-inch, and 2-inch (15-cm, 10-cm, and 5-cm) ring to make the cuts as shown in the tutorial photos at right.

bake it like you mean it

Chapter 4

SMOOTH & CREAMY

CHEESECAKES and MOUSSE CAKES

CHEESECAKES AND MOUSSE CAKES WERE REQUIRED ADDITIONS TO MY

pastry repertoire at Gesine Confectionary. There is an inherent drama to both, the challenge of baking the cheesecake without cracking it. The layering of mousses in kaleidoscope colors in a tower so high, we held our breath when we slid them into the refrigerated case for fear they'd be too tall to fit. These creamy delicacies are also a boon to have in your pastry repertoire when only something light and fresh will do.

What's even better is that these creamy elements can be used as filling for towering layer cakes or placed in rings to create kaleidoscopic rounds of mousse. A mousse also has the very convenient advantage of being a great "make-ahead" dessert, as it is perfectly happy to be left frozen until you need it!

SUNSHINE CREAMSICLE CHEESECAKE

Makes 1 (8-inch / 20-cm) cheesecake

NOTHING SCREAMS SUMMER LIKE A CREAMSICLE, that orange-and-vanilla frozen treat that combines citrus zing with opulent yet mellow creaminess. I have re-created this beloved flavor combination in a cheesecake, piping orbs of sunshine inside the batter, and the classic summer treat has risen to new heights.

FOR THE CRUST:
1 cup (125 g) all-purpose flour
½ cup (60 g) cornstarch
¼ cup (50 g) granulated sugar
zest of 1 orange
½ teaspoon salt
¾ cup (170 g) unsalted butter, cut into small cubes, cold
1 egg
1 tablespoon sweetened condensed milk
1 teaspoon vanilla bean paste

FOR THE FILLING:
4 (8-ounce / 225-g) packages cream cheese, at room temperature
¼ cup (60 ml) heavy cream
1½ cups (300 g) granulated sugar
½ teaspoon salt
5 eggs
1 tablespoon vanilla extract
¼ cup (30 g) all-purpose flour
zest of 1 orange
1 teaspoon orange extract
2 or 3 drops orange gel food coloring

TO ASSEMBLE:
¼ cup (60 ml) smooth apricot preserves
4 oranges, supremed (see page 172)

Make the crust:

Preheat the oven to 350°F (175°C). Spray an 8-inch (20-cm) springform pan or cake ring with nonstick baking spray and place on a parchment-lined sheet pan.

In the bowl of a food processor fitted with the blade attachment, combine the flour, cornstarch, granulated sugar, orange zest, and salt. Pulse until well combined.

Add the butter and pulse until the mixture resembles coarse cornmeal.

In a separate bowl, whisk together the egg, condensed milk, and vanilla bean paste. While pulsing the flour mixture, slowly add the egg-milk mixture. Pulse until the dough just comes together. Turn the dough out onto a large piece of plastic wrap and press it together into a loose round. Refrigerate for 20 minutes.

Press the crust dough onto the bottom and 1 inch (2.5 cm) up the sides of the pan or ring. Bake for 10 minutes and set aside to cool.

Make the filling:

In the bowl of a stand mixer fitted with the paddle attachment, add the cream cheese, cream, granulated sugar, and salt. Mix on high speed until very smooth. Add the eggs, one at a time, mixing after each addition just until the egg is fully incorporated. Add the vanilla extract, then the flour, and gently mix until just combined.

Transfer one-third of the batter to a large bowl and stir in the orange zest, orange extract, and food coloring until

the orange color is uniform. Chill the orange batter until firm, 30 minutes to 1 hour. Leave the plain batter at room temperature.

Pour the plain batter onto the crust in the cake ring or springform pan.

Transfer the orange batter to a large pastry bag fitted with a large open tip. Insert the tip about halfway down into the middle of the plain batter (do not touch the bottom of the pan with the tip). Uniformly squeeze out about one-eighth of the batter and carefully remove the tip.

Pipe 8 smaller dollops of the remaining batter halfway into the batter evenly along the perimeter of the cake, making sure that none of the dots touch.

Lower the oven temperature to 300°F (150°C) and immediately place the cheesecake in the oven.

Bake for 1½ to 2 hours, until the cake slightly shimmies in the middle. Turn the oven off and open the door slightly. If the cake hasn't pulled away from the sides of the pan when you first turn off the oven, quickly remove the cake from the oven, run a sharp paring knife around the edge of the cake to release it, and return the cake to the oven. Allow the cake to rest in the cooling oven for 20 minutes. Remove the cake from the oven and allow it to rest for 10 minutes before carefully releasing it from the pan. Allow to cool completely at room temperature.

To assemble:

In a small saucepan, combine the apricot preserves with 2 tablespoons water and stir over low heat until the preserves have dissolved and the mixture is smooth.

Arrange the orange segments in a fan over the top of the cake. Using a pastry brush, gently brush the slices with apricot glaze. Refrigerate the cake for 1 hour, or overnight.

Serve immediately or refrigerate, covered, for up to 5 days.

A NOTE FROM THE SWEET TALKER: You could just slice an orange, with the membrane and skin still clinging onto the pulpy, succulent pieces, but why not take a few extra minutes to make them "supreme"? To supreme an orange is to create perfect orange segments without any pith, skin, membrane, or seeds sullying your gorgeous half moon of citrus. Using a very sharp paring knife, trim off the top and bottom of the orange. Place a now flat end of the orange on a cutting board and, using the paring knife, carefully carve off the remaining skin in strips (why not save them to make some candied orange peel?). Follow the curve of the peel so you retain as much of the orange flesh as possible. Place the orange on its side and slice in between the layers of membrane to create perfect segments of orange.

MEYER LEMON AND BLACKBERRY ZEBRA CHEESECAKE

Makes 1 (8-inch / 20-cm) cheesecake

OKAY, MAYBE NOT "ZEBRA"—THIS CAKE isn't black and white. So let's call it a pastel zebra cake. This stripey and creamy, fruity and zesty treat is packed with tremendous flavor while delivering a full dose of fun. The chèvre will give this cheesecake both a little tang and a cloudlike texture, while the small dose of cream cheese will give it body. You can play with flavor and color combinations to your heart's content.

FOR THE CRUST:

1 cup (125 g) all-purpose flour
½ cup (60 g) cornstarch
¼ cup (50 g) granulated sugar
½ teaspoon salt
¾ cup (170 g) unsalted butter, cut into small cubes, cold
1 egg
1 tablespoon sweetened condensed milk

FOR THE FILLING:

1 pound (455 g) chèvre (goat cheese), at room temperature
1 (8-ounce / 225-g) package cream cheese, at room temperature
1 cup (200 g) granulated sugar
5 eggs
¼ cup (30 g) all-purpose flour
½ teaspoon salt
¼ cup (60 ml) blackberry purée
zest and juice of 1 Meyer lemon
1 teaspoon lemon extract

FOR THE ASSEMBLY:

1 pint (250 g) fresh blackberries
¼ cup (25 g) confectioners' sugar

Make the crust:

Preheat the oven to 350°F (175°C). Line a sheet pan with parchment paper. Spray an 8-inch (20-cm) springform pan or cake ring with nonstick baking spray and place it on the parchment-lined sheet pan.

In the bowl of a food processor fitted with the blade attachment, combine the flour, cornstarch, granulated sugar, and salt. Pulse until well combined.

Add the butter and pulse until the mixture resembles coarse cornmeal.

In a bowl, whisk together the egg and condensed milk. While pulsing the flour mixture, slowly add the egg-milk mixture. Pulse until the dough just comes together. Turn the dough out onto a large piece of plastic wrap and press it together into a loose round. Refrigerate for 20 minutes.

Press the crust dough onto the bottom and 1 inch (2.5 cm) up the sides of the pan or ring. Bake for 10 minutes and set aside to cool.

Make the filling:

In the bowl of a stand mixer fitted with the paddle attachment, combine the chèvre, cream cheese, and granulated sugar. Mix until completely smooth; this is crucial to the integrity of the stripes. If you find that there are any lumps, run the batter through a fine-mesh sieve. Add the eggs, one at a time, mixing after each addition until the egg is just incorporated, and continue mixing until smooth. Add the flour and salt and mix until just combined. Do not overmix.

Transfer one-third of the batter to a clean bowl and add the blackberry purée to it; stir until combined. To the batter in the stand mixer bowl, add the lemon zest, juice, and extract. Stir until combined.

To assemble:

In the very center of the crust, add 2 tablespoons of the Meyer lemon batter, and right in the middle of the lemon batter, add 1 tablespoon of the blackberry batter. Continue in this manner, adding 2 tablespoons of lemon batter and then 1 tablespoon blackberry batter to the same spot (creating layers), until all the batter is used. If the batter has not spread to fill up the cake pan, resist the urge to tap the pan or to spread the batter. The batter will even out in the pan as it's baking (as my friend Agnes asked as she was layering the batters, "Is this supposed to look like Jabba the Hutt?"). You may have a teetering mound that looks as if it will never spread—just put it in the oven and let the heat do its work.

Bake the cake for 1 hour to 1 hour 15 minutes, until the middle of the cheesecake shimmies very slightly. Turn the oven off and open the oven door slightly. If the cake hasn't pulled away from the sides of the pan when you first turn off the oven, quickly remove the cake from the oven, run a sharp paring knife around the edge of the cake to release it, and return the cake to the oven. Allow the cake to rest in the cooling oven for 20 minutes. Remove the cake from the oven and allow it to rest for 10 minutes before carefully releasing it from the pan. Allow to rest in the refrigerator for about 2 hours before serving.

Arrange the blackberries on top of the cake to cover completely. Serve immediately, or refrigerate for up to 5 days.

OPTIONS!

THE REAL ZEBRA: Add 1 tablespoon vanilla bean paste to the larger (two-thirds) portion of batter instead of the lemon zest, juice, and extract. Add 3 tablespoons cocoa powder to the smaller (one-third) portion of batter and stir until combined.

THANKSGIVING SURPRISE: To the larger portion of batter, add the zest and juice of ½ orange along with 1 teaspoon orange extract. To the smaller portion, add ¼ cup (60 ml) cranberry purée (1 cup / 125 g frozen cranberries simmered with ¼ cup / 60 ml water and ½ cup / 100 g sugar until the sugar has dissolved, then puréed in a food processor until smooth and cooled completely). Reserve the remaining purée to top the cake.

BLACK PEPPER AND BLACK CHERRY MARBLE CHEESECAKE

Makes 1 (10-inch / 25-cm) cheesecake

IT SOUNDS STRANGE, I KNOW. What the hell is black pepper doing in a cheesecake? But I promise you, the addition of pepper gives this dense, luscious cake a slight kick while melding effortlessly with the lush juiciness of the black cherries. The tart undertones of the chèvre blend all the flavors effortlessly, while the chocolate—well, it's chocolate, and it goes with pretty much anything.

FOR THE CRUST:

3 ounces (85 g) bittersweet chocolate, finely chopped

¼ cup (55 g) unsalted butter

1 tablespoon coffee, very hot

1 egg

¼ cup (50 g) granulated sugar

¼ cup (20 g) Dutch-process cocoa powder

½ teaspoon salt

FOR THE FILLING:

1 pound (455 g) fresh cherries

4 ounces (115 g) bittersweet chocolate, finely chopped

2 pounds (910 g) chèvre (I use Vermont Butter & Cheese)

1 cup (200 g) granulated sugar

½ teaspoon salt

½ teaspoon black pepper, finely ground

4 eggs

3 tablespoons cornstarch

2 tablespoons kirsch

½ teaspoon almond extract

FOR THE ASSEMBLY:

1 cup (240 ml) heavy cream

¼ cup (25 g) confectioners' sugar

1 ounce (30 g) bittersweet chocolate, for shaving

1 egg white

¼ cup (50 g) granulated sugar

For the crust:

Preheat the oven to 325°F (165°C). Spray a 10-inch (25-cm) springform pan or cake ring liberally with nonstick baking spray.

In a double boiler, combine the chocolate, butter, and coffee and heat over gently simmering water until the chocolate is melted.

In the bowl of a stand mixer fitted with the whisk attachment, combine the egg, granulated sugar, cocoa powder, and salt and whisk together. Scrape the sides and bottom of the bowl to ensure that the cocoa powder has not clumped together in a dry mass. Continue to mix and scrape until you are sure that the cocoa powder is well and truly mixed into the batter.

With the mixer on low speed, slowly pour the melted chocolate mixture into the egg mixture. Continue to mix until the batter is smooth.

Pour the batter into the prepared pan or ring and bake for 10 minutes, or until barely baked through.

For the filling:

Pit half of the cherries and place them in a large bowl.

Place the chocolate in a heatproof bowl and place over a bain marie (a large saucepan half filled with gently simmering water), stirring constantly until the chocolate is just melted. Turn off the heat but keep the chocolate over the saucepan to keep it warm.

In a stand mixer fitted with the paddle attachment, combine the chèvre, granulated sugar, salt, and pepper and beat until smooth. Add the eggs, one at a time, mixing after each addition until just combined. Gently stir in the cornstarch.

Transfer one-third of the batter to a separate bowl and quickly stir in the melted chocolate.

To the plain batter in the stand mixer bowl, add the kirsch, almond extract, and any juice that has collected in the bowl containing the pitted cherries.

Pour the kirsch-laced batter carefully on top of the prepared crust.

Transfer the chocolate batter to a large pastry bag fitted with a large open pastry tip.

Insert the pastry tip halfway down into the kirsch batter and pipe generous dollops of chocolate batter into the kirsch batter all along the perimeter of the cake. Pipe a few more evenly spaced dollops onto the middle of the cake. Drag a skewer through the batters in a swirling motion to create a marble effect. Gently insert the pitted cherries into the batter, using a wooden skewer to guide them in.

Bake for 1 to 1½ hours, until the middle of the cheesecake shimmies very slightly. Turn the oven off and open the door slightly. If the cake hasn't pulled away from the sides of the pan when you first turn off the oven, quickly remove the cake from the oven, run a sharp paring knife around the edge of the cake to release it, and return the cake to the oven. Allow the cake to rest in the cooling oven for 20 minutes.

Cool the cake completely in the refrigerator, about 1 hour.

To assemble:

In the bowl of a stand mixer fitted with the whisk attachment, combine the cream and confectioners' sugar and whisk until stiff peaks form, being careful not to overwhip. Swirl the whipped cream atop the cheesecake.

Using a vegetable peeler, shave curls and shards from the chocolate onto the whipped cream.

Gently dip the reserved whole cherries, with pits and stems still intact, into the egg white to coat, then dip them into the granulated sugar. Arrange them over the whipped cream.

Serve immediately.

bake it like you mean it

DULCE DE LECHE–NUTELLA CREAM TORTE

Makes 1 (10-inch / 25-cm) torte

THE OUTSIDE OF THIS ELEGANT TORTE hints at the glory within. It has an understated beauty, with chopped hazelnuts gracing the sides of the cake, while the top is glazed with glistening dark chocolate. Cut inside to find rings of vanilla, Nutella, and chocolate cream.

NOTE: This cake requires three cake rings of increasing size to create the alternating flavor rings inside. I use 10-, 8-, and 6-inch rings (25-, 20-, and 15-cm rings). You can also use springform pans to make the rings, leaving the bottom of the 10-inch (25-cm) pan on but just using the side rings to make the remaining layers.

FOR THE HAZELNUT CAKE:
12 ounces (340 g) chopped hazelnuts
1 cup (200 g) granulated sugar, divided
2 teaspoons baking soda
1 teaspoon salt
6 eggs, separated
1 teaspoon vanilla bean paste

FOR THE DULCE DE LECHE:
1 (14-ounce / 400-g) can sweetened condensed milk

FOR THE FILLING:
2 (8-ounce / 225-g) packages cream cheese, at room temperature
1 tablespoon vanilla bean paste
pinch salt
2¼ cups (540 ml) heavy cream
1 teaspoon gelatin
½ cup (120 g) Nutella
6 ounces (170 g) bittersweet chocolate, finely chopped

FOR THE GLAZE:
8 ounces (225 g) bittersweet chocolate, finely chopped
½ cup (120 ml) heavy cream
3 tablespoons unsalted butter

FOR THE ASSEMBLY:
2 cups (230 g) chopped hazelnuts, lightly toasted and cooled

Make the hazelnut cake:

Preheat the oven to 325°F (165°C). Spray the bottom (but not the sides) of a 10-inch (25-cm) cake pan, cake ring, or springform pan with nonstick baking spray, and place on a parchment-lined sheet pan.

In the bowl of a food processor fitted with the blade attachment, combine the hazelnuts and ½ cup (100 g) of the sugar. Pulse until the mixture resembles a fine flour. Add the baking soda and salt. Pulse to combine. Add the egg yolks and vanilla bean paste and pulse until a smooth paste forms. Transfer the batter to a large bowl.

In the bowl of a stand mixer fitted with the whisk attachment, add the egg whites and whisk until foamy. Slowly add the remaining sugar and whisk on high speed until soft peaks form. Gently fold the egg whites into the batter until no white streaks remain.

Transfer the batter to the prepared pan. Bake for 1 hour to 1 hour 20 minutes, just until the cake is golden and springs back when you touch it.

Allow the cake to cool. Run a sharp paring knife around the edge of the cake to release it. Using a long, very sharp serrated knife, split the cake in half horizontally to create two even cake rounds.

Make the dulce de leche:

Puncture two holes in the top of the can of condensed milk. Place the can in a tall saucepan and fill the saucepan with water so that it reaches two-thirds of the way up the side of the can.

Simmer for 2 hours, checking the water level often so that it never drops below halfway down the side of the can. Allow the metal can to cool a bit before handling.

Carefully remove the hot can from the water and allow to cool completely. When cool, stir the dulce de leche well.

Make the filling:

In the bowl of a stand mixer fitted with the paddle attachment, cream together the cream cheese and condensed milk (now dulce de leche). Add the vanilla bean paste and salt. Divide the mixture evenly among three bowls.

Place ¼ cup (60 ml) of the heavy cream in a microwave-safe bowl. Sprinkle the gelatin over the cream and allow to sit until the gelatin has bloomed and looks soggy. Microwave the cream at 50% power in 10-second bursts, swirling the bowl between blasts, until the gelatin has completely dissolved. Transfer one-quarter of the cream cheese mixture from one of the bowls into the gelatin mixture and stir to combine. Transfer the gelatin–cream cheese mixture into the remaining cream cheese and stir well.

In the bowl of a stand mixer fitted with the whisk attachment, whip the remaining 2 cups (480 ml) of cream to stiff peaks. Carefully fold one-third of the whipped cream into the gelatin–cream cheese mixture. Place a 6-inch (15-cm) round cake ring on a parchment-lined sheet pan. Fill the ring to the rim with the plain cream cheese mixture. Use a large offset spatula to even the top of the filling at rim level. Freeze until set, about 2 hours. Place the leftover whipped cream and the two remaining bowls of cream cheese mixture in the refrigerator.

Using a kitchen torch or blow dryer, gently heat the sides of the ring to remove. Leave the round of plain filling on the sheet pan. Place an 8-inch (20-cm) cake ring on the sheet pan to surround the plain round, making sure it's evenly spaced around the smaller round.

Stir the Nutella into one of the remaining bowls of filling until completely combined. Gently fold in half of the remaining whipped cream. Transfer the filling to a large pastry bag fitted with a large open tip. Pipe the filling between the cake ring and the plain round in its center. Freeze until set, about 2 hours.

Place the chocolate in a heatproof bowl over a bain marie (a large saucepan half filled with gently simmering water) and stir occasionally until completely melted. Allow to cool just a bit.

Stir the chocolate into the last bowl of filling and refrigerate until cool. Fold the remaining whipped cream into the chocolate mixture.

Gently heat the 8-inch (20-cm) ring with a kitchen torch or blow dryer to release the ring, leaving the set fillings on the parchment-lined sheet pan. Place the 10-inch (25-cm) cake ring around the set fillings, making sure it's evenly spaced around the smaller Nutella round.

Transfer the chocolate-filling mixture to a large pastry bag fitted with a large open tip. Pipe the filling between the cake ring and the set Nutella filling. Spread any remaining chocolate filling on top. Freeze for 2 hours, or until set.

Place one of the hazelnut cake layers on a cooling rack placed over a parchment-lined sheet pan. Center the set fillings, ring still attached, on top of the cake layer. Gently warm the sides of the cake ring to release. Center the second layer of cake on top of the filling. Refrigerate until needed.

Make the glaze:

Place the chocolate in a heatproof bowl.

In a heavy saucepan, combine the cream and butter and bring to a simmer. Pour the hot mixture over the chocolate, making sure the chocolate is completely covered, and allow to sit undisturbed for 2 minutes. Whisk clockwise until smooth.

Immediately pour the glaze over the cake, using a large offset spatula to smooth it over the top and to adhere it to the sides.

To assemble:

Press the chopped hazelnuts on the sides of the cake. Refrigerate until the glaze is set, about 20 minutes.

MOCHA RICOTTA TOWER

Makes 1 (8-inch / 20-cm) cake

IF YOU'RE LOOKING FOR A shockingly impressive cake, one that's built on a grand scale, towers above all other cakes, and, when sliced, reveals decadent earth-toned layers ranging from a warm latte to a bittersweet cocoa black, this is the cake for you. That each mouthful contains the moist chocolate cake of your dreams and a creamy filling from heaven is a wonderful bonus.

FOR THE CAKE:

2 cups (170 g) Dutch-process cocoa powder

2 tablespoons instant espresso powder

1 teaspoon salt

½ cup (120 ml) strong coffee

2 eggs

2 egg whites

2½ cups (500 g) granulated sugar

1½ cups (360 ml) canola oil

1 tablespoon vanilla bean paste

2 cups (250 g) all-purpose flour

1 teaspoon baking powder

1 teaspoon baking soda

¾ cup (180 ml) buttermilk

FOR THE FILLING:

1 pound (455 g) bittersweet chocolate, finely chopped
   (I use Lindt 70%)

3 cups (720 ml) heavy cream, divided

¼ cup (55 g) unsalted butter

2 (15-ounce / 430-g) containers ricotta

2 (8-ounce / 225-g) containers mascarpone

1 tablespoon vanilla bean paste

½ teaspoon salt

2 tablespoons very strong coffee, cold

5 tablespoons confectioners' sugar, divided

FOR THE ASSEMBLY:

coffee simple syrup (1 cup / 240 ml coffee and 1 cup / 200 g
   sugar heated together until the sugar is dissolved)

Make the cake:

Preheat the oven to 350°F (175°C). Prepare six 8-inch (20-cm) round cake pans by lining the bottom of each with a round of parchment paper and spraying with non-stick baking spray. (If you have only two or three pans, work in batches once the batter is ready.)

In a large bowl, combine the cocoa powder, espresso powder, and salt. Whisk until combined. In a separate bowl, whisk together the coffee, eggs, and egg whites. Add the coffee mixture to the cocoa powder and stir until smooth.

In the bowl of a stand mixer fitted with the whisk attachment, combine the granulated sugar, oil, and vanilla bean paste and whisk until smooth. Add the cocoa mixture and continue whisking until completely smooth.

In a bowl, whisk together the flour, baking powder, and baking soda. Add one-third of the flour mixture to the cocoa mixture, then one-third of the buttermilk, and whisk on low speed until just combined. Continue alternating additions of flour and buttermilk until both are incorporated and completely combined.

Divide the batter evenly among the prepared pans and bake until the cake springs back when touched, about 20 minutes. Allow to cool completely.

Make the filling:

In a large heatproof bowl, combine the chocolate, ½ cup (120 ml) of the cream, and butter. Place the bowl over a bain marie (a large saucepan half filled with gently simmering water). Stir until completely melted and smooth. Set aside to cool.

Mocha Ricotta Tower

Dulce de Leche–Nutella Cream Torte

In the bowl of a food processor fitted with the blade attachment, combine the ricotta, mascarpone, vanilla bean paste, and salt.

Divide the ricotta mixture evenly among 5 large bowls.

In the first bowl, add half of the chocolate mixture. In the second bowl, add half of the remaining chocolate mixture. In the third bowl, add half of the remaining chocolate mixture, and in the fourth bowl, add half the remaining chocolate and 1 tablespoon confectioners' sugar. In the fifth bowl, add 2 tablespoons confectioners' sugar. (The first bowl will have the most chocolate, the second will have half as much as the first, and the third will have half as much as the second.) Refrigerate the remaining chocolate mixture. Stir each bowl until just combined. Each bowl should get gradually lighter and you should have a bit of chocolate left. Add more chocolate to any bowl that looks too light so the colors graduate naturally.

In a clean bowl of a stand mixer fitted with the whisk attachment, whisk together the remaining 2½ cups (600 ml) cream, the coffee, and the remaining 2 tablespoons confectioners' sugar until stiff peaks form. Divide the whipped cream evenly among each of the five bowls and gently fold into each of the mixtures.

To assemble:

Place a cake round on a cake platter. With a pastry brush, brush an even layer of coffee simple syrup onto the cake layer. Spread the most-chocolaty filling evenly on the layer and place in the freezer for 15 minutes, or until firm.

Place the second cake round over the filling and press gently to adhere. Brush with coffee simple syrup and spread the second-most chocolaty filling evenly on this layer. Freeze again for 15 minutes, or until firm.

Place the third cake round over the filling and press gently to adhere. Brush with coffee simple syrup and spread the filling with the third amount of chocolate evenly on this layer. Freeze for 15 minutes, or until firm.

Place the fourth cake round over the filling and press gently to adhere. Brush with coffee simple syrup and spread the filling with the least amount of chocolate evenly over this layer. Freeze for 15 minutes, or until firm. Place the fifth cake round over top of the filling and press gently to adhere. Brush with coffee simple syrup and spread the plain filling evenly over this layer. Top with the last layer, press gently to adhere, then brush the top layer with coffee simple syrup. Freeze until firm, about 15 minutes.

Wrap the sides of the cake tightly with parchment paper (this may take a few pieces) and use tape to keep the parchment cocoon in place. Refrigerate until set, at least 2 hours or overnight.

To finish:

Carefully remove the parchment wrap. Remove the reserved chocolate mixture from the refrigerator and stir to a spreadable consistency. With a small offset spatula, spread a thin, even layer of the chocolate along the sides and top of the cake.

BUILDING TALL CAKES WITH CAKE RINGS AND PARCHMENT

Tall cakes can be a hassle to build. The layers easily list over to one side, and loose fillings like mousse spill out between the layers before having had time to set. But get yourself a cake ring—or two or three—and your problems will be miraculously solved. Cake rings come in a dazzling array of sizes, from 2-inch (5-cm) petite rounds to 12-inch (30.5-cm) heart shapes. And even if the shape isn't quite round, the moniker "ring" still applies in the pastry world. What distinguishes rings from pans is that they are bottomless. This is why I keep tomato soup, tuna, cat food, and coffee cans—I remove the top and bottoms, wash them thoroughly, and put them to use!

First, decide what size and shape cake you'll be making. Let's assume it's a very traditional 8-inch (20-cm) round. You can bake 8-inch (20-cm) round layers in an 8-inch (20-cm) round cake pan or in a cake ring, or you can bake rectangular layers in a sheet pan and stamp out the rounds with your 8-inch (20-cm) cake ring as if you were stamping out dough with a cookie cutter. Once you have your layers and filling, place your 8-inch (20-cm) cake ring on a sheet pan lined with parchment. Place your first layer inside your ring, making sure it's nestled safely on the bottom. When you add filling, you'll see already how this is going to help because the ring is there to stop any filling from spurting out the sides and you can bring the filling all the way to the edge of the layer without fear.

You can continue layering cake and filling until you've reached your final layer, then refrigerate or freeze until the filling is set. But what's this? You've noticed that only the bottom few layers and filling have been confined within the secure side of that ring! So while the bottom layers are stable and even, the top layers may be making their way over to the floor. This is where multiple rings come in handy—just stack one on top of the other in a continuous ring so that every layer and every bit of filling is contained. You can use the top ring as a guide to smoothing the top of the frosting perfectly. Or, once you've started your first few layers, wrap two pieces of parchment around the side of the cake ring to create a parchment cocoon that will hold your cake beautifully.

PUMPKIN PULLMAN SURPRISE

Makes 1 (13-by-4-inch / 33-by-10-cm) cake

ON THANKSGIVING, IT'S A WONDER we ever have room for dessert, but we always manage to shove a few pieces of pie into our bellies, if only out of sheer obligation to the hardworking bakers. But why not take the chore out of eating Thanksgiving pie and turn our greedy stomachs to this delightful pumpkin-mousse dessert? The filling is so light and creamy, you'll barely notice it in your turkey-clogged belly. The outer wrapping is beautiful and inviting, and at the very core is a spiral of luscious chocolate and almond to bring the flavors—and our gluttony—to a happy denouement.

FOR THE TUILE STRIPES:

¼ cup (55 g) unsalted butter, softened

¼ cup plus 1 tablespoon (30 g) confectioners' sugar

2 tablespoons egg white, from 1 egg

2½ tablespoons bread flour

1 tablespoon Dutch-process cocoa powder

FOR THE JOCONDE SPONGE CAKE:

⅔ cup (90 g) almond flour

¼ cup (35 g) bread flour

½ teaspoon salt

3 eggs

1 egg yolk

⅓ cup (35 g) granulated sugar

2 egg whites

2 tablespoons unsalted butter, melted

FOR THE CAKE BOTTOM:

1 cup (230 g) unsalted butter

8 ounces (225 g) bittersweet chocolate

6 eggs

¾ cup (150 g) granulated sugar

½ cup (40 g) Dutch-process cocoa powder (I use Cacao Barry Extra Brute)

1 teaspoon cinnamon

½ teaspoon ground ginger

½ teaspoon nutmeg

¼ teaspoon ground cloves

pinch salt

FOR THE ROULADE:

2 (7-ounce / 200-g) tubes almond paste

9 eggs, separated, at room temperature

½ teaspoon salt

¼ teaspoon cream of tartar

¾ cup (150 g) granulated sugar

1 tablespoon vanilla extract

¾ cup (65 g) Dutch-process cocoa powder

⅔ cup (70 g) confectioners' sugar

coffee simple syrup (½ cup / 120 ml coffee and ½ cup / 100 g sugar heated together until the sugar is dissolved), or ½ cup (120 ml) Amaretto

FOR THE MOUSSE:

5 egg whites

1 cup (200 g) granulated sugar

½ teaspoon salt

½ cup (115 g) mascarpone

2½ cups (600 ml) heavy cream

1 tablespoon powdered gelatin

1½ cups (360 ml) pumpkin purée

1 teaspoon cinnamon

½ teaspoon ground ginger

½ teaspoon nutmeg

¼ teaspoon ground cloves

Make the tuile stripes:

In the bowl of a stand mixer fitted with the paddle attachment, cream together the butter and confectioners' sugar until smooth. Add the egg white and stir until just combined. The mixture should look ropey and a bit curdled. Add the flour and cocoa powder and mix until a smooth paste forms.

Spread the tuile paste in an even layer on a half sheet pan lined with a silicone baking mat. Drag a decorating comb down the paste to create stripes. Continue until the entire surface is striped. Freeze the tuile until rock hard, at least 2 hours.

Make the joconde sponge cake:

Preheat the oven to 425°F (220°C).

In the bowl of a food processor fitted with the blade attachment, combine the almond flour, bread flour, and salt. Pulse until well combined.

In a large metal bowl, combine the whole eggs, yolk, and half the granulated sugar. Set the bowl over a bain marie (a saucepan half filled with gently simmering water), whisking constantly until the sugar has completely melted.

With the food processor running, pour the egg mixture into the almond flour until just combined.

In the clean bowl of a stand mixer fitted with the whisk attachment, add the egg whites and whisk until just foamy. Slowly add the remaining granulated sugar and whisk until medium-stiff peaks form.

Transfer the flour-egg mixture to a large bowl and use a large rubber spatula to fold in the egg whites until just combined. Fold in the butter. Remove the tuile stripes from the freezer and carefully spread the joconde batter over the frozen tuile. Bake for about 4 minutes, just until the middle of the cake is no longer tacky to the touch and before the edges brown. Allow to cool completely.

Make the cake bottom:

Preheat the oven to 325°F (165°C). Line a half sheet or jelly roll pan with parchment.

In a metal bowl, combine the butter and chocolate. Place the bowl over a bain marie to melt the ingredients.

Meanwhile, in the bowl of a stand mixer fitted with the whisk attachment, add the eggs, granulated sugar, cocoa powder, cinnamon, ginger, nutmeg, cloves, and salt and whisk until combined. With the mixer running on low speed, slowly add the melted chocolate. Transfer the batter to the prepared pan in a layer that's a little less than ½ inch (12 mm) thick. (You'll have batter left over; reserve it for another use.) Bake for 10 to 15 minutes, checking often—the batter tends to bubble up in a shocking manner. Don't let that worry you. Just make sure it's cooked through and let it cool. It will return to normal.

Make the roulade:

Line a half sheet pan with parchment paper and spray with nonstick baking spray.

Roll the almond paste between two sheets of parchment paper into a 9-by-14-inch (23-by-35.5-cm) rectangle. Set aside.

In the bowl of a stand mixer fitted with the whisk attachment, combine the egg whites, salt, and cream of tartar and whisk until just foamy. Slowly add ½ cup (100 g) of the granulated sugar and whisk on high speed until stiff peaks form, being careful not to overbeat to the point of dryness or clumping. Transfer the egg whites to a large, clean bowl.

In the same stand mixer bowl (you needn't clean it), combine the egg yolks, the remaining granulated sugar, and the vanilla extract and whisk on high until the yolks are pale yellow and the batter ribbons when you lift the whisk.

Stir one-third of the egg whites into the yolk mixture. Using a large rubber spatula, gently fold in the remaining egg whites. Sift the cocoa powder over the egg mixture and fold into the batter until just combined. Using a large offset spatula, spread the batter evenly into the prepared pan and bake for 25 minutes.

While the cake is still warm, run a sharp paring knife along the sides of the cake to release it. Sprinkle confectioners' sugar over a clean kitchen towel and turn the cake out onto the towel. Peel the parchment paper off the cake.

Place the rectangle of almond paste on one end of the cake. Using the kitchen towel to help you, roll the cake into a jellyroll and allow to cool completely.

Make the mousse:

In a metal bowl of a stand mixer fitted with the whisk attachment, combine the egg whites, granulated sugar, and salt. Place the bowl over a bain marie and whisk constantly until the sugar is melted (dip your finger in the mixture and rub to see if particles remain). Attach a candy thermometer and heat until the mixture reaches 160°F (72°C), the temperature at which bacteria are killed. Transfer the bowl to the stand mixer and whisk until the egg whites have doubled to tripled in volume and stiff peaks form. Transfer the mixture to a metal bowl and set aside.

In a mixing bowl, combine the mascarpone and cream and beat until stiff peaks form. Fold the whipped cream into the egg white mixture and set aside in the refrigerator.

Meanwhile, in a microwave-safe bowl, sprinkle the gelatin over 2 tablespoons water. Allow to bloom until the gelatin is saturated and looks soggy. Microwave at 50% power for 9 to 11 seconds at a time, swirling in between.

Place the pumpkin purée in a large bowl. Add the ground spices and stir to combine. Add a small amount of the pumpkin purée to the gelatin to temper it. Quickly add the gelatin mixture to the purée and stir to combine. Then gently fold the chilled egg white mixture into the purée until incorporated.

To assemble:

Line a 13-inch (33-cm) Pullman loaf pan with plastic wrap so that the plastic hangs over all the edges.

Measure the décor side of the joconde and trim the width of the sides to 12 inches (30.5 cm). Carefully transfer the décor side, pattern-side down, to the loaf pan. Carefully center the décor side in the loaf pan, gently pressing so that the pan is fully lined. Trim any joconde that is draping over the edge of the pan.

Place half of the mousse in the décor-lined loaf pan. Trim the roulade to 12½ inches (32 cm) in length and lower it into the loaf pan to rest on the mousse. Spread the remaining mousse over the roulade and gently smooth with a small offset spatula.

Trim the bottom cake layer to 13 by 4 inches (33 by 10 cm) and gently press the layer onto the mousse.

Freeze until set, at least 4 hours or overnight.

To release, invert the loaf pan onto a cake platter. Gently shimmy the pan and pull lightly on the plastic wrap to release the cake. Place in the refrigerator for 2 hours to allow the mousse to thaw. Serve immediately.

THE VERMONTER

Makes 1 (10-inch / 25-cm) cake

VERMONT IS KNOWN AS THE GREEN MOUNTAIN STATE, but when I think of my adopted home, I think in shades of aubergine, not moss. Without fail, if you drive through an average town in Vermont, you'll see a cavalcade of violets and deep purples. From T-shirts to winter puffers, the royal hue is queen in our parts. And so it is that I created "the Vermonter" in homage to my beautiful state and the lovely people who inhabit it. I've combined a lovely, tart, black currant mousse with shades of green gooseberry and dark chocolate to evoke the colors that make the Green Mountains sing. When you slice into the cake, you'll discover that a peaked mountain of tart green gooseberry rises from within the confines of the gemlike currant mousse. A treat for all the senses.

FOR THE COOKIE BASE:

1 cup (125 g) all-purpose flour

10 tablespoons (140 g) unsalted butter, cut into cubes, slightly cooler than room temperature

¼ cup (50 g) granulated sugar

½ teaspoon salt

FOR THE CAKE BASE:

¼ cup (55 g) unsalted butter

4 ounces (115 g) bittersweet chocolate

1 tablespoon strong coffee

¼ cup (50 g) granulated sugar

¼ cup (20 g) Dutch-process cocoa powder

¼ teaspoon salt

2 eggs

1 teaspoon vanilla extract

FOR THE GOOSEBERRY AND BLACK CURRANT MOUSSES:

1½ cups (360 ml) heavy cream

1 tablespoon powdered gelatin

3 egg whites

½ cup (100 g) granulated sugar

4 ounces (115 g) white chocolate, melted

½ cup (120 ml) black currant purée (see page 48)

¼ cup (60 ml) gooseberry purée (see page 48)

1 drop green food coloring (optional)

FOR THE ASSEMBLY:

2 tablespoons black currant preserves

FOR THE GLAZE:

1 tablespoon powdered gelatin

½ cup (120 ml) simple syrup (¼ cup / 60 ml water and ¼ cup / 50 g sugar simmered until the sugar has completely melted)

¼ cup (60 ml) black currant purée

Make the cookie base:

Preheat the oven to 350°F (175°C). Line the bottom of a 10-inch (25-cm) cake pan with a round of parchment paper and spray with nonstick baking spray.

In a large mixing bowl, combine all the ingredients. Using your fingers, gently rub the butter into the mixture until the texture resembles cornmeal. Press the dough in an even layer into the prepared pan. Bake for 10 to 15 minutes, until the base just begins to turn golden brown. Allow to cool completely.

Make the cake base:

Preheat the oven to 325°F (165°C). Line the bottom of a 10-inch (25-cm) cake pan with a round of parchment paper and spray with nonstick spray.

In a heatproof bowl, combine the butter, chocolate, and coffee. Place the bowl over a bain marie (a large saucepan half filled with gently simmering water) and stir until melted and completely smooth.

In the bowl of a stand mixer fitted with the whisk attachment, whisk together the granulated sugar, cocoa powder, and salt. Add the eggs, one at a time, and continue whisking until smooth. Add the vanilla extract. Scrape down the sides of the bowl. With the mixer running on low speed, carefully pour the chocolate mixture down the side of the bowl into the egg mixture and mix until completely smooth.

Transfer the batter to the prepared pan. Bake for 15 to 20 minutes, until the cake is slightly firm to the touch and bubbles a bit in the center. Cool completely.

Make the gooseberry and black currant mousses:

In the bowl of a stand mixer fitted with the whisk attachment, whisk the heavy cream until stiff peaks form. Refrigerate until needed.

Pour ½ cup (120 ml) water into a shallow microwave-safe bowl. Sprinkle the gelatin over the water in an even layer. Allow to bloom for several minutes, until the gelatin is saturated and looks soggy.

In a heatproof bowl of a stand mixer fitted with the whisk attachment, combine the egg whites and granulated sugar. Place the bowl over a bain marie and whisk until the sugar has completely melted and the mixture feels warm; attach a thermometer to ensure the mixture reaches 160°F (72°C), the temperature that kills any bacteria in raw eggs. Transfer the bowl to the stand mixer and whisk on high speed until the egg whites form stiff, glossy peaks and the bowl is cool to the touch.

Stir one-quarter of the white chocolate into the gooseberry purée and add the drop of green food coloring. Stir the remaining white chocolate into the black currant purée.

Microwave the gelatin mixture at 50% power in 5-second intervals, swirling the bowl in between, until the gelatin is completely dissolved. Quickly stir one-quarter of the gelatin mixture into the gooseberry mixture and the remainder into the black currant mixture. Stir each until combined.

Fold one-quarter of the egg white mixture into the gooseberry mixture and the remainder into the black currant mixture. Add one-quarter of the whipped cream to the gooseberry mixture and the remainder to the black currant mixture, folding each until no white streaks remain. Place both mousses in the refrigerator to firm.

To assemble:

Place the cookie crust on a half sheet pan lined with parchment paper. Using a small offset spatula, smooth 2 tablespoons of the preserves over the entire top of the crust. Place the chocolate cake layer atop the preserve layer and press gently to adhere. Place a 10-inch (25-cm) cake ring snugly around the layers.

Make sure that the mousses are both very stiff. If they aren't, refrigerate for 20 minutes more until they can hold their shape when piped.

Transfer the gooseberry mousse to a large pastry bag fitted with a large open tip. Starting in the center of the cake and spiraling outward, pipe an even layer of mousse over the cake until you reach the middle of the cake. Pipe another spiral on top of the first, but stop about ½ inch (12 mm) from the edge of the mousse. Make another spiral on top of the second and again stop about ½ inch (12 mm) from the edge. Continue until all the gooseberry mousse is piped and you've created a peak. Using a small offset spatula, gently smooth the sides of the mousse mountain. Freeze until set.

Transfer the black currant mousse to a large pastry bag fitted with a large open tip. Pipe the black currant mousse around the gooseberry dome until all the mousse is piped. Gently smooth the mousse along the sides and top until even and smooth. Freeze the cake until set, about 2 hours or overnight.

Make the glaze:

Pour ¼ cup (60 ml) water into a microwave-safe bowl and sprinkle the gelatin over the water in an even layer. Allow to bloom for several minutes, until the gelatin is saturated and looks soggy. Microwave the gelatin mixture at 50% power in 5-second intervals, swirling the bowl in between, until the gelatin is completely dissolved.

Quickly stir the simple syrup and black currant purée into the gelatin and stir until combined. Allow to cool a bit but don't allow to harden. Pour over the top of the cake and tilt the cake back and forth until the glaze evenly coats the top of the mousse (don't use a spatula to smooth the glaze because it will leave marks).

To finish:

Allow to set, about 20 minutes. Gently warm the sides of the cake ring with a kitchen torch or blow dryer and carefully remove the ring. Serve immediately.

A NOTE FROM THE SWEET TALKER: Cheesecakes are notorious for cracking. The causes vary. First, over-beating the batter will give you large air pockets that create fissures in the finished cake. To remedy this, make sure to blend the cheese and sugar until very smooth before adding the eggs. And when you add the remaining ingredients, do it just until combined, without any extra stirring. Second, bake at a gentle temperature. I like to bake low and slow (at 300°F to 325°F / 149°C to 165°C) to prevent cracks, and I cool gently. Third, the surfeit of proteins in a cheesecake batter leads to a great deal of shrinkage during baking. Therefore, it's very important to grease the sides of your baking vessel liberally so that the cake can release from the sides of the pan. If the cake clings to the sides as it's baking and shrinking, the cake will tear in the middle, but if it's allowed to release from the sides, the top will stay unsullied. Fourth, if you are using a springform pan, you can use a water bath to create a gentle and even baking element. To do this properly, you need to thoroughly cover your springform pan with aluminum foil to prevent moisture from seeping inside the pan. You then bake the springform gently in a larger vessel that's filled with enough hot water to reach just over halfway up the sides of the springform. (I bake cheesecakes in cake rings. They don't have bottoms, so a water bath is an impossibility.) Fifth, don't overbake. Allow the cheesecake to start cooling when there's still a slight shimmy in the middle. Cheesecakes continue cooking as they're cooling; that shimmy will go away and the cake will firm beautifully once cooled. If you find that the cheesecake is still sticking to the sides of the pan at this point, carefully run a very sharp paring knife between the pan and the cake to release the sides. Continue to cool as directed in the recipe.

CARAMEL MACADAMIA CAROUSEL

Makes 1 (10-inch / 25-cm) cake

THIS CAKE COMBINES TEXTURES, FLAVORS, and optical illusion all in one. The buttery crunch of macadamia and the lush mouthfeel of caramel cream dance in the rings of this whimsical cake.

FOR THE MERINGUE BOTTOM:
2 ounces (55 g) blanched slivered almonds
½ cup (100 g) granulated sugar
2 tablespoons cornstarch
¼ cup egg whites
¼ teaspoon salt

FOR THE SPONGE CAKE:
7 eggs
1 cup (100 g) granulated sugar
1 teaspoon salt
1 cup (140 g) cake flour
¼ cup (30 g) cornstarch
½ cup (40 g) Dutch-process cocoa powder

FOR THE CARAMEL CREAM:
½ cup (100 g) granulated sugar
½ teaspoon lemon juice
½ teaspoon salt
2½ cups (600 ml) heavy cream

FOR THE GANACHE:
4 ounces (115 g) bittersweet chocolate, finely chopped
¼ cup (60 ml) heavy cream
1 tablespoon unsalted butter

FOR THE MACADAMIA FLORENTINE:
½ cup (115 g) unsalted butter
1 cup (120 g) finely chopped macadamia nuts
1 cup (220 g) light brown sugar, firmly packed
1 egg
1 tablespoon vanilla bean paste
½ teaspoon salt

FOR THE FINISH:
12 whole macadamia nuts

Make the meringue bottom:

Preheat the oven to 300°F (150°C). Line a half sheet pan with parchment paper. Draw a 10-inch (25-cm) circle on the parchment and flip the parchment over onto the pan so the circle is visible but will not transfer onto the meringue.

In the bowl of a food processor fitted with the blade attachment, combine the almonds, one-third of the granulated sugar, and the cornstarch. Pulse until the mixture resembles a fine meal.

In the bowl of a stand mixer fitted with the whisk attachment, combine the egg whites and salt. Whisk on high speed until the whites are foamy and increased in volume. Slowly add the remaining sugar and whip on high speed until very stiff, white glossy peaks form.

Using a large rubber spatula, fold the macadamia mixture into the egg whites. Transfer the batter to a large pastry bag fitted with a large open tip.

Starting in the center of the drawn circle and spiraling outward to the edge, pipe a 10-inch (25-cm) round of meringue onto the parchment. Place a dab of batter under each corner of the parchment to keep it from curling up in the oven.

Bake for 30 to 35 minutes, until golden brown. Set aside to cool completely.

Make the sponge cake:

Preheat the oven to 400°F (205°C). Place a parchment round in the bottom of a 10-inch (25-cm) cake pan. Line a half sheet pan with parchment paper. Do not spray either with nonstick spray.

In a heatproof bowl of a stand mixer, combine the eggs, granulated sugar, and salt. Place the bowl over a bain marie (a large saucepan half filled with gently simmering water) and whisk constantly until the sugar has completely melted and the mixture is smooth (rub a bit between your fingers to see if it still feels grainy).

Transfer the bowl to a stand mixer fitted with the whisk attachment and whisk on high speed until the eggs have quadrupled in volume and the bowl is cool to the touch.

Sift the flour, cornstarch, and cocoa powder over the egg mixture. Using a large rubber spatula, fold the flour mixture into the eggs.

Spread one-third of the batter into the cake pan and spread the remaining batter in the half sheet pan. Bake the cakes for 15 to 20 minutes, until they just spring back when you touch them. Set aside to cool completely.

Make the caramel cream:

Don't start the caramel cream until all your cake elements are completely cool!

In a large saucepan, combine the granulated sugar, ¼ cup (60 ml) water, the lemon juice, and salt. Stir over low heat until the sugar has completely melted. Dip a pastry brush in water and brush it along the sides of the pan to remove any lingering sugar crystals.

Stop stirring, raise the heat to medium-high, and cook the syrup until it turns a light amber. Remove the sugar from the heat and add ½ cup (120 ml) of the cream. Be careful, because the mixture will bubble vigorously for a moment. Once the caramel has calmed, stir until smooth. Refrigerate until cool.

Whisk the remaining cream to stiff peaks. Fold one-third of the cream into the caramel to lighten it. Using a large rubber spatula, transfer the lightened caramel cream into the bowl with the remaining whipped cream and gently fold until completely incorporated. Refrigerate immediately.

Make the ganache:

Place the chocolate in a heatproof mixing bowl. In a saucepan, combine the cream and butter and bring to a simmer. Pour the cream mixture over the chocolate, making sure the chocolate is completely covered. Allow to sit undisturbed for a few minutes. Whisk until the chocolate is completely melted and the mixture is smooth.

To assemble:

Transfer the meringue layer to a half sheet pan lined with parchment paper. Spread one-third of the ganache in an even layer over the meringue layer. Reserve the remaining ganache in the refrigerator.

Place a 10-inch (25-cm) cake ring atop the meringue layer. (There's a very good chance that the meringue is slightly larger than the ring and we don't want to trim it while it's still brittle. So just rest the ring on top of the meringue if it doesn't fit snugly inside.)

Cut the cake in the sheet pan lengthwise into strips 2 inches (5 cm) wide. Line the inside of the cake ring by pressing a cake strip around the outer edge (you may need to use more than one strip to go all the way around, trimming the strips as necessary to fit).

Make four more concentric rings of cake strips, starting slightly in from the outside ring and working your way toward the center. Leave enough space between rings for filling to be piped.

Transfer the caramel cream to a large pastry bag fitted with a large open tip. Pipe the cream in between the standing cake rings. Spread any extra cream along the top in an even layer.

Place the round sponge layer atop the cream and press gently to adhere. Refrigerate until set, 2 hours or overnight.

Make the macadamia Florentine:

Preheat the oven to 350°F (175°C). Spray a 10-inch (25-cm) cake ring with nonstick baking spray and place on a parchment-lined half sheet pan.

In a small saucepan, melt the butter over low heat until it separates and starts to brown. Set aside.

In the bowl of a food processor fitted with the blade attachment, combine the macadamia nuts, brown sugar, egg, vanilla bean paste, and salt and pulse until a slightly chunky paste forms. Still pulsing, pour in the butter until combined.

Spread the batter evenly inside the cake ring and bake until just golden brown, about 15 minutes. Remove the ring and score the Florentine into 12 even wedges while still warm.

To finish:

Warm the reserved ganache over gently simmering water until just spreadable.

Carefully remove the cake ring by gently heating it with a kitchen torch or blow dryer. With a sharp paring knife, trim the meringue to be flush with the cake layers.

Spread the ganache in an even layer over the top and sides of the cake. Allow to set, about 20 minutes.

Spread a thin layer of the remaining ganache over the scored Florentine. Spread the remaining ganache in an even layer over the top and sides of the cake.

Fan the Florentine wedges over the top of the cake, placing a macadamia nut under each wedge to prop it up. Serve immediately.

FOURTH OF JULY BERRY MOUSSE

Makes 6 mousse towers

THIS IS AN ALTERNATIVE TO the ubiquitous holiday sheetcake with strawberries, whipped cream, and blueberries standing in for the red, white, and blue of the American flag. That's a lovely cake, to be sure. I'm not belittling it, by any means, but I ask that you take a little more time celebrating the birthday of our beloved country by making a cake that's as spectacular as the fireworks we set off to commemorate our Declaration of Independence. This recipe combines very American-looking stripes of bright-red raspberry mousse and white chocolate mousse under a field blackberry mousse, if a little more pastel. Your guests will slice into a culinary celebration worthy of these United States.

FOR THE COOKIE BASE:

1 cup (125 g) all-purpose flour

10 tablespoons (140 g) unsalted butter, cut into cubes, slightly cooler than room temperature

¼ cup (50 g) sugar

½ teaspoon salt

FOR THE BERRY AND WHITE CHOCOLATE MOUSSES:

1½ cups (360 ml) heavy cream

1 tablespoon powdered gelatin

3 egg whites

½ cup (100 g) granulated sugar

4 ounces (115 g) white chocolate, melted

¼ cup (60 ml) raspberry purée

2 drops red food coloring

¼ cup (60 ml) blackberry purée

2 drops blue food coloring

¼ cup (60 ml) key lime juice

FOR THE GLAZE:

1 tablespoon powdered gelatin

½ cup (120 ml) simple syrup (¼ cup / 60 ml water and ¼ cup / 50 g sugar simmered until the sugar has completely melted)

¼ cup (60 ml) blackberry purée

Make the cookie base:

Preheat the oven to 350°F (175°C). Line a half sheet pan with parchment paper. Spray six 3-inch-tall-by-2-inch-wide (7.5-cm-tall-by-5-cm-wide) cake rings with nonstick baking spray. Alternately, use six empty 15-ounce metal cans as rings. Make sure the tops and bottoms of the cans have been removed with a can opener, the label has been taken off, and the can has been cleaned thoroughly.

In a large mixing bowl, combine all the ingredients. Using your fingers, gently rub the butter into the mixture until the texture resembles cornmeal. Roll the dough out about ¼ inch (6 mm) thick and stamp out six rounds of dough with your cake ring or can. Place the rounds of dough on the prepared sheet pan. Bake for 10 to 15 minutes, until the bases just begin to turn golden brown. Allow to cool completely.

Make the berry and white chocolate mousses:

In the bowl of a stand mixer fitted with the whisk attachment, whisk the cream until stiff peaks form. Refrigerate until needed.

Pour ½ cup (120 ml) water into a shallow microwave-safe bowl. Sprinkle the gelatin over the water in an even layer. Allow to bloom for several minutes, until the gelatin is saturated and looks soggy.

In a heatproof bowl of a stand mixer, combine the egg whites and granulated sugar. Place the bowl over a bain marie (a large saucepan half filled with gently simmering water) and whisk until the sugar has completely melted and the mixture feels warm. Transfer the bowl to a stand mixer fitted with the whisk attachment and whisk on high speed until the egg whites form stiff, glossy peaks and the bowl is cool to the touch.

Microwave the gelatin mixture at 50% power in 5-second intervals, swirling the bowl in between, until the gelatin is completely dissolved. Quickly mix the gelatin mixture into the white chocolate.

Divide the gelatin–white chocolate mixture among 3 mixing bowls. Add the raspberry purée and red food coloring to one, the blackberry purée and blue food coloring to the other, and the key lime juice to the third. Stir to combine. If the white chocolate in any of the bowls isn't completely melted, place the bowl over a bain marie and stir until completely melted.

Fold the egg whites into the whipped cream and divide evenly among the 3 bowls. Use a large rubber spatula to fold the mixture into each of the bowls of purée/juice mixture.

To assemble:

Place the cake rings over the cookie bases so that the cookie base is nestled in he bottom of the ring.

Transfer each of the mousse mixtures to separate large, disposable pastry bags. Cut the tip off each bag to create a 1-inch (2.5-cm) opening. Pipe the raspberry mousse evenly into the bottom of each of the rings on top of the cookie crust and gently shimmy them to even the mousse. Pipe the key lime mouse evenly among the 6 rings atop the raspberry layer and gently shimmy to even the layer. Pipe the blackberry mousse evenly among the 6 rings atop the key lime mousse and gently shimmy to even the layer.

Freeze the mousses until firm and set, at least 4 hours to overnight.

Make the glaze:

Pour ¼ cup (60 ml) of water into a microwave-safe bowl and sprinkle the gelatin over the water in an even layer. Allow to bloom for several minutes, until the gelatin is saturated and looks soggy. Microwave the gelatin mixture at 50% power in 5-second intervals, swirling the bowl in between, until the gelatin is completely dissolved.

Quickly stir the simple syrup and blackberry purée into the gelatin until combined. Allow to cool a bit but don't allow to harden. Spoon over the tops of the mousse and tilt the towers back and forth until the glaze evenly coats the top of the mousse (don't use a spatula to smooth the glaze because it will leave marks). Allow to set, at least 10 minutes.

Remove the rings by gently heating their sides with a blow dryer or heat gun, then carefully slipping the ring off. Serve immediately.

A NOTE FROM THE SWEET TALKER: Here's a helpful little hint for assembling mini desserts like these. Get your hands on a load of cat-food, tomato sauce, or tuna-fish cans that have been thoroughly cleaned and have had both tops and bottoms removed. This gives you a set of lovely metal rings. You could buy professional cake rings, but why bother? This is so much cheaper and works just as well.

PUMPKIN-MOUSSE CRULLER TART

Makes 1 (10-inch / 25-cm) tart

WHAT HAPPENS WHEN YOU CROSS a cruller, that delightfully airy fried donut–cream puff hybrid, with one of the most famous tarts in all of pastrydom, the St. Honoré? You get something fan-freaking-tastic, that's what. When you combine a gorgeous cruller with pumpkin mousse, you have a dessert that is slightly crisp, with a soupçon of chew and a grand dollop of creamy.

FOR THE CAKE:

1 cup (230 g) unsalted butter
8 ounces (225 g) bittersweet chocolate
6 eggs
¾ cup (150 g) granulated sugar
½ cup (40 g) Dutch-process cocoa powder
pinch salt
1 teaspoon cinnamon
½ teaspoon ground ginger
½ teaspoon nutmeg
¼ teaspoon ground cloves

FOR THE MOUSSE:

5 egg whites
1 cup (200 g) granulated sugar
½ cup (115 g) mascarpone
2½ cups (600 ml) heavy cream
¼ cup (60 ml) warm water (105°F to 115° / 41°C to 46°C)
3 teaspoons powdered gelatin
1½ cups (360 ml) pumpkin purée
1 teaspoon cinnamon
½ teaspoon ground ginger
½ teaspoon nutmeg
¼ teaspoon ground cloves

FOR THE CRULLERS:

1 cup (240 ml) 2% milk
½ cup (115 g) unsalted butter
3 tablespoons sweetened condensed milk
½ teaspoon salt

1 cup (125 g) all-purpose flour
5 eggs
¼ teaspoon baking powder

FOR THE ASSEMBLY:

1 quart (960 ml) vegetable oil, for frying
¼ cup (25 g) confectioners' sugar

Make the cake:

Preheat the oven to 325°F (165°C). Spray a 10-inch (25-cm) round cake pan with nonstick baking spray and line the bottom with a round of parchment paper.

In a metal bowl, combine the butter and chocolate. Place the bowl over a bain marie (a large saucepan half filled with simmering water) and stir until melted.

In the meantime, in the bowl of a stand mixer fitted with the whisk attachment, combine the eggs, granulated sugar, cocoa powder, salt, and spices and whisk until combined. With the mixer running on low speed, slowly pour the chocolate mixture down the side of the bowl into the egg mixture. Transfer the batter to the prepared pan in a layer a little less than ½ inch (12 mm) thick. (You'll have batter left over. Reserve for another use.) Bake for 10 to 15 minutes, checking often, until the cake is slightly firm to the touch. The batter tends to bubble up in a shocking manner while baking. Don't let that worry you. Just make sure it's baked through and let it cool. It will return to normal.

Make the mousse:

In a heatproof bowl of a stand mixer fitted with the whisk attachment, combine the egg whites and granulated sugar and whisk to just combine. Then place the bowl over a bain marie and whisk constantly until the sugar is

dissolved (dip your finger in the mixture and rub to see if particles remain). If you wish, attach a candy thermometer to the side of the saucepan to ensure that the mixture reaches 160°F (72°C), the temperature at which bacteria are killed. Transfer the bowl to the stand mixer and mix until the mixture has doubled or tripled in volume and is a thick, white, stiff cloud of goodness. Transfer the meringue to a clean metal bowl and set aside.

In the same stand mixer bowl (you needn't clean it), combine the mascarpone and cream and whisk until stiff peaks form. Fold the whipped cream into the egg whites and set aside in the refrigerator.

Place the warm water in a microwave-safe bowl and sprinkle the gelatin evenly over the surface of the water. Allow to bloom for several minutes, until the gelatin is saturated and looks soggy. Microwave at 50% power in 10-second intervals, swirling the bowl in between, until the gelatin is completely dissolved.

Place the pumpkin purée in a bowl and stir in the spices. Add a small amount of the pumpkin to the gelatin to temper it. Quickly combine the remaining purée with the gelatin mixture. Using a large rubber spatula, gently fold the egg-cream mixture into the pumpkin mixture until completely combined.

Transfer the chocolate cake layer to the bottom of a cake ring and spoon the mousse over the cake. Smooth the top with an offset spatula.

Freeze until set, 2 hours or overnight.

Make the crullers:

In a large saucepan over medium heat, combine the milk, butter, sweetened condensed milk, and salt. Stir until the butter has completely melted and the mixture has come to a gentle simmer.

Add the flour to the milk mixture all at once and mix, stirring constantly with a wooden spoon until the mixture thickens and pulls away from the sides of the pan.

Transfer the flour-milk mixture to the bowl of a stand mixer fitted with the paddle attachment. Mix on low for 1 minute to allow the paste to cool slightly. Add 1 egg and mix until fully incorporated. (You may not need all the eggs, so crack them just before using them.) Add the baking powder and mix to incorporate. Continue adding eggs until a smooth paste forms; it should flow easily from the paddle of the stand mixer but still hold its shape when piped.

Transfer the batter to a large pastry bag fitted with a large star tip. Line sheet pan with parchment paper. Pipe the batter onto the prepared sheet pan in small S shapes.

Freeze the unbaked crullers until firm, at least 2 hours.

To assemble:

In a deep-fryer or large heavy skillet, heat the oil to 350°F (175°C). Line a sheet pan with parchment and place a wire rack on top.

Using a wide spatula, slide the crullers into the hot oil, in batches as necessary. Turn them over as they rise to the surface. Fry on each side until golden brown, about 2 minutes per side. Transfer the crullers to the wire rack to drain and cool.

Sift the confectioners' sugar over the crullers.

Remove the cake from the freezer and gently heat the sides of the cake ring with a kitchen torch or blow dryer. Carefully remove the ring. Place the cake in the refrigerator for 1 hour to thaw. Line the perimeter of the cake with the crullers. Serve immediately.

Chapter 5

SPRINGY
&
YUMMY

YEASTIES

IN AMERICAN CULINARY TRADITION, YEASTED PASTRIES ARE RELEGATED

to the breakfast table, coated in a sodden mass of sugary glaze. That's all well and good, but cakes and confections leavened with fresh yeast have a spectacular history in other parts of the world, most notably in Europe. Yeast even makes a frequent appearance in layer cakes. One of my childhood favorites, the *Bienenstich* ("bee-sting" cake), is a prime example. The cake layers are sweet yeast rounds filled with a lovely custard. Or there's the *Gerbeaud*, a delightful cake composed of very thin yeasted layers. Expand your horizons! Learn to think of the yeast beasts as agents of pastry beauty and innovation.

If you have a single brioche recipe under your belt, you have an ability to make rolls, buns, cake layers, and coffeecake rings. And croissant dough can be transformed into chocolate, almond, cinnamon, or savory treats. Adding yeasted pastries to your repertoire will expand your offerings a thousandfold.

BRIOCHES

Makes 12 brioches

BRIOCHE IS THE MOTHER of all yeasted pastry doughs. It's a rich, slightly sweet, smooth dough. In its traditional form, with a petite topknot of dough nestled in a larger orb, this simple treat takes on the dignity of a mini cathedral. Used as the base for a *pain perdu* or in layers in a cake, it keeps its subtle sweetness and lovely texture. But when married with other ingredients, brioche realizes its true potential as a luscious foundation to cakes and pastries of all kinds.

FOR THE SPONGE:

1 cup (240 ml) warm whole milk

¼ cup (60 ml) honey

2 ounces (55 g) dry active yeast

2 cups (280 g) bread flour

FOR THE DOUGH:

¾ cup (150 g) granulated sugar

4 teaspoons salt

8 eggs

2 pounds (910 g) all-purpose flour

1 cup plus 2 tablespoons (260 g) unsalted butter, at room temperature

egg wash (1 egg whisked with 2 tablespoons water)

¼ cup (50 g) turbinado sugar

Make the sponge:

Preheat the oven to 400°F (205°C). Line a 12-cavity muffin tin with cupcake liners. Spray the liners with nonstick baking spray.

In the bowl of a stand mixer fitted with the dough hook, combine the milk and honey. Dissolve the yeast in the mixture and allow to bloom (*blooming* is the term for letting the yeast become active and bubbly in a liquid). Add the flour and mix on slow speed until the sponge is smooth.

Cover and let rise until it has doubled in volume, about 1 hour.

Make the dough:

Add the granulated sugar, salt, and eggs to the sponge and mix until incorporated. Add the flour and mix to combine. Add the butter, a bit at a time. Once the butter is added and the dough has mixed for just a bit, the dough will look shaggy. This is normal; it is an indication that the dough requires more mixing to develop the glutens. Continue mixing until the dough isn't sticking to the sides of the bowl, forms a ball, and looks shiny. This can take quite some time, up to 15 minutes. Make sure to take the time for the dough to develop to this texture. Cover the dough and set aside until doubled in volume, about 1 hour.

Punch the dough down and transfer to a floured work surface. Cut the dough into 12 equal pieces.

Using your hand in a karate-style motion, "chop" one piece of the dough as if you were trying to sever one-quarter of the piece from the rest of it. But instead of cutting this small portion off, gently saw back and forth with your hand so that you form a spindly neck with a large bottom on one side and a tiny dough ball on the other. Place the fatter portion of dough into a muffin cavity (the little head should still be attached). With your thumb, gently press into the middle of the fat piece of dough, making a little bowl into which you will then press the smaller dollop of dough. Repeat with the remaining pieces of dough and allow the brioche to proof (or double in size) for about 30 minutes.

Brush the brioches with the egg wash and sprinkle with the turbinado sugar. Bake for 20 to 30 minutes, until the brioches are golden brown.

Serve with lovely pats of butter and preserves.

ALL ABOUT YEAST

Sourdough starter. Fresh yeast. Cake yeast. Active yeast. Instant yeast. All are versions of *Candida milleri*, and all of them help make your lovingly made pastries rise, but they aren't all used in the same manner. Sourdough starter, also known as a mother sponge, is a "captured" live culture: It's a liquid yeast made by harvesting the yeast that's all around us, floating in the air, and coaxed into growing in a container through regular feeding until it is transformed into a liquid natural "starter." Fresh yeast, which is alternatively known as cake or compressed yeast, is a refrigerated brick of fresh yeast that's composed of 30% live active cultures and 70% water. The stuff doesn't live very long: Remember, yeast is a living organism. Fresh yeast stays active for only three weeks. Dry active yeast is what you find in the little packets on your grocery shelves. It's dehydrated (dormant) yeast and needs to be "bloomed," or brought back to life with a measure of water, before being added to other ingredients. Instant yeast can be added straight to the dry ingredients of a bread formula; it doesn't need to be brought back to life through blooming and has a heartier shelf life than other yeasts. Now you know the differences among all those living beasts!

PAIN PERDU WITH RUMMED-UP APPLES

Makes 2 pain perdu

YOU'VE HEARD OF FRENCH TOAST, the breakfast staple that elevates stale bread to a higher plane. But did you know that there's another way, in fact a better way, to make this already delicious treat? And did you know that it isn't just for breakfast? And to top it all off, could you have imagined that this original version is actually beautiful? *C'est vrai!*

FOR THE SPONGE:

1 cup (240 ml) warm whole milk

¼ cup (60 ml) honey

2 tablespoons dry active yeast

2 cups (280 g) bread flour

FOR THE DOUGH:

½ cup plus 2 tablespoons (225 g) granulated sugar

4 teaspoons salt

8 eggs

2 pounds (910 g) all-purpose flour

1 cup (230 g) unsalted butter, at room temperature

FOR THE CRÈME ANGLAISE:

1 cup (240 ml) heavy cream

1 cup (240 ml) whole milk

6 egg yolks

¾ cup (150 g) granulated sugar

2 teaspoons vanilla extract

FOR THE APPLES:

2 tablespoons unsalted butter

¼ cup (55 g) light brown sugar, firmly packed

1 tablespoon apple brandy, such as Calvados

2 tart apples, cored, peeled, and thinly sliced

FOR THE ASSEMBLY:

2 tablespoons unsalted butter

1 cup (100 g) confectioners' sugar, for sprinkling

1 small stencil

vanilla bean ice cream, for serving

Make the sponge:

In the bowl of a stand mixer fitted with the dough hook, combine the milk and honey. Dissolve the yeast in the mixture and allow to bloom (*blooming* is the term for letting the yeast become active and bubbly in a liquid). Add the flour and mix on slow speed until the sponge is smooth. Cover and let rise until it has doubled in volume, about 1 hour.

Make the dough:

For perfect results, have two cleaned coffee cans handy in which to bake your brioches. Place the cans, closed side down, on a parchment-lined sheet pan and spray them liberally with nonstick baking spray.

Add the granulated sugar, salt, and eggs to the sponge and mix until incorporated. Add the flour and mix to combine. Add the butter, a bit at a time. Mix until the dough forms a ball; the dough should look shiny and shouldn't stick to the sides of the bowl.

Cover the dough and set aside until doubled in volume.

Punch down the dough and transfer to a floured work surface.

Pat the dough into a rough rectangle and divide in half. Roll each half into a neat ball and place one ball at the bottom of each of the prepared coffee cans. Let the dough rise until it reaches the tops of the cans, 1 to 1½ hours.

Preheat the oven to 325°F (165°C). Bake the dough balls until the tops are brown, about 20 minutes.

Make the crème anglaise:

In a heavy saucepan, heat the cream and milk until scalding.

Meanwhile, in a heatproof bowl of a stand mixer fitted with the whisk attachment, combine the egg yolks, granulated sugar, and vanilla extract and whisk until fluffy. Decrease the mixer speed to low and slowly pour the hot cream mixture down the side of the bowl into the eggs until fully combined.

Transfer the bowl of still rather watery custard to a bain marie (a large saucepan half filled with gently simmering water) and whisk until the mixture thickens enough to coat the back of a spoon, about 15 minutes. Transfer to a clean bowl and cover with plastic wrap, pressing the plastic directly onto the surface of the custard to prevent a skin from forming. Refrigerate.

Prepare the apples:

In a sauté pan, melt the butter over low heat. Add the brown sugar and brandy and stir to combine. Add the apples and sauté until tender. Set aside to cool completely.

To assemble:

Remove the brioches from the coffee cans and slice each into 4 pieces, each 1¼ inches (3 cm) thick. Pour 2 cups (480 ml) of the crème anglaise into a shallow bowl large enough to hold 4 pieces of brioche. Place 4 pieces in the crème anglaise and soak for 5 minutes, flipping them halfway through so they are coated evenly. (I'll sometimes ladle crème anglaise over the naked sides to hasten the process.)

In a nonstick sauté pan, melt the butter over low heat. Add the 4 pieces of brioche and cook over medium-low heat until golden, 4 to 5 minutes. Flip the pieces to cook the other side, 4 to 5 minutes. Transfer to a serving platter while you soak and cook the remaining pieces.

Place a stencil over the top and sift confectioners' sugar over the stencil. Serve with the remaining crème anglaise, a bowl of rummed-up apples, and vanilla ice cream.

A NOTE FROM THE SWEET TALKER:
Viennoiserie: What the heck is it? What is the meaning of this word? The most easily deciphered portion of it is "Vienna." That beautiful city, the capital of Austria, plays a part in the definition, but the word does not refer to the inhabitants of that city. Instead, it refers to the doughs that are identified as coming from her hallowed bakeries. Those doughs include laminated doughs like croissants, and sweet, enriched doughs like brioches. Surprised? Thought those beauties were created by the French? Think again. Although the French have certainly developed their share of glorious pastries and have spectacularly riffed off Viennesse goodies, *Viennoiserie* are firmly within the bragging rights of the Austrians.

KRAPFEN

Makes 20 Krapfen

FASCHING IS THE GERMAN VERSION of Carnivale or Mardi Gras. Fasching is a week of splendid masquerade balls and extravagant food and drink. Not at all surprising is that this bacchanal leads up to the spiritual deprivation that is Lent, so why not binge like you mean it?

And the food I think about when all bets are off, when I'm staring down the reality of my last sugar-and-fat-laden hurrah before I repent? Donuts. More specifically *Krapfen*, the official guilty pleasure of the Fasching season. They are extra special because they are traditionally filled to the rim with glorious jam filling! I prefer apricot, but it's your kitchen, so choose a filling of pastry cream laced with melted bittersweet chocolate if you like. And for parties, I like to tip my hat to the genius of the French *croquembouche*, that tower of cream puffs, and build a *Krapfen* tower.

FOR THE SPONGE:

¾ cup (180 ml) warm whole milk

2 teaspoons dry active yeast

pinch granulated sugar

1¼ cups (175 g) bread flour

FOR THE DOUGH:

2 teaspoons dry active yeast

¼ cup (60 ml) warm whole milk

3 egg yolks

1 teaspoon vanilla extract

zest of ½ lemon

½ teaspoon salt

⅓ cup (65 g) granulated sugar

6 tablespoons (85 g) unsalted butter, very soft

2 cups (280 g) bread flour

FOR THE ASSEMBLY:

vegetable oil (enough to fill a stockpot 4 inches / 10 cm deep for frying)

1 cup (240 ml) apricot jam (or the jam or filling of your choice)

confectioners' sugar, for dusting

Make the sponge:

Place the warm milk (not hot—you don't want to kill the yeast) in a small bowl and sprinkle with the yeast and granulated sugar. Let sit undisturbed 3 to 5 minutes to bloom the yeast (*blooming* is the term for letting the yeast become active and bubbly in a liquid).

In the bowl of a stand mixer fitted with the dough hook, add the yeast mixture and flour and mix until smooth. Cover with a damp kitchen towel and allow the sponge to rise at room temperature. Proceed to the dough stage just as the sponge starts to fall, which takes about 1 hour.

Make the dough:

In the bowl of a stand mixer fitted with the dough hook, sprinkle the yeast over the warm milk and allow to bloom. Add the sponge and mix at low speed.

Meanwhile, in a small bowl, stir together egg yolks, vanilla extract, lemon zest, salt, and granulated sugar. Add to the sponge mixture. Add the butter, small pieces at a time, mixing until incorporated. Slowly add the flour and mix until the dough is smooth, shiny, and elastic, 15 to 20 minutes.

Spray the dough with a light coating of nonstick baking spray and cover with plastic wrap. Allow to rest for 1 hour at room temperature.

Divide the dough in half. Roll each piece into a rope and cut each into 10 shorter ropes. Roll each rope into a tight round bun, using no flour on your surface (to avoid flour

burning in the hot oil). Place the buns on a parchment-lined sheet pan and allow them to rise in a warm place until slightly less than doubled in volume. Place a moist dish towel over the buns while they're resting to prevent them from developing dry skins.

Add at least 4 inches (10 cm) of vegetable oil to a large stockpot and heat to 360°F (180°C).

Add the *Krapfen* to the oil, one at a time, gently placing them in the oil seam side up. Six per batch is usually the perfect amount. Allow to brown for 4 to 5 minutes, then flip the *Krapfen* and cook the other side for 3 to 4 minutes, until brown. Transfer the *Krapfen* to a cooling rack or a paper towel–lined sheet pan to allow oil to drain off and the *Krapfen* to dry. Repeat with the remaining dough.

To assemble:

Fit a pastry bag with an open tip (large enough to allow jam to flow freely but small enough not to create a huge hole) and fill with the jam or filling of your choice. Insert the pastry tip into the *Krapfen* and gently fill.

Sift confectioners' sugar on top of your *Krapfen*. Serve immediately.

KING'S CAKE

Makes 1 coffee cake

MY VERSION OF THE TRADITIONAL KING'S CAKE is a lush, sweet roll intertwined with bourbon- and cinnamon-laced pastry cream. I make it every year, a few days before Mardi Gras, so that we may snack on this feast of sweetness up until the very last moments before Lent. This also gives us plenty of time to discover the lucky pecan (I add a pecan instead of a plastic baby for obvious choking-hazard reasons). But let me just say that this is a great treat at any time of the year, not just around "Fat Tuesday."

FOR THE PASTRY CREAM:
1 cup (240 ml) whole milk
1 cup (240 ml) heavy cream
6 egg yolks
½ cup (100 g) granulated sugar
2 tablespoons bourbon
1 tablespoon cinnamon
¼ cup (30 g) cornstarch
pinch salt
½ cup (115 g) bittersweet chocolate chips (I use Callebaut/
    Cacao Barry 60/40)

FOR THE DOUGH:
5 to 6 cups (700 to 840 g) bread flour
1 tablespoon instant yeast
2 teaspoons salt
2 eggs
¼ cup (60 ml) maple syrup
1¾ cups (420 ml) whole milk
zest of 1 lemon
1 tablespoon vanilla bean paste
¼ cup (55 g) unsalted butter, at room temperature

FOR THE ASSEMBLY:
2 egg whites, whisked
1 pecan
3 tablespoons granulated sugar

FOR THE GLAZE:
1½ cups (150 g) confectioners' sugar
3 to 6 tablespoons (45 to 90 ml) whole milk, divided
green, yellow, and purple decorating sugar balls

Make the pastry cream:

In a large saucepan, combine the milk and cream. Bring to a simmer.

In the bowl of a stand mixer fitted with the whisk attachment, combine the egg yolks, granulated sugar, bourbon, cinnamon, cornstarch, and salt. Whisk until light and fluffy.

Slow the mixer speed to medium and carefully pour the simmering milk-cream mixture down the side of the bowl into the whisking egg yolks. Whisk until well combined.

Transfer the pastry cream back to the saucepan and whisk constantly over medium heat until the mixture thickens to the consistency of mayonnaise. Transfer the pastry cream to a large bowl and cover with plastic wrap, pressing the plastic directly onto the surface to prevent a skin from forming. Refrigerate until completely cool, at least 2 hours.

Make the dough:

Place 5 cups (700 g) flour, the yeast, and salt in the bowl of a stand mixer fitted with the dough hook attachment. Stir to combine.

In a bowl, whisk together the eggs, maple syrup, milk, lemon zest, and vanilla bean paste. With the mixer running on low speed, add the egg mixture to the flour mixture. When just combined, slowly add the butter in small bits until incorporated.

Mix the dough until it starts to pull from the sides of the bowl and is very shiny. The mixing process can take up to 15 minutes. Be patient. If the dough is very sticky, slowly add more flour from the extra cup.

Spray a large bowl with nonstick cooking spray. Transfer the dough to the bowl and let rest until it doubles in volume, about 1 hour.

Punch down the dough. Transfer the dough to a lightly floured work surface and roll it out into a rough rectangle, approximately 24 inches (61 cm) long and 10 to 12 inches (25 to 30.5 cm) wide.

To assemble:

Remove the pastry cream from the refrigerator and stir until the mixture is smooth. Spread the pastry cream evenly over the rectangle of dough.

Roll the dough, starting with the long edge closest to you, into a jelly roll and slice the roll of dough in half lengthwise. Turn the cut sides so they are facing outward and twist the two strands of dough together. On a sheet pan, form the jelly-roll twist into a ring, pinching the cut ends together gently to seal. Every few inches, make a cut in the top layer of the cake, just deep enough to expose the pastry cream. Brush the entire top and sides with egg white. Allow to rise until doubled in volume, about 1 hour.

Preheat the oven to 350°F (175°C).

Brush the cake again with egg white and sprinkle with granulated sugar. Bake for 30 to 40 minutes, until the crust is golden brown. Allow to cool completely.

Hide a pecan in the cake by sticking it gently in one of the cut openings.

Make the glaze:

Combine the confectioners' sugar and milk in a small bowl and stir until smooth. Drizzle the glaze over the cake and sprinkle the colored decoration balls randomly over the wet glaze.

King's Cake

Tangerine
Dream Ring

Anglai

GERBEAUD SLICES

Makes 1 (8-by-12-inch / 20-by-30.5-cm) cake

EMIL GERBEAUD WAS ONE OF the preeminent confectioners of the nineteenth century, creating countless delicacies from pastries to bonbons in his eponymous café located on Vörösmarty Square in Budapest. The most famous of his creations was the Gerbeaud Slice, layers of delicate yeasted cake schmeared liberally with walnut cream and tart apricot preserves. All are then baked together, resulting in a deeply flavorful pastry with an otherworldly texture. Sadly, Chef Gerbeaud left this pastry plane many years ago, but his great works in sweetness live on in his café, and possibly in your very own kitchen.

FOR THE CAKE:

3 cups (375 g) all-purpose flour plus ½ cup (60 g) extra

2 teaspoons instant yeast

1 teaspoon salt

3 eggs

½ cup (120 ml) whole milk

¼ cup (60 ml) honey

1 teaspoon vanilla bean paste

6 tablespoons (85 g) unsalted butter,
    cut into small pieces, softened

FOR THE FILLING:

2 cups (200 g) finely chopped walnuts

¾ cup (150 g) granulated sugar

3 tablespoons unsalted butter, softened

1 teaspoon vanilla bean paste

FOR THE ASSEMBLY:

1 cup (240 ml) apricot preserves

FOR THE APRICOT GLAZE:

¼ cup (60 ml) apricot preserves

2 tablespoons rum

FOR THE CHOCOLATE GLAZE:

8 ounces (225 g) bittersweet chocolate, finely chopped

½ cup (120 ml) heavy cream

1 tablespoon unsalted butter

1 tablespoon corn syrup

Make the cake:

Spray a half sheet pan with nonstick baking spray and line with parchment paper. Set aside.

In the bowl of a stand mixer fitted with the dough hook, combine the 3 cups (375 g) flour, the yeast, and salt. Stir until combined.

In a small bowl, whisk together the eggs, milk, honey, and vanilla bean paste. With the mixer running on low speed, add the egg mixture to the flour mixture and mix until just combined. Add the butter, a few pieces at a time, and continue mixing until a smooth dough forms, 10 to 15 minutes. If after 5 minutes, the dough is still so sticky that it's sticking in streaks to the side of the bowl, add a little more flour from the ½ cup (60 g) of reserve flour. Add only a little at a time until the dough is still very soft but not extremely sticky. Continue mixing until the dough pulls away from the sides of the bowl.

Spray a large mixing bowl with nonstick spray and transfer the dough to the bowl. Spray the top of the dough with nonstick spray and cover the bowl with plastic wrap. Allow the dough to proof (rest) on your work surface until doubled in volume, about 1 hour.

Make the filling:

In the bowl of a food processor fitted with the blade attachment, combine the walnuts, granulated sugar, butter, and vanilla bean paste. Process until a paste forms.

To assemble:

Turn the dough out onto a lightly floured work surface and divide it into 3 pieces. With a rolling pin, roll each dough piece out into a rectangle measuring approximately 8 by 12 inches (20 by 30.5 cm).

Transfer one dough rectangle to the prepared sheet pan, using your fingers to press the rectangle in place so that it's even. Spread half of the walnut filling over the entirety of the first dough sheet. Spread half of the apricot preserves over the walnut paste. Carefully transfer the second sheet of dough to cover the preserves and press gently to adhere. Spread the remaining walnut filling, then the remaining apricot preserves, over the second layer. Top with the final layer of dough and press gently to adhere.

Cover the sheet pan with a barely moist kitchen towel and allow to rest until the cake is slightly puffy, about 1 hour.

Preheat the oven to 375°F (190°C). Bake the cake for 30 minutes, checking frequently to make sure the top layer of dough doesn't burn. If it begins to brown too deeply, cover the top of the cake with aluminum foil.

Allow the cake to cool completely. If the cake has adhered to the sides of the sheet pan, gently run a very sharp paring knife along the edges of the pan to release it, then unmold it onto a cooling rack set over a parchment-lined sheet pan. Cut the cake in half lengthwise to make 2 rectangles, approximately 12 by 8 inches (30.5 by 20 cm).

Make the apricot glaze:

In a small saucepan, combine the apricot preserves and rum and cook over low heat, stirring constantly, until the preserves melt completely and create a shiny glaze.

With a pastry brush, brush the warm glaze evenly over the surface of both pieces of the cake. Stack one half of the cake on top of the other.

Refrigerate the cake to allow the glaze to set, 10 to 15 minutes.

Make the chocolate glaze:

Place the chocolate in a heatproof mixing bowl.

In a small saucepan, combine the cream, butter, and corn syrup and bring to a simmer. Pour the hot cream mixture over the chocolate, making sure the cream completely covers the chocolate. Allow to sit undisturbed for 2 minutes. Whisk clockwise until the chocolate is completely melted and the mixture is smooth and shiny.

Using a large offset spatula, spread the chocolate glaze evenly over the top of the cake. Allow the glaze to set completely at room temperature, about 30 minutes.

Run a sharp knife under scalding water and quickly dry. Cut the cake in half lengthwise. Running the knife under scalding water and drying before each slice, cut each half into six slices.

Serve immediately, or store in the refrigerator, tightly wrapped, for up to 4 days.

TANGERINE DREAM TEA RING

Makes 1 coffee cake

THIS IS A SWEET BREAD that will take you from brunch to midnight snack, that's how damned good it is. It's not at all cloying, but it's addictive. And although it's terribly elegant, it brings to mind the most wonderful of childhood summer treats: Creamsicles.

FOR THE DOUGH:

5 cups (700 g) bread flour plus 1 cup (140 g) extra

1 tablespoon instant yeast

½ cup (50 g) granulated sugar

2 teaspoons salt

2 eggs

1¼ cups (300 ml) whole milk

¼ cup (60 ml) tangerine (or orange) juice, from about
   4 tangerines

zest of 1 tangerine

1 tablespoon orange extract

¼ cup (55 g) unsalted butter, at room temperature

FOR THE FILLING:

1 cup (100 g) confectioners' sugar

1 cup (250 g) quark or farmer's cheese (ricotta is a fine substitute
   but make sure to drain it until relatively firm and dry)

1 (8-ounce / 225-g) package of cream cheese,
   at room temperature

¼ cup (30 g) all-purpose flour

1 egg yolk, at room temperature

1 teaspoon vanilla bean paste

zest of 1 tangerine

pinch salt

2 to 3 drops orange food coloring (optional)

FOR THE ASSEMBLY:

egg wash (1 egg whisked with 2 tablespoons water)

FOR THE GLAZE:

1 cup (100 g) confectioners' sugar

¼ cup (60 ml) whole milk

Make the dough:

Place 5 cups (700 g) of the flour, the yeast, granulated sugar, and salt in the bowl of a stand mixer fitted with the dough hook attachment. Stir to combine.

In a bowl, whisk together the eggs, milk, tangerine juice, tangerine zest, and orange extract. With the mixer running on low speed, add the egg mixture to the flour mixture. When just combined, slowly add the butter in small bits until incorporated.

Mix the dough until it starts to pull from the sides of the bowl and is very shiny. The mixing process can take up to 15 minutes. Be patient. If the dough is very sticky, slowly add more flour from the extra cup.

Spray a large bowl with nonstick cooking spray. Transfer the dough to the bowl and let rest until it doubles in volume, about 1 hour.

Punch down the dough. Transfer the dough to a lightly floured work surface and roll it out into a rough rectangle, approximately 24 inches (61 cm) long and 10 to 12 inches (25 to 30.5 cm) wide.

Make the filling:

In the bowl of a stand mixer fitted with the paddle attachment, combine all the ingredients. Mix until smooth.

To assemble:

Preheat the oven to 350°F (175°C). Line a half sheet pan with parchment paper.

Turn the dough out onto a lightly floured work surface. Roll the dough into a 15-by-25-inch (38-by-63.5-cm) rectangle. Transfer the filling to a large pastry bag fitted with a large open tip. Pipe the filling over the entire surface of the dough, leaving only a 1-inch (2.5-cm) border on one long side. Spread the filling over the filling.

Brush the exposed border with egg wash. Starting with the long edge of the dough with the filling, gently roll the dough into a long log; pinch the dough together at the seam to seal. Gently transfer the dough log to the prepared sheet pan, seam side down, and form the log into a circle. Press the ends together, gently pinching the edges of dough to seal.

Using a very sharp serrated knife, cut gashes three-quarters of the way through the dough at 1-inch (2.5-cm) intervals. Slightly rotate each half-slice so that the attached slices are fanned out, slightly overlapping one another. Lightly cover the ring and allow to rise until doubled in volume, about 1 hour.

Brush the ring with egg wash. Bake for 30 minutes, or until the ring is golden brown.

Make the glaze:

Whisk together the confectioners' sugar and milk until smooth.

Remove from the oven and spoon the glaze over the entire ring while it's still very warm. Serve warm or cooled.

CROISSANTS

Makes 2 dozen croissants

IT TOOK TEN YEARS OF trial and error, but at long last I discovered my all-time favorite croissant formula. It might seem ridiculous that a few changes in ratio among flour, butter, sugars, and yeast would have such a significant impact on a recipe, but when you're striving for the perfect croissant, one that mimics or perhaps surpasses the paragons in France, then microscopic changes in measurements can absolutely make the difference between merely wonderful and outrageously heavenly. For the first time ever, I am releasing my recipe into the wild. Be patient. Be meticulous. But above all, be ready for some buttery, flaky deliciousness.

If you've done any research on croissant dough, you'll have noticed that there are options when it comes to liquid ingredients. Some doughs are leaner than others, using only water. Some use milk, while others use a combination of the two. I've found that I prefer whole milk above all else. You'll also notice that I use barley-malt syrup, available in health food stores, instead of sugar. I love the subtle sweetness and depth of flavor that malt brings to the equation, but feel free to substitute sugar if you wish.

FOR THE DOUGH:

3½ cups (840 ml) whole milk, at room temperature

¼ cup (60 ml) barley malt syrup (or ¼ cup / 50 g granulated sugar)

1 tablespoon salt

8½ cups (1 kg) all-purpose flour (plus a few more ounces)

2 tablespoons instant yeast

FOR THE BUTTER BLOCK:

2 pounds (910 g) unsalted European butter (see page 228), cut into small pieces, at room temperature

½ cup (60 g) all-purpose flour

1 tablespoon fresh lemon juice

FOR THE ASSEMBLY:

egg wash (1 egg whisked with 2 tablespoons water)

ice cubes

Make the dough:

In the bowl of a stand mixer fitted with the dough hook, combine the milk, barley malt syrup (or granulated sugar), and salt and stir until just combined. Add the flour and yeast and mix on low speed until a smooth, shiny dough forms, about 15 minutes. If the air conditions are very humid and the dough is very wet, you may need a few more ounces of flour. If conditions are dry and the dough is looking very "shaggy," add a few ounces of water. The dough should pull away from the sides of the bowl.

Spray a large bowl with nonstick cooking spray and add the dough. Spray the top of the dough with nonstick spray as well. Cover the bowl with plastic wrap and place in a warm corner of your kitchen to proof until the dough doubles in volume, about 1 hour.

Line a half sheet pan with plastic wrap and spray with nonstick spray. Turn the dough out onto the plastic wrap. Using the tips of your fingers, gently press the dough down to deflate it and press it outward to fit the contours of the sheet pan. Spray the top of the dough with nonstick spray and cover the dough-lined sheet pan in plastic wrap. Refrigerate for at least 1 hour but no more than 2 hours.

Make the butter block:

In the bowl of a stand mixer fitted with the paddle attachment, combine the butter, flour, and lemon juice. Mix on low speed until the mixture forms a smooth paste.

Transfer the butter mixture to a large piece of parchment paper and spread into a rough rectangle approximately 14 by 10 inches (25 by 35.5 cm).

Wrap the butter block tightly in the parchment and then again securely in plastic wrap, then use a rolling pin to shape the dough more evenly into a 14-by-10-inch (35.5-by-25-cm) rectangle. Refrigerate for no more than 20 minutes, until cool and firm but not hard. Check the butter block after 10 minutes to ensure that it has not become too hard—when you bend it, it shouldn't crack. (This is crucial. If the butter cracks when you bend it, it is too cold and will not roll out properly. If it is too warm, it will escape from the sides of the sealed dough and won't form a proper layer.)

The lamination process:

Remove the dough and the butter block from the refrigerator. The dough should feel cool and slightly firmer than when it first went into the fridge, and it may have risen just a little. The butter should be firm enough to handle in your hands without sagging, but you should be able to bend it as well.

Sprinkle a generous, even layer of flour onto your work surface. Turn the dough out onto the surface. Sprinkle the top of the dough with flour as well. Roll the dough out into a 16-by-22-inch (40.5-by-55-cm) rectangle. Place the butter block on the center of one half of the dough, leaving about ½ inch (12 mm) around the edges, and fold the second half of the dough over the butter block to seal it in. This is called the "lock-in." Press along the edges of the dough to seal the butter block in tightly. (Can you see why this process is called "lamination" now? Just as when you laminate a sheet of paper between two sheets of plastic, you are laminating a block of butter between two sheets of dough.)

Make the first letter turn: Turn the dough a quarter turn so the long end now faces you. Check underneath the dough to ensure there's sufficient flour still on the table; replenish

if necessary. Roll the dough into a 20-by-24-inch (50-by-61-cm) rectangle. Fold one-third of the dough over toward the middle and fold the other third over as if you were folding a business letter. Place the dough on a parchment-lined sheet pan and cover with plastic wrap. Refrigerate for 20 minutes to rest. (You must allow the dough to rest because the rolling and handling has activated the gluten and will make any more rolling very difficult—20 minutes in the refrigerator allows the gluten to relax, allows the butter to firm up a bit, and makes rolling a cinch. Don't refrigerate for more than 20 minutes, however, or the butter will become too firm and will crack when you continue rolling.)

Make the second letter turn: Remove the dough from the refrigerator and turn it out onto your floured work surface, with the long side facing you. Roll it out into a 20-by-24-inch (50-by-61-cm) rectangle and execute another letter turn, folding the sides over as directed previously. Cover the dough and refrigerate for 20 minutes again.

Execute this process two more times to make a total of four letter turns. Once you've finished your last turn, cover the dough again, but this time with extra plastic wrap to secure it very tightly (the dough might rise and want to bust out of its protective wrap, so make sure it's secure). Refrigerate for at least 2 hours or overnight.

To form traditional croissants:

Cut the dough in half lengthwise. Wrap one half in plastic wrap and return to the refrigerator.

Place the other half of the dough on a floured work surface. Roll the dough into a rough rectangle ¼ inch (6 mm) thick, 15 inches (38 cm) wide, and 21 inches (53 cm) long. Trim the edges with a very sharp knife or a pastry wheel. Cut the dough in half lengthwise, into 2 pieces, each 7½ by 21 inches (17 by 52.5 cm).

Mark the top edge of the first piece of dough by making a slight indentation every 4 inches (10 cm). Along the bottom edge of the dough, make your first indentation at

2 inches (5 cm) and then continue marking every 4 inches (10 cm). Using a ruler, connect the first mark on the top with the first mark on the bottom and gently score the dough with the ruler's edge. With the ruler, connect that same first top mark with the second bottom mark and score with a knife. Continue marking triangles on the dough. Once you have marked the length of dough, use a very sharp pastry wheel to cut along the scores to separate the triangles.

Place a triangle of dough in front of you, the narrowest point facing away. Cut a ½-inch (12-mm) notch in the middle of the bottom edge. Grabbing the outer corners, gently tug to stretch the bottom of the dough. Now place your left palm on the bottom portion of dough and gently tug at the narrow point with your right hand to elongate the triangle just a smidge. Still holding on to the point of the dough, use the flat of your palm to roll the bottom edge up to the tip. Place the croissant with the tip tucked under on a parchment-lined sheet pan.

Repeat with the remaining triangles and cover with plastic wrap. (If you don't cover the croissants during the rise, they will form a skin and this will keep them from rising.) Then score, cut, and roll the remaining dough and place on additional sheet pans. Allow the croissants to proof on a cool kitchen counter until they have almost doubled in volume, 2 to 3 hours. You should be able to gently press them and they will spring back. (The best temperature for proofing is about 70°F / 21°C.) If your kitchen is too warm, the butter may leak from the croissants).

Preheat the oven to 400°F (205°C).

Brush the croissants very gently with the egg wash. (Brush with extreme care so you don't deflate the rise.)

Before you place the croissants in the oven, quickly open the doors and toss a handful of ice cubes onto the bottom of the oven and immediately close the door to create steam. Immediately lower the temperature of the oven to 375°F (190°C) and place the croissants in the oven. Bake

for 20 minutes, or until the croissants are a deep golden brown.

OPTIONS!

ALMOND CROISSANTS: Proceed exactly as you would for plain croissants, but before you roll the croissants, you will place a roll of almond paste at the bottom of the triangle and roll it up as you would a traditional plain croissant.

CHOCOLATE CROISSANTS: Instead of cutting the rolled piece of dough lengthwise, keep the dough whole and cut it into 3-by-15-inch (7.5-by-38-cm) strips. Place 3 tablespoons of chopped bittersweet chocolate 2 inches (5 cm) from the end of the dough and fold the shorter end of the dough over the chocolate. Fold the remaining longer piece of dough over the shorter end until you have a nice square packet. Proof until doubled in size. Brush with egg wash and bake until golden brown. Drizzle with melted chocolate.

CINNAMON SWIRLS: Instead of cutting the dough in half and then cutting again into triangles, slather the rolled length of dough with ½ cup (115 g) room-temperature unsalted butter. Sprinkle with 1 cup (200 g) sugar and 1 teaspoon cinnamon that have been stirred together. Press gently on the sugar to adhere to the butter. Roll the dough into a jelly roll and cut it into 1½-inch (4-cm) rounds. Place the rolls on a parchment-lined sheet pan, a few inches apart, and tuck the loose end of the dough underneath each roll. Sprinkle each with another 1 tablespoon sugar. Bake at 350°F (175°C) for 45 minutes.

SCRAP TARTLETS: You'll find that in trimming the dough and in making plain croissants, you'll be left with pretty large chunks of dough. This may leave you bereft: After all that work, these swaths of glorious dough that are too small and too wonky to shape are to be thrown away? Of course not! Who do you think I am? Instead, I cut the scraps into small pieces, about ½ inch (12 mm) in size. Then I either toss them with 1 tablespoon melted and

*Plain
Croissants*

*Scrap
Tartlets*

Almond Croissant

Cinnamon Swirls

Chocolate Croissants, or pain au chocolat

cooled unsalted butter, 2 tablespoons sugar, and a small handful of raisins or currants, or, if you happen to have some pastry cream lying about, with 2 tablespoons pastry cream, 1 teaspoon rum, and a small handful of raisins. Scatter the dough into 4-inch (10-cm) tart forms sprayed with nonstick baking spray. Cover with a clean dish towel and allow to proof for about 45 minutes. (Sprinkle turbinado sugar on top of the pastry cream version after proofing.) Bake for 10 to 15 minutes. Voilà! An ersatz *pain aux raisins* that's painfully delicious and has put all that extra gorgeous dough to use.

A NOTE FROM THE SWEET TALKER: European butter. You've seen it in your grocery store and have been immediately taken by the fancy gold wrapping. And then you saw the price, laughed your tush off, and went for the Land O'Lakes or Cabot instead. In most circumstances, I stick with American butter. But when it comes to laminated doughs, as for croissants and *kouign-amann*, I use European butter exclusively. Why? Because it has a high butterfat content and is lower in moisture. This all makes for flakier and more buttery doughs. If you're spending the time on laminating, why not spend just a wee bit more money on a butter that can elevate your hard work enormously? So go for the gold-wrapped nugget and have no regrets.

BIENENSTICH

Makes 1 (12-inch / 30.5-cm) cake

BIENENSTICH, OR "BEE STING," IS a cake deceptive in its simplicity. It's composed of layers of yeasted cake infused with honey (Get it? Bee sting!) sandwiching a single layer of rich custard. With toasted, sweetened almonds atop, you've got the perfect midafternoon snack. The type of honey you use makes a difference in the taste. Lavender honey is my favorite.

FOR THE FILLING:

½ cup (120 ml) lavender honey

6 egg yolks

5 tablespoons (40 g) cornstarch

1 cup (240 ml) heavy cream

1 cup (240 ml) whole milk

FOR THE CAKE:

2½ cups (310 g) all-purpose flour

2 teaspoons instant yeast

1 teaspoon salt

3 eggs

½ cup (120 ml) whole milk

¼ cup (60 ml) lavender honey

1 teaspoon almond extract

6 tablespoons (85 g) unsalted butter, cut into pieces, softened

4 tablespoons (55 g) unsalted butter, melted

FOR THE TOPPING (OPTIONAL):

1 cup (240 ml) heavy cream

½ cup (115 g) unsalted butter

½ cup (120 ml) lavender honey

1 teaspoon almond extract

1 cup (90 g) sliced almonds

FOR THE ASSEMBLY:

¼ cup (20 g) cocoa powder

1 (7-ounce / 200-g) package almond paste (I use Odense)

4 ounces (115 g) melted chocolate

½ cup (45 g) sliced almonds

Make the filling:

In the bowl of a stand mixer fitted with the whisk attachment, combine the lavender honey, egg yolks, and cornstarch. Whisk until fluffy, about 5 minutes.

Meanwhile, in a saucepan, combine the cream and milk and bring to a simmer.

With the stand mixer running on medium speed, slowly pour the hot cream mixture down the side of the bowl into the egg mixture. Continue mixing until well combined.

Transfer the mixture back to the saucepan and whisk over medium heat until it thickens to the consistency of mayonnaise.

Transfer the filling to a large bowl and cover with plastic wrap, pressing the plastic directly onto the surface to prevent a skin from forming. Refrigerate until cool, about 2 hours.

Make the cake:

Spray a 12-inch (30.5-cm) round cake pan with nonstick baking spray and line it with a round of parchment paper.

In the bowl of a stand mixer fitted with the dough hook, combine the flour, yeast, and salt. Stir until combined.

In a small bowl, whisk together the eggs, milk, lavender honey, and almond extract. With the mixer running on low speed, add the egg mixture to the flour mixture and stir until just combined. Add the softened butter, a few pieces at a time, and continue mixing until a smooth dough forms, 5 to 10 minutes.

Spray a large mixing bowl with nonstick cooking spray and transfer the dough to the bowl. Spray the top of the dough with nonstick spray. Cover the bowl with plastic wrap and allow to proof at room temperature until doubled in volume, about 1 hour.

Turn the dough out onto a lightly floured work surface. Gently form it into a neat round. Use a rolling pin to roll the round to approximately 12 inches (30.5 cm) in diameter. Transfer the round to the prepared pan. Brush the top with the melted butter. Cover the pan with a moist kitchen towel and allow to rest until doubled in volume, about 45 minutes.

Make the topping (optional):

About 15 minutes before the cake dough is ready, preheat the oven to 375° (190°C).

In a large saucepan, combine the cream and butter and stir over medium heat until the butter has melted. Add the honey and almond extract. Attach a candy thermometer to the side of the saucepan and continue stirring until the mixture reaches 245° (120°C). Remove from the heat and immediately stir in the almonds. Set aside to cool so that the topping isn't scalding hot when you add it to the top of the cake.

Quickly spread the almond topping evenly over the top of the cake. Bake for 30 minutes, or until the almond top is golden brown and the cake begins to pull away from the sides of the pan. Let cool completely.

To assemble:

Give the custard filling a good stir with a wooden spoon to loosen it up because it will have stiffened and set in the refrigerator.

Using a serrated knife, cut the cake into 2 even layers. Spread all of the filling on one layer of cake and place the second layer on top of the filling. Press gently to adhere.

Place a stencil over the top of the cake and gently dust with the cocoa powder. Carefully remove the stencil.

Divide the almond paste into 20 even pieces. Roll each piece in your hand to make a rough oval, like a jelly bean. These will be the bees' bodies.

Transfer the melted chocolate to a small pastry bag fitted with a small open tip or a coronet (see page 51). Pipe stripes along the top of each oval. At one end of each oval, pipe two dots for eyes and a smiley face (if you want happy bees).

Using the chocolate as glue, place two almond slices on top of each oval to act as wings and gently set the bees on a piece of parchment to set.

Carefully skewer the underside of each bee with a toothpick so that the end goes just to the middle of the bee body. Place the other end of the toothpick firmly into the top layer of cake. Arrange the bees willy-nilly on the surface.

KOUIGN-AMANN

Makes 8 individual pastries

IF YOU'VE HAD THE PLEASURE of spending time in Brittany, no doubt you have had a taste of a *kouign-amann*. If you've had the pleasure of spending time in Brittany and you didn't eat *kouign-amann*, then you never really went to Brittany at all because you can't fully appreciate the place and her people until you take a bite of that crispy, sweet, buttery, slightly-chewy-in-the-center-and-caramelized-on-top-and-on-the-edges pastry.

2¼ cups (450 g) granulated sugar, divided
2 teaspoons salt
5 cups (625 g) all-purpose flour, plus extra for dusting
  the work surface
2 tablespoons instant yeast
1 pound (455 g) unsalted European butter, at room temperature

In the bowl of a stand mixer fitted with the hook attachment, combine 1½ cups (360 ml) water, ¼ cup (50 g) granulated sugar, and the salt. Add the flour and yeast and mix until a smooth, shiny dough forms, about 10 minutes. If the air conditions are very humid, you may need to add a bit more flour. If dry, add a few tablespoons of water. The dough should be smooth and pull away from the sides of the bowl.

Spray a large bowl with nonstick cooking spray. Place the dough in the bowl and turn it over a few times to coat thoroughly. Cover with plastic wrap and place in a warm area of your kitchen to allow to proof until doubled in volume, about 1 hour.

In the bowl of a stand mixer fitted with the paddle attachment, combine the butter and ½ cup (100 g) sugar. Mix until the two are well blended and the butter is smooth but not soft. Transfer the mixture to a piece of plastic wrap and shape into a rough 8-by-11-inch (20-by-28-cm) rectangle. Cover completely with plastic wrap and, using a rolling pin, gently even out the butter into an even block. Refrigerate for 20 minutes.

Turn the dough out onto a lightly floured work surface. Lightly dust the top of the dough with flour as well. Roll the dough into a rough rectangle, approximately 12 by 18 inches (30.5 by 46 cm). Place the butter block on one side of the dough and fold the second half over the dough block. Press along the edges of the dough block to secure the butter inside the dough.

Sprinkle the work surface evenly with ¼ cup (50 g) sugar. Place the dough on the sugar and roll out into a rectangle approximately 12 by 18 inches (30.5 by 46 cm). Sprinkle the top with ¼ cup (50 g) sugar. Fold one short half toward the middle and fold the other half over on top of that, as if you were folding a business letter. Cover with plastic wrap and chill for 20 minutes.

Again, sprinkle your work surface with ¼ cup (50 g) sugar, and sprinkle ¼ cup (50 g) sugar over the top of the dough in an even layer. Roll out the dough into a rectangle 12 by 18 inches (30.5 by 46 cm) and fold into a business letter again. Cover and refrigerate for 45 minutes.

Preheat the oven to 400°F (205°C). Line a half sheet pan with parchment paper.

Sprinkle ¼ cup (50 g) sugar onto the work surface and roll the dough into a rectangle 8 by 16 inches (20 by 40.5 cm). Using a very sharp pastry wheel, cut the dough into eight (4-inch / 10-cm) squares. Prepare each pastry by folding each corner of the square toward the center and pressing the corner to seal into place (you've just created a smaller square). Continue until you've finished folding all the squares. Sprinkle the squares with the remaining ¼ cup (50 g) sugar. Cover with plastic wrap and allow to rest for 20 minutes.

Bake for 20 minutes, or until the top is a deeply golden brown and caramelized. Eat while warm!

CONVERSION CHARTS

Weight Equivalents: The metric weights given in this chart are not exact equivalents, but have been rounded up or down slightly to make measuring easier.

Volume Equivalents: These are not exact equivalents for American cups and spoons, but have been rounded up or down slightly to make measuring easier.

AVOIRDUPOIS	METRIC
¼ oz	7 g
½ oz	15 g
1 oz	30 g
2 oz	60 g
3 oz	90 g
4 oz	115 g
5 oz	150 g
6 oz	175 g
7 oz	200 g
8 oz (½ lb)	225 g
9 oz	250 g
10 oz	300 g
11 oz	325 g
12 oz	350 g
13 oz	375 g
14 oz	400 g
15 oz	425 g
16 oz (1 lb)	450 g
1½ lb	750 g
2 lb	900 g
2¼ lb	1 kg
3 lb	1.4 kg
4 lb	1.8 kg

AMERICAN	METRIC	IMPERIAL
¼ tsp	1.2 ml	
½ tsp	2.5 ml	
1 tsp	5.0 ml	
½ Tbsp (1.5 tsp)	7.5 ml	
1 Tbsp (3 tsp)	15 ml	
¼ cup (4 Tbsp)	60 ml	2 fl oz
⅓ cup (5 Tbsp)	75 ml	2.5 fl oz
½ cup (8 Tbsp)	125 ml	4 fl oz
⅔ cup (10 Tbsp)	150 ml	5 fl oz
¾ cup (12 Tbsp)	175 ml	6 fl oz
1 cup (16 Tbsp)	250 ml	8 fl oz
1¼ cups	300 ml	10 fl oz (½ pint)
1½ cups	350 ml	12 fl oz
2 cups (1 pint)	500 ml	16 fl oz
2½ cups	625 ml	20 fl oz (1 pint)
1 quart	1 liter	32 fl oz

OVEN MARK	F	C	GAS
Very cool	250-275	130-140	½-1
Cool	300	150	2
Warm	325	170	3
Moderate	350	180	4
Moderately hot	375	190	5
	400	200	6
Hot	425	220	7
	450	230	8
Very hot	475	250	9

WEIGHT EQUIVALENTS

All-Purpose Flour: It's critical to weigh certain ingredients for successful baking. Dry ingredients—especially flour—compress easily into a cup measure, making the scoop-and-level method inaccurate. The most accurate way to measure flour is to weigh it after sifting. Here are the weight equivalents for common volume measurements of all-purpose flour.

WEIGHT	VOLUME
1 ounce	3 tablespoons
2 ounces	¼ cup + 2 tablespoons
3 ounces	½ cup + 1 tablespoon
4 ounces	¾ cup + ½ teaspoon
5 ounces	1 cup
6 ounces	1 cup + 1 tablespoon
7 ounces	1¼ cups + 2 tablespoons
8 ounces	1½ cups + 1 tablespoon
9 ounces	1¾ cups + ½ teaspoon
10 ounces	2 cups
11 ounces	2 cups + 1 tablespoon
12 ounces	2¼ cups + 2 tablespoons
12½ ounces	2½ cups
13 ounces	2½ cups + 1 tablespoon
13½ ounces	2½ cups + 3 tablespoons
14 ounces	2¾ cups + ½ teaspoon
14½ ounces	2¾ cups + 1 tablespoon +1 teaspoon
15 ounces	3 cups

Superfine Granulated Sugar: Superfine granulated sugar, the sugar generally used in this book, weighs about 8 ounces per cup. (Standard table sugar, or typical granulated sugar, weighs 7 ounces per cup. It has a larger crystal than extra-fine granulated, so less mass fits into a one-cup measure.)

WEIGHT	VOLUME
1 ounce	2 tablespoons
2 ounces	¼ cup
3 ounces	6 tablespoons
4 ounces	½ cup
5 ounces	½ cup + 2 tablespoons
6 ounces	¾ cup
7 ounces	¾ cup + 2 tablespoons
8 ounces	1 cup
12 ounces	1½ cups
16 ounces	2 cups
20 ounces	2 ½ cups
24 ounces	3 cups

Other Ingredients

INGREDIENT	WEIGHT	VOLUME
butter	4 ounces	8 tablespoons (1 stick)
confectioners' sugar	4¼ ounces	1 cup
cocoa powder	1 ounce	¼ cup

index

page references in italic refer to illustrations

ACKNOWLEDGMENTS

A huge thank you to all my students and "bake it like you mean it" followers who inspire me to share and teach the fun stuff every day.

A big hug and thanks to Laura Nolan, an agent, a champion, and a voice of reason.

To the glorious gang at ABRAMS, from editorial to design, you guys are the tops.

And a big hug and kiss to my Raymo. For every cake I include in a book, you've had to eat at least four versions. Your sacrifices make me better.

And to my Schwester and Neffe, you make life sweet.

BAKE IT
like you
MEAN IT